# THE GREEN GUIDE
# TO LONDON

# THE GREEN GUIDE TO LONDON

*Written and edited by*

## BILL BRECKON

# SIMON AND SCHUSTER

LONDON • SYDNEY • NEW YORK • TOKYO • SINGAPORE • TORONTO

**In association with *Friends of the Earth***

First published in Great Britain by
Simon & Schuster Ltd in 1990

**Simon & Schuster Ltd**
**West Garden Place**
**Kendal Street**
**London W2 2AQ**

Simon & Schuster of Australia Pty Ltd, Sydney

British Library CIP data is available for this title
ISBN 0-671-69719-6

Text design and diagrams by Tony Short
Cover design by ATS Design
Cartoons by Funny Business Ltd.
Typeset in Palatino by Simon & Schuster/ATS
Printed and bound in Great Britain
by Guernsey Press Co.Ltd, Guernsey,
Channel Islands

Impression 10 9 8 7 6 5 4 3 2 1

# CONTENTS

# Acknowledgements

This book has been a team effort and many people have contributed with their time, effort and expertise.

Particular thanks must first go to Margaret Downes, who has not only co-ordinated all the research, encouraging, chivvying and cajoling contributors to all our surveys and sections, but also masterminded the massive task of collating, processing and organising the vast amount of data we have collected in our surveys and investigations.

Nicolette Fox also did a highly-professional job in background research for some of the Capital Issues chapters and Tara Emmerson helped in ferreting out additional material for our area-by-area guide to green shops, businesses and services.

In our guide to the environmental activities of the 33 London boroughs – the most detailed and comprehensive survey yet carried out – we asked many searching questions of council members and officers. To all those who took so much time and effort to provide us with the answers we would also like to say a big 'thank you'.

Much of the work on the area-by-area guide was done by local Friends of the Earth groups, whose enthusiasm and expertise is largely responsible for the success of this section of the Green Guide. We also received invaluable advice from, among others, the Vegetarian Society, the Vegan Society, the Henry Doubleday Research Trust, the London Cycling Campaign and from whole-food wholesalers and charitable organisations. Members of the public also wrote in with their suggestions, which we investigated. To all: many thanks.

My sincere thanks, too, to the staff at Friends of the Earth headquarters, who helped at every stage in the preparation of the Green Guide, from planning and research to checking and augmenting the final copy. Particular thanks to Mary Blake, Sarah Tisdall, Rupert Harwood and Pippa Hyam who also helped greatly with the Capital Issues on air pollution, rubbish and recycling and traffic and roads. The expertise is theirs; the opinions (and any mistakes) are mine.

# INTRODUCTION

London is my favourite city. It offers much in beautiful buildings and marvellous parks; in art galleries, museums, concert halls and theatres; in an amazing diversity of restaurants, pubs and bars, and an infinite variety of shops selling just about anything anyone could ever want. It is hustling, bustling, vibrant, alive.

But what of the quality of life in the capital? Just how good **is** it to live in London in the 1990s? There is no denying that when we look at such things as the cost of living, the availability of good, reasonably priced housing, swift and efficient transport systems, safety and cleanliness in the streets, easy access to green space and recreational activities, Londoners are less well off than people who live in many other towns and cities in Britain, or in the major cities of the continent.

Our local environment is under threat, with 'development' eating away at our green spaces; our roads and streets are clogged with traffic, the fumes polluting the air; our public transport services are overcrowded and unreliable; too many of our streets are litter-strewn and dirty, and unsafe to walk at night.

More than that, the sheer numbers of people living and working in the capital make a significant contribution to the wider environmental problems which now threaten the very fabric of the planet itself. It is **our** cars that clog the streets and pour out their pollutants, **our** rubbish that accumulates in ever-growing mountains, **our** requirements for convenience foods and convenience shopping that have spurred the overuse of pesticides and fertilisers, additives and preservatives and, perhaps above all, **our** apparently insatiable demand for energy, which we often use extremely wastefully, that has helped to create major universal problems such as global warming.

Increasing numbers of people, however, are aware of these 'green' issues – and they want to try to do their bit to overcome the problems, not just to improve their own quality of life but to help create a better world for their children. The problem is: how best to go about it? Sometimes the issues appear so complex, and the problems so large, that individual action would seem a mere drop in the ocean. Global issues require global solutions: isn't this something that is best left to governments and international agencies?

While it is certainly true that we do need concerted, co-operative worldwide effort on environmental problems, and a practical commitment by local and national government, individual
actions, multiplied by the million, can and do have a significant
effect. It is public purchasing power that brings about changes in
the products we buy and the way that they are grown or manufactured; it is public opinion that makes manufacturers and retailers re-examine their practices and their policies; it is public
pressure that forces local and national government to act more
firmly to conserve, protect and enhance the environment. Much,
much more remains to be done, but a start has been made and the
moves, slow and small as they may be, are in the right direction.

There are those who argue that green consumerism is not enough
and the problems lie not so much in our greenness, but in our
consumption. We must consume less of everything, particularly
energy, they say, rather than simply trying to lessen the harmful
effects of the products we buy. Sometimes, it seems, they want
to lead us into a Brave Old World of declining living standards
and no economic or technological progress. Certainly we have to
examine our 'needs'– all the foods we eat, the products we buy
and the energy we consume, – but everyday life, like politics, is
the art of the possible and the changes we seek should be within
a framework of economic growth and individual prosperity.

Another important aspect of green consumerism is the increasing awareness that seeking out products less damaging to the
environment gives us of the wider issues. The green consumer
will also demand that industry and commerce, local authorities
and national government play their proper role. Of course, green
**is** the fashionable colour of the 1990s, for politicians and business-
men alike: fine words win votes and sell goods. At the moment
we hear many fine words; the early 1990s will see how much of
the rhetoric is turned into radical action. The government has
promised tough new measures in the new Environment Bill and
many London local authorities have drawn up, or are drawing
up Environmental Strategies to place these issues at the forefront
of their activities. In the next few years we shall see how effective
their plans have been.

On the commercial side too, there have been welcome changes,
with manufacturers and retailers trying to gear more and more
of their products to our demands for more wholesome foods and
goods that are less damaging to the environment in their manufacture, use and disposal. These we commend, but at the same

time, the marketing men and the advertising agents have leapt on to the green bandwagon and pushed growing numbers of their products as 'green' and 'environmentally-friendly.' Often this is sheer nonsense. It is reasonable, for instance, to label an aerosol that doesn't contain propellants which damage the ozone layer as 'ozone-friendly' but its a perversion of the truth to describe such products, with the high demand for energy and raw materials in their manufacture and the great difficulties in their disposal, as 'environment-friendly'. Clearly, they are not. There is a pressing need for an objective, universal system of environmental labelling so that we can properly assess the products we buy and make an informed choice. Further, it is nonsense too, that many of our electrical domestic appliances use twice as much energy to do the same job as others. Not only would using energy-efficient appliances reduce our personal bills, it was also have a significant effect in reducing the output of the greenhouse gas, carbon dioxide from our power stations, lessening the dangers of global warming. Yet at the moment we have no proper energy-efficiency labelling system. Green consumers want to make an informed choice. At present it is often difficult for them to do so.

# Using *The Green Guide to London*

More and more Londoners are expressing their concerns by trying to buy products that cause the least possible damage to the environment, yet it is still not easy to know what to look for and where to buy it. That is where *The Green Guide to London* comes in. As the first comprehensive Londonwide guide we offer listings of more than 1,000 'green' shops and services, showing you area by area where you can buy a wide range of foods, meals, cleaning materials, cosmetics and toiletries, electrical goods, timber and so on which do the least damage to the environment.

In addition we have questioned every one of the 33 London boroughs about their environmental practices and policies to enable you to find out just how well, or badly, your council is doing. Our survey reveals vast differences in approach and activity: by comparing your council with others you will be able to see what needs to be done and where.

We have also produced the most comprehensive up-to-date guide to recycling services in the capital. Much of what we throw away in our dustbins every day could be re-used, with great savings in money, energy and raw materials, yet most of it is simply wasted and buried, with increasing problems, in the ground. Recycling schemes in Britain are still way behind those in many other countries, but they are growing rapidly. By taking individual action on what we throw away as well as what we buy, we can again help to make a significant contribution to the quality of the environment.

There are many environmental issues that do not just affect a borough or a locality, but rather the whole of the capital. In this first edition of *The Green Guide*, we have concentrated on three of them – the scourge of traffic and roads, the mounting rubbish and litter on our streets, and the insidious problems of air pollution, again largely caused by traffic. In each of our three chapters on Capital Issues, we examine the problems, suggest some solutions and give positive ideas as to how individual action can effect much-needed change. Other issues, such as the quality of our food, the protection of green and open spaces and the purity of our water supplies (particularly after privatisation) will be investigated in subsequent editions.

Although we have scoured the whole of the greater London area to find environmentally-sensitive shops and services, there are bound to be omissions. To those left out, we apologise. At the back of the guide you will find forms for nominations for inclusion in the 1991 edition. All these will be investigated for next year.

We hope you find *The Green Guide to London* useful, interesting and stimulating and that it will help you to reflect your concern for the quality of the world we live in by 'thinking globally, acting locally.'

Bill Breckon
*London*
*February 1990*

# CAPITAL ISSUES 1:
# TRAFFIC AND ROADS

# TRAFFIC AND ROADS

At 6.25 on the morning of February 27th 1989 there was an accident on the elevated section of the M4 in Brentford, west London. After a blowout, a Ford Sierra estate car crashed into the barriers and ended up across the motorway. The traffic could not get past and the car was so badly damaged that the police were unable to tow it away quickly.

Within an hour and a half the traffic tailed back eleven miles, to Slough in Berkshire. It was the beginning of one of the worst days ever on London's roads, 'The day,' as *The Times* reported, 'the cars stood still'.

Soon adjoining routes to the capital, notably the A4 and the A40, became clogged as frustrated drivers sought diversions, but this was only the beginning: drivers coming in from the south-west along the M3 and A3 also became stuck in long queues as broken-down vehicles and traffic light failures added to the normal morning congestion. From the north and east, *The Times* reported, drivers were delayed by problems on the A1, A41 and A13. Motorists using the A21, one of the busiest routes from Kent, were delayed by an accident outside Farnborough Hospital which blocked the road for nearly two hours.

Meanwhile, the first of two 'minor incidents' which brought the A40 to a halt occurred. An explosion at a junction box in Devonshire Street in the West End extinguished the traffic lights over a wide area, including the Marylebone Road, linking the A40 in the West with the City in the East. Then just before nine o'clock, a workman in Paddington Street punctured a gas main with his digger. 2,000 people had to be evacuated from their homes and offices and Baker Street was closed. It was 12.35 before it re-opened, by which time the traffic jam stretched down the Marylebone Road and along the entire three miles of the elevated Westway. The tailback there was still one-and-a-half miles long at two o'clock.

Russell Kane, who provides 'flying eye' traffic reports from his plane for Capital Radio said of that Monday morning: 'It surpassed the normal levels of ghastliness', yet Gary Meadows, the AA's road services manager in London, thought is 'unexceptional, just the normal pattern of events which occur on any Monday morning'.

## Strangled to death

Jams in London **are** nothing new, of course: traffic in the centre, crawls and fumes at an average of some 11 miles an hour...but the jams today spread wider and last longer than they used to. And they are no longer confined to the rush hours in the city centre, but are increasingly frequent in off-peak hours and in the suburbs. For if London's roads are its arteries, the capital already suffers from severe arteriosclerosis: one thrombosis and circulation all but ceases. How much longer before the condition becomes terminal?

As the Department of Transport itself admits, London's road system continually operates close to maximum capacity and any disruption, through accident, say, or burst water main, or traffic light failure, 'leads to widespread and long-lasting jams'. Mixing the medical metaphor, the prognosis from the Confederation of British Industry is much more blunt. London, said a recent CBI report, is simply 'strangling itself to death'.

The ordinary Londoner hardly needs telling that his city's transportation systems are near to breaking point, with congestion and crush the order of the day, every day. And it is not just on the roads, but on the railways, too, both above and below the ground. Crammed into commuter trains, squeezed into tubes, jammed in buses and their private cars in fume-filled streets, Londoners know only too well the profound effect that transport has on the quality of life – or rather the lack of it. Others see their homes threatened with destruction, their communities wrecked, by grandiose road-improvement schemes that seem to do little or nothing to relieve the overall congestion.

While complaints have undoubtedly increased and grumbles become more vociferous (remember the tube travellers who refused to leave a train which stopped at a station short of its final destination and who stayed put until it eventually continued?), many people seem to accept discomfort and delay as an inevitable part of the daily round. The capital's problems seem insolubly complex and decision-making so remote from the average man and woman in the street (or car, or bus, or train) as to be beyond their reach. What commuter, they ask, change the policies of British Rail? What shopper, those of London Regional Transport? What families can save their homes as another Department of Transport traffic plan blights their area?

But while it is true that too many decisions are still taken without proper consultation or direct democratic control, there are welcome signs of change. Opposition to road-building and road-widening schemes, for example, is spreading rapidly. Local groups, acting singly or in concert, **have** forced the planners and the bureaucrats to abandon schemes that would have killed their communities and consumer pressures **are** beginning to influence the decisions of the transport bosses, making them aware of the needs of people as well as profits.

It is true, however, that many of the changes have been local, piecemeal or cosmetic: a protected street or two here, a pelican crossing there; a face-lift for the stations, some prettily-painted rolling stock. While neighbourhood group action is essential to ensure that the immediate environment is not destroyed and that local services do not continue to deteriorate, there is also a desperate need for a radical rethinking of transport policies, both public and private, throughout the whole of the greater London area.

Individual influence over such London-wide strategic planning is far less easy to achieve, but equally as important as local action. The problems **are** undoubtedly complex, but they are by no means insoluble: what is needed is the political will to tackle them. With the capital's transportation in such a sorry state, however, the time has never been riper for informed individuals to push for a major shift in transport policies.

In this chapter we examine the issues, look to the solutions and suggest how each of us can contribute towards making travelling in London more pleasant and more efficient, safer and less damaging to the environment.

## Jam yesterday and jam today

Look at early photographs of Victorian London and you will see that horse-drawn traffic jams were as commonplace as those created by motor vehicles. They were less polluting perhaps, although there is the well-known anecdote about a turn-of-the century analysis which suggested that if the current trends were to continue, London's traffic would become literally bogged down by the 1960s, since all the streets would be under three feet of horse dung.

The invention of the internal combustion engine removed that risk, but did little or nothing to relieve congestion or improve speeds in the centre of the city. Surveys in the early years of this century showed that both the new motor vehicles and the old horse-drawn ones continued to travel at the same slow pace, about eight miles an hour. The Post Office, worried about its collections and deliveries, conducted its own survey in 1911 and concluded gloomily: 'Whether it will ever be possible to obtain an average reliable speed of over eight miles an hour during ordinary business hours in Central London, even with motor vans, is a matter of extreme doubt'. How right they were: after the Great War, when the motor vehicle almost completely replaced the horse, the traffic remained as congested as ever.

There are difficulties in making direct and specific comparisons of speed and congestion then and now, because of differences in survey methods and the areas covered. But if we look at journey times – the time taken between a number of random points in a given area – we can see that average door-to-door speeds in the Central area (a 10km square centred on Horse Guards Parade) average today, yes, just eight miles an hour!

Another way of assessing the problem is to measure the average speeds on various parts of the road network. Definitive surveys were begun in 1947 by the Road Research Laboratory and later taken over by the Greater London Council and they again showed that speeds had not changed appreciably over a 40 year period.

Analyses by the Department of Transport show that in recent years the problem has actually been getting worse, not just in the central area but notably in suburban areas too. Measuring average speeds on London's roads (which are clearly faster than door-to-door journey speeds), they show a distinct decline between 1968 and today. On ordinary roads in the central area during the evening peak period was 11.8 miles an hour in 1968/70; by 1974/76 is had risen slightly, to 13.2 mph, but by 1986 it had dropped once more, to 11 mph. In the inner suburbs there was an even more marked decline in average speeds on the roads, from 14.6 mph in 1968 to 12.5 mph in 1986 and there was a similar slowing down in the outer suburbs. While the morning rush was slightly less congested than the evening crush, also of significance was the fact that congestion was increasingly being experienced throughout the day.

In its recent publication on 'Transport in London', the Department of Transport notes: 'Traffic speeds have been falling in all areas at all times of day, though the change has been

# AVERAGE TRAFFIC SPEEDS IN LONDON SINCE 1968

| | Primary/ Trunk Roads | Other Roads Central Area | Inner Area | Outer Area | All Areas | All Roads |
|---|---|---|---|---|---|---|
| | mph | mph | mph | mph | mph | mph |
| **Morning Peak Period** | | | | | | |
| 1968-1970 cycle | 24.3 | 12.7 | 14.4 | 19.4 | 17.3 | 18.1 |
| 1971-1973 .. | 25.0 | 12.9 | 13.8 | 18.7 | 16.8 | 17.7 |
| 1974-1976 .. | 24.1 | 14.2 | 15.3 | 18.0 | 17.0 | 17.9 |
| 1977-1979 .. | 23.0 | 12.3 | 13.3 | 17.6 | 15.9 | 16.9 |
| 1980-1982 .. | 26.2 | 12.1 | 13.5 | 18.0 | 16.2 | 17.5 |
| 1983-1986 .. | 24.9 | 11.8 | 12.9 | 17.2 | 15.6 | 16.9 |
| 1987 .. | | 11.5 | | | | |
| **Daytime Off Peak Period** | | | | | | |
| 1968-1970 cycle | 32.1 | 12.1 | 17.4 | 24.6 | 20.2 | 21.3 |
| 1971-1973 .. | 34.2 | 12.6 | 17.7 | 24.2 | 20.3 | 21.6 |
| 1974-1976 .. | 36.9 | 12.9 | 17.7 | 23.6 | 20.1 | 21.7 |
| 1977-1979 .. | 35.5 | 12.6 | 16.4 | 22.6 | 19.1 | 20.9 |
| 1980-1982 .. | 36.3 | 11.6 | 16.3 | 22.4 | 18.6 | 20.6 |
| 1983-1986 .. | 36.5 | 11.9 | 15.4 | 22.7 | 18.9 | 20.9 |
| 1987 .. | | 11.0 | | | | |
| **Evening Peak Period** | | | | | | |
| 1968-1970 cycle | 26.9 | 11.8 | 14.6 | 20.5 | 17.6 | 18.6 |
| 1971-1973 .. | 26.9 | 12.7 | 13.9 | 20.0 | 17.3 | 18.3 |
| 1974-1976 .. | 30.4 | 13.2 | 14.8 | 18.7 | 17.0 | 18.3 |
| 1977-1979 .. | 27.2 | 11.9 | 12.9 | 18.3 | 15.9 | 17.2 |
| 1980-1982 .. | 29.8 | 12.2 | 13.6 | 18.7 | 16.4 | 18.0 |
| 1983-1986 .. | 27.6 | 11.5 | 12.5 | 18.2 | 15.8 | 17.2 |
| 1987 .. | 11.0 | | | | | |

*Source: The Department of Transport*

most marked in the outer areas'. And all this is despite decades of 'traffic management' and 'road improvement'. Increasing car ownership might be thought to be the root of the problem, and there certainly are many more cars on the roads. The numbers rose from just over two million car-owners in London in 1983 to nearly 2.2 million in 1987. Interestingly, however, while traffic entering outer London was up by a hefty eight per cent in the same period, that entering the inner areas rose by only two per cent and that entering central London increased by only 0.4 per cent. So the question ought to be: given the massive rise in car ownership over the last few decades, why don't car owners drive into central London in greater numbers?

The answer, of course, is the traffic jams. When their journey is slow and horrendous, people turn to other forms of transport (although other factors, such as the price of petrol and rail, tube and bus fares also play their part). There has been a sharp up-turn, for instance, in the numbers of people using the Underground: the number of journeys on the tube rose from 560 million in 1983 to 800 million in 1987, by which time 36 per cent of all London commuters arrived by tube. There were similar, though less dramatic rises for the trains and the buses.

In part this reflects a recovery in London's economy, leading to an overall rise in demand for transport, and while central London occupies only a small area of the capital, it provides one-third of all the jobs. Curiously, there are actually fewer jobs available there than there were in the 1960s, but as *The Economist* noted in February 1989: 'They are different jobs. The stevedores, meat-handlers and machine operators who have all but disappeared did far less commuting than the salesmen, advertising managers and word-processor operators who replaced them. They travelled around to fewer business meetings, lunches and dinner parties. Neither did they have to share their city with 24 million tourists every year'.

Behind the bald statistics of ever-increasing demand for transport, lie the human costs for the millions who work, shop, go to school, play sport and seek pleasure in the capital. These are immeasurable, but clearly London's crowded and creaking transport systems have a serious, deleterious effect on the 'quality of life' and the stresses created undoubtedly lead to ill-health as well. The pollution caused by motor vehicles and its effects on health, the atmosphere and the global environment are another cause for concern, and are examined in the chapter on air pollution.

The economic costs of congestion, however, can be measured, or at least estimated, and in its report on 'The Capital at Risk' in 1989, the Confederation of British Industry put them at billions of pounds per year. The dilapidation and inadequacy of the transport system throughout Britain, said the CBI, may be costing nearly £15 billion a year, almost two-thirds of which is due to extra costs incurred in London and the South-east. Every British household has to spend at least £5 a week more than necessary on goods and services to meet the costs to businesses of congestion on the road and rail systems. No wonder the CBI warns that the capital is strangling itself to death.

Where, then, do the solutions lie, particularly for London's jam-packed roads? We suffered jam yesterday and we suffer jam today. Will it still be jam tomorrow?

## Jam tomorrow?

'Jam yesterday, jam today and jam tomorrow?' was the title of a fascinating and influential lecture given a few years ago by Dr Martin Mogridge, one of Britain's leading transport experts. Dr Mogridge, from the Transport Studies Group at University College, London, sees the solution to improving traffic speeds in central London not in trying to improve the roads, but rather in speeding up public transport. 'Only by speeding up bus and rail,' he contends, 'will it be possible to speed up cars and lorries'. How can this be?

All the results of traffic surveys, Dr Mogridge says, 'show that speeds have not changed appreciably in central London over the last 40 years, although traffic volumes have doubled with all the sophistication of modern traffic measures, one-way systems, automatic traffic control, junction improvements and so on.' There may be short-term fluctuations but there is a long-term stability in speeds, unaffected by road building and traffic improvement schemes. The reason is simple: 'Traffic will distribute itself all over a network, even one as complex as Central London in such a way as to ensure that speeds are fairly uniform – with faster stretches of roads leading to a higher level of congestion at junctions and more direct routes being at lower speeds than more tortuous routes'.

No-one who has ever driven in London will doubt the veracity of that, but the analysis of door-to-door journey times throws up another significant fact: speeds for both car and rail journeys in the central area are almost the same, at just under eight miles an hour. Although the average speed rises with distance from the centre, it rises in exactly the same way for both road and rail travellers.

As we have seen, many car-owners who have the choice of using their car, choose to travel by rail instead, leading to what the planners call 'suppressed demand'.

In such conditions, say Dr Mogridge and other transport analysts, 'the speed of the road network is determined by the speed of the high-capacity network,' that is, the trains and the buses. There seems always to be a balance between them. What happens when we try to alter that balance?

Dr Mogridge says: 'In conditions of suppressed demand, increasing the capacity of the road network merely shifts sufficient car-owning high-capacity network users on to the roads until road speeds are in equilibrium again... This has an interesting corollary, that things can actually get worse if you try to improve them in the wrong way and draw passengers off the more efficient system to the less efficient – efficient in the sense of the use of land for moving a given flow of people. 'If services are then reduced on the high-capacity system, road speeds in equilibrium will be lower than before'.

So the solution is to improve the high-capacity public transport systems in order to speed up the roads. Improving the roads and reducing public transport will only lead to more congestion. Dr Mogridge's arguments, which are shared by many other traffic experts, planners and local councils, not only conform to the scientific facts, but fit in with our own common sense and daily experience. Yet in seeking solutions to London's chaotic and collapsing transport systems, official policies proceed in precisely the opposite direction: major 'road improvement' schemes for the capital and declining support for its public transport.

## Roads to ruin?

The Government is already committed to spending £1 billion on major road-building schemes in London. And in the late 1980s it began considering new proposals which could have led to the construction of up to another 40 miles of 'urban trunk roads', costing as much as £3.5 billion, in four areas of inner London. These plans could have meant the demolition of as many as 8,000 homes and they threatened to destroy many acres of parkland, playing fields and open spaces.

The proposals were contained in The London Assessment Studies, commissioned by the Department of Transport in 1984. Private firms of consultants were asked to investigate four notoriously congested areas: in west London, where the M4 comes in; in the south, along the A23; in the east, from Archway to Docklands; and along the South Circular Road. In the summer of 1988 the consultants produced a series of proposed options to relieve congestion in these areas which, although they made a few suggestions for improving public transport, were unquestionably biased towards new urban expressways – motorways in all but name. Of the 40 proposed options more than half involved major road building and could have meant up to 40 miles of four- and six-lane highways being carved through the capital.

Because the assessment study options covered such wide swathes of London, they caused widespread 'planning blight': uncertainty as to exactly where the new roads were to be built meant a sharp drop in the prices of some 100,000 homes and many became simply unsaleable. Some 200 parks and open spaces were under threat, 30 of them of great ecological importance, and eight designated Sites of Special Scientific Interest.

Opposition to the plans was widespread, with more than 100 local groups fighting against them. They banded together to form ALARM (All London Against Road-building Menace) and the campaign was supported by a wide variety of other groups and organisations, right across the political spectrum. Both the Conservative London Boroughs Association and the Labour Association of London Authorities has joined the battle, as did virtually every London MP.

In December 1989, however, the Transport Secretary, Cecil Parkinson, announced that the Government had ruled out the most extreme road-building proposals, abandoning most of those which involved wide-scale demolition of residential property. It was a partial victory for the campaigners and meant an apparent reprieve for areas like Parkland Walk in North London, although other parts of the capital, like Archway, were still under threat. The new options were open to public discussion and the final decisions were due to be made at the end of March 1990.

Only the Department of Transport and its consultants, it seems, are keen on new road–building schemes and, according to Friends of the Earth, the terms of reference for the assessment studies meant that the reports were bound to have a built-in road-building bias. FoE says: 'The instructions the Government gave to their consultants make it clear that the studies were designed to provide a justification for more major road-building. In particular the methodology adopted for evaluating alternative options is profoundly biased in favour of road building; and of course fails to take account of generated traffic. In fact it seems likely that the studies were set up to take advantage of the impending abolition of the Greater London Council and the consequent trunking (taking under Government control) of 70 miles of former GLC roads. All the studies are closely related to major roads which the Government intended to trunk'.

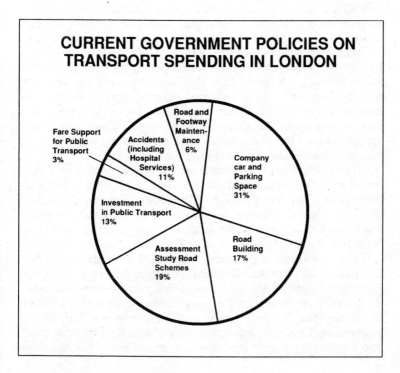

## CURRENT GOVERNMENT POLICIES ON TRANSPORT SPENDING IN LONDON

Fare Support for Public Transport 3%

Accidents (including Hospital Services) 11%

Road and Footway Maintenance 6%

Company car and Parking Space 31%

Investment in Public Transport 13%

Assessment Study Road Schemes 19%

Road Building 17%

FoE criticises the Government for its 'consistent commitment to environmentally-damaging urban road schemes', such
as the East London River Crossing, now approved, which will
cut through the 8,000 year-old Oxleas Wood, a designated Site
of Special Scientific Interest, and the A13 improvements through
Rainham Marshes. One of the reasons why the Department of
Transport is keen to run roads through important open spaces
is the way in which the costs and benefits of road-building
schemes are assessed: the costs include the acquisition of land
and property, construction and maintenance, to be weighed
against benefits including time-saving and accident reduction.
If the benefits outweigh the costs, the scheme is said to have
a 'positive Net Present Value' and to make economic sense.

Rupert Harwood, Friends of the Earth's London Roads Campaigner says: 'The method would perhaps make some sense if
realistic values were attributed to the various factors on the
cost and benefit sides'. He says, as we have seen, that values
placed on time-saving are unrealistic, as they take no account
of traffic generation, while on the other side, the Department
appears to put a zero or marginal value on important open
spaces to be acquired for road schemes. The reasoning appears
to be that an asset should be valued at its 'opportunity cost',
that is, the value of the land when put to its most profitable
alternative use. Rupert Harwood says: 'As it is protected, it
may be impossible to get planning permission for a commercial development, and therefore it has no opportunity cost.
Indeed, if it wasn't used as a road, it would have to be maintained and so its opportunity cost may be considered to be
negative and equal to the cost of maintenance.'

'This institutionalised contempt for countryside has a profound effect on traffic policy in Britain. If a realistic value were
put on, say, Barnes Common, Wimbledon Common, Parkland
Walk or other threatened sites, there is no way that the major
road-building options in the London Assessment Studies would
be given the go-ahead'.

The road safety arguments, also often put forward to justify new roads, are also dubious. As Rupert Harwood argues:
'Building roads is not a cost-effective way of reducing accidents. Most of the reductions occur because the new roads are
too dangerous for pedestrians and cyclists to use. Experience
suggests that traffic-calming measures, including speed humps,
and improving public transport are much more cost-effective

ways of reducing accidents. 'And, of course, unlike road-building, they have the advantage of improving rather than destroying the environment and of enhancing rather than undermining people's freedom to move around in their own communities'.

Despite all the arguments against them, new and bigger roads still seem to be the Government's choice in trying to overcome our colossal congestion problems. While pushing ahead with its mammoth spending on roads, not only in the capital but throughout the country, the Government continues to neglect the railways and public transport, insisting increasingly that they should 'pay their way'. Government subsidy for the day-to-day running costs of London Regional Transport, for instance, was cut back from £195 million in 1984/5 to zero in 1989/90 and the lack of financial help is reflected in increased costs to the traveller: fares in London, in real terms, are higher than in any other European capital. In Milan, for example, a ticket costs the passenger just 29 per cent of its true cost, in Paris, some 65 per cent, yet the London underground travellers pays 85 per cent of the actual cost – and public transport continues to become more overcrowded and unreliable.

Meanwhile the crush and chaos on the roads continues. But if building new ones or widening old ones is not the answer, what is?

## Shaping the future

A major argument against the London Assessment Studies, and indeed against all the other 'traffic improvement' schemes proposed by both national and local government, is that they are piecemeal and each fails to relate to the others proposals. What is needed is a London-wide plan which takes into account the needs of everyone living in, working in and using the capital.

One suggestion, from the CBI, is that there should be a Minister of Transport for London and that the capital should be designated a transport priority zone under the direction of a Department of Transport task force. The involvement of the Department, with its penchant for road-building, is unlikely to find favour with the environmental groups, unless there are very clear terms of reference which place an emphasis on public transport and the reduction of traffic demand.

It has to be said, however, that the setting up of any organisation to plan, oversee and finance the desperately needed solutions to London's transportation problems, will require an act of national political will – and there is little sign of any movement in that direction at present. (However, following 'green' pressures, the Secretary of State for the Environment, Chris Patten, announced in October 1989, that there is to be a study by senior ministers to evolve a more environmentally-sensitive overall government strategy, which will include higher investment in public transport – though not necessarily at the expense of the roads programme.)

Further pressure for change will have to continue to come from groups of informed and committed individuals arguing their case, campaigning for change and persuading their elected representatives, local and national, of the need for radical action. There will continue to be debate about the form of that action, but planners, pressure groups and environmental organisations have come up with a variety of positive suggestions for improving transport in London and getting the capital moving again.

One of the top priorities is for major improvements in the public transport system: more and better trains, more and quicker buses. As we have seen, improving the efficiency and the journey speeds of the high-capacity networks will in itself improve congestion on the roads by tempting more drivers away from them.

One of the best ways to improve the rail system would be through a number of strategic through-running schemes, rather than by building more slow underground-type railways with short station spacings, although there are some areas, like Chelsea, Hackney and Peckham, where they could be valuable. Linking up the South, West and North London lines, to form a new Outer Circle with high frequency services would also bring great improvements.

But proposed cross-rail links – Paddington to Liverpool Street, Chelsea to Hackney; and the Thameslink line linking north and south London – have been ditched by the Department of Transport. While the go-ahead has been given for an extension of the Jubilee tube line into the Docklands and to Stratford, this is the scheme that will probably do least to reduce road congestion – and it will cost the taxpayer at least £600 million.

On the roads themselves, we need to switch more and more

from single-occupancy cars to multiple-occupancy buses: an average peak time bus carries the occupants of 22 cars and in central London the bus is far and away the biggest load carrier for short distances. Yet London buses are planning to carry two per cent fewer passengers in 1989/90 than they did in 1988/9. They should carry more passengers, not fewer, and to speed them on their way we need a far more comprehensive bus lane system and more bus priority schemes, such as fixing the traffic lights to favour buses. (There has been a welcome move here, in new plans to equip some of London's buses with a device which enables the driver to turn the traffic lights to green.)

There is a need too for more staff to improve safety, security and efficiency on the public transport network. A 1989 survey showed that half the women in Britain try to avoid public transport after dark because they feel unsafe. Ninety per cent of buses are now driver only, and they take four times longer picking up passengers than ones with a conductor, again adding to traffic congestion.

Direct action as far as clogged roads is concerned means first, a removal of the hidden subsidy that encourages too many cars. Some 80 per cent of all the vehicles coming into central London in the morning rush hour are company cars, or their capital and running costs have in some way been subsidised by the drivers' employers: ending such subsidies would encourage many of these drivers to switch to public transport. So would charging motorists to use certain roads at certain times and channelling the money raised into public transport improvements. Enforcing parking regulations would also be of immense benefit. At present there are around 500,000 parking violations every day in London, of which only two per cent are detected. Clamping has reduced illegal parking in some areas by as much as 40 per cent, although a clamped vehicle itself can add to congestion.

There are now government plans for a new crackdown on illegal parking by designating some 300 miles of roads in the capital as 'red routes' on which parking and loading during rush hours will be banned, with much heavier fines for offenders and regular patrols by traffic wardens with new enforcement powers. Loading and unloading is one of the major causes of hold-ups and a ban on key routes in the rush hours would certainly help. (Government researchers recently filmed a van unloading in Streatham on the A23. It caused traffic congestion that was still being felt two-and-a-half hours later.)

Many of the new proposals will require legislation, including possible government control of 330 miles of designated roads run by local authorities. That is likely to provoke disputes, since many local authorities believe that their boroughs are being invaded by commuter traffic and that 'red routes' will only make the problem worse. There are plans, too, to enforce better consultation between the utility companies so that they do not keep digging up the same bit of road in quick succession; delays caused by gas, water, electricity and telephone roadworks cost an estimated £70 million a year.

Perhaps the most efficient machine ever invented for inner city transport is the bicycle. It is not only non-polluting, but also provides much-needed healthy exercise. In many other countries it is one of the most popular means of getting to work: in Denmark, for example, some 40 per cent of people travel to work by bike and in The Netherlands, 30 per cent of all urban journeys are by pedal power. A National Travel Survey in Britain found that about three-quarters of all the trips we make are less than five miles long, ideal for a bicycle, yet all too often they are made by car.

While there has been a considerable increase in the use of bicycles in Britain since the 1970s (between 1974 and 1984 there was a 300 per cent increase in cycle traffic entering central London) many people are still reluctant to take to the streets, not least because of concerns over safety. Cyclists are certainly more at risk than other road users, 17 times more vulnerable than car drivers per mile travelled, according to Department of Transport figures, and the risks to them have been increasing, rising by five per cent in the last ten years while the risks for other road users have fallen by 25 per cent.

Clearly new legislative and engineering measures are needed to encourage cycling, including the provision of more cycle routes and lanes and 'traffic calming' measures. Such calming will help to eliminate 'rat runs' of commuter cars rushing through side-streets in an attempt to beat the jams. Measures include the closing of streets to cars, the provision of 'pinch points' to prevent the incursion of large vehicles and road humps to slow motorists down.

Pedestrians, too, are often badly catered for in Britain's towns and any sensible planning should integrate their needs with those of the motorist. As well as pedestrianised areas and traffic calming measures there is a need for well-thought out walking routes in towns, to avoid interruption and delay from motor traffic, for the sensible siting of bus stops near safe crossing points, and for clearer signals and simplified layouts at major route crossings, to help pedestrian and motorist alike.

The principle of traffic calming, as opposed to traffic restraint (which has traditionally been an isolated approach leading to migration of the traffic elsewhere) is to treat whole blocks of streets including the main roads. In Germany, the most advanced country in this respect, the concept has been further expanded to city-wide traffic calming measures.

## Taking action

The best advice for any concerned individual keen to play his or her part in improving London's transport and traffic and enhancing the local environment is: join a group. There are now literally hundreds of them, campaigning locally and nationally, not only against the horrendous possibilities thrown up by the road-building options in the assessment studies, but for a more positive approach to the provision of public transport, the taming of the motor car and better facilities for pedestrians and cyclists.

A word of caution, though, from Rupert Harwood at Friends of the Earth. He says: 'In the past anti-roads campaigns have tended to be rather parochial. Instead of opposing the principle of building a road, groups have often suggested that it would be a much better idea to build it in somebody else's neighbourhood. If there is a whole series of groups opposing and supporting alternative alignments, the Department of Transport can present this as indicating that everybody supports the principle of building a new road, but that they differ as to exactly what detailed route it should take. Then can then simply choose their own preferred route.'

'Fortunately the cry of NIMBY (Not In My Back Yard) is being supplanted by the cry of Not In My City. There are over a hundred local groups across London which have formed themselves into ALARM (All London Against Road-building Menace). Their message is quite simple; major road-building will only make London's problems worse and is therefore totally unacceptable in any part of London'.

Writing to your local MP (names can be found in the parliamentary guides available in the local library) will help, and if a small group of you can arrange to meet him at the House of Commons to air your views, so much the better. Lobbying the local council is a worthwhile exercise, too. While almost every council is opposed to the options in the London Assessment Studies, some are doing very little actively to oppose them. The organisation of local government sometimes seems rather complicated and transport matters are often dealt with by a number of different committees (such as Planning, Civil Engineering, Technical Services), although some do have a Transport Committee, or sub-committee. The council's information office should be able to tell you who deals with what. It is important to meet the councillors who sit on these committees, to provide them with alternative sources of information to augment (and possibly disagree with) that which they receive from the council's officers.

Using the local papers is a valuable way of getting a message across and the provision of salient facts, such as local features and activities that are under threat, as well as the staging of events, will provide good 'copy'.

If you are particularly interested in making your streets safer and more pleasant to live in, the 'Friends of the Earth Guide to Traffic Calming in Residential Areas' provides essential information on how to go about this.

## Useful names and addresses

Department of Transport
2 Marsham Street
London SWIP 3EB
(071) 276 3000
Public Enquiries Unit: (071) 276 0990

Association of London Authorities
36 Old Queen Street
London SW1H 3JF
(Labour-dominated local authorities association)

London Boroughs Association
c/o Westminster City Hall
Victoria Street
London SW1E 6QP

(071) 828 8070
(Conservative-dominated local authorities association)

London Planning Advisory Committee
Eastern House
8/10 Eastern Road
Romford RM1 3PN
(0708) 45997
(Statutory London wide committee on transport and planning)

London Ecology Unit
Berkshire House
168/173 High Holborn
London WC1V 7 AG
(071) 379 4352
(For information on the impact of road schemes on open spaces)

Capital Transport Campaign
308 Gray's Inn Road
London WC1X 8DP
(071) 833 4022
(Experts on public transport)

Friends of the Earth
26/28 Underwood Street
London N1 7JQ
(071) 490 1555
(For information on traffic policy and campaigns, traffic calming, cycling etc, plus details of local groups fighting London
Assessment Studies options)

Planning Aid for London
100 Minories
London EC3N 1JY
(071) 702 0051
(For advice on planning matters)

Transport 2000
Walkden House
10 Melton Street
London NW1 2EJ
(071) 388 8386
(For research and information on transport policies in general)

London Cycling Campaign
Tress House
3/7 Stamford Street
London SE1 9NT
(071) 928 7220
(For information and support on improving cycling facilities)

The Pedestrians Association
1 Wandsworth Road
London SW8 2LJ
(071) 735 3270
(For information and advice on pedestrians' rights)

## Useful publications

(Addresses above)

*Transport in London*,
     from the Department of Transport

*Getting There, a Transport Policy*;
*Roads to Ruin: Stopping the London Road Schemes*;
*Guide to Traffic Calming in Residential Areas*;
*Pro-bike, a Cycling Policy for the 1990s*;
*Roads to a Better Economy*;
*London's Green Spaces: What are they worth?*
     all from Friends of the Earth

*Jam Yesterday, Jam Today and Jam Tomorrow, or How to Improve
Traffic Speeds in Central London*, by Dr Martin Mogridge,
     available from Transport 2000

*Feet First: Putting people at the Centre of Planning*,
     from Transport 2000

*On Your Bike: The Guide for London Cyclists*,
     from the London Cycling Campaign

# CAPITAL ISSUES 2:
# RUBBISH, LITTER AND RECYCLING

# RUBBISH, LITTER AND RECYCLING

When it comes to the quality of their environment, nothing, it seems, causes people more concern than rubbish, litter and dirty streets.

While they may occasionally present a health hazard, their consequences in ecological terms pale in comparison with those of depletion of the ozone layer and global warming due to the greenhouse effect. But our daily experience of litter-strewn streets, and pavements piled high with bulging, breaking black plastic bags, offends us more than anything else. A recent survey by the Tidy Britain Group found that nineteen people out of twenty cited litter as a major problem, a far higher proportion than for any other environmental issue.

There is no denying that Britain is a dirty country and that we cast aside our litter - from fast food containers to fag packets, from paper bags to newspapers, from sweet wrappings to drinks cans - with a careless abandon. But although some nations are clearly inherently tidier than we are (the Swiss spring immediately to mind) we are not unique in our untidy habits. There's no suggestion that the French, for instance, or the Italians are intrinsically a cleaner people. Yet the filthy streets of London are in sharp contrast to those of Paris and Milan which, if not exactly litter-free, are subjected to a regular and rigorous clean-up by the municipal authorities. Despite Prime Ministerial pronouncements; despite innumerable campaigns, official, voluntary, national and local; despite the provision of litter bins by the thousand; despite constant exhortation to 'keep it clean', London remains one of the dirtiest capitals in Europe. Why?

## A Tale of Two Cities

In a recent television film my colleagues and I compared and contrasted the efforts made in London and Paris to keep our respective capitals clean. The differences in approach, in attitudes, in investment in manpower and machines and above all, in political will and commitment, are very instructive.

Undoubtedly, the Presidential aspirations of Jacques Chirac, the Mayor of Paris have much to do with the transformation of the French capital. Until 1977 Paris was run by a Government prefect and 20 separate arrondissements, each responsible for street cleaning and rubbish collection in its own area, as London's 33 boroughs are today. When Chirac was elected mayor all Paris (the first since the Commune of 1871) he inaugurated an ambitious clean-up plan, involving both the municipal authorities and private companies. Said Chirac: 'Cleanliness is the well-being, the harmony, the beauty, the security, the health – in brief, the pleasure – of living in Paris.'

There has been a major investment, not only in manpower but in an incredible variety of new machines to lift the litter, scour the streets: from the Lily, a small trolley that zooms along the pavement, pushing rubbish into the gutter, to the benne, a small truck with giant scouring brushes and directional hoses, to a giant vacuum cleaner, looking like a baby elephant, sucking up litter with its trunk, to graffiti trucks, summoned by radio from motorcycle spotter patrols, to scrub walls clean almost before the paint has dried.

In 1989 Paris spent some £83 per head on rubbish collection and street cleaning, with central government making, through grants, a hefty 25 per cent contribution, while in inner London, we spent £47 per person, little more than half the French figure. With their tight budgets and heavy demand for other services, many London councils are hard pressed to find as much as they may like too. One of the French firms which has won a contract to clean up part of Tower Hamlets, for example, admits that it cannot do as good a job as in Paris because the budget precludes the optimum investment in manpower and machines.

The sheer scale of the Parisian operation makes possible those large investments in state-of-the-art technology for speedy and efficient cleaning up and rubbish removal – and in publicity. The recent announcement of a 15-million-franc Paris Propre poster campaign brought a wry smile from the deputy leader of Lambeth Council, Jon Davies, who has lived in both capitals. He said: 'That would be half our annual street cleaning budget. I tried to get a poster campaign here in Lambeth and failed to get £5000.' Lambeth would like to double its street cleaning budget, but the accumulated effects of five years of rate-capping mean no increase, but rather a 25 per cent cutback in services this year.

But it is more than just money. It is no co-incidence that the improvement in Paris dates from the establishment of a centralised city government thirteen years ago, while in London the 33 boroughs must each still fight alone to try to keep their local streets clean. And, of course, once a place is clean, it is more likely to remain so, while litter-strewn streets invoke no civic pride or incentive not to drop even more litter.

## *Towards a cleaner London*

In its legislative programme for 1990 the government has proposed new action on litter, including raising the maximum fine under the 1973 Litter Act from £400 to £1,000. It also wants councils to introduce fixed penalty 'on the spot' fines, to be handed out to offenders by litter wardens. Westminster already has such a scheme, under the City of Westminster Act, 1988, with a £10 fixed penalty for offenders. After a year of monitoring, it is acknowledged that the scheme works well in terms of education and deterrence: most approaches by wardens result in litter being picked up, rather than a ticket being issued. Westminster itself would like to see tougher laws, resulting in the issuing of more 'on the spot' tickets for an even greater deterrent effect.

The government also proposes that the responsibilities of local councils should be extended to a general duty 'clear and keep clear of litter' all land in their ownership or control, open to the air and to which the public have access. Councils may be taken to court if they fail in these duties. Many councils, however, see no point in being given extra responsibilities if they are not given extra resources to do the job – and that will inevitably mean more help from central government, rather than an extra burden on the poll tax payer. While no specific provision has yet been made for this, the Environment Minister David Trippier told me (in October 1989) that the Government will consider providing extra for councils needing more money for clean up campaigns. It still remains to be seen how much the political rhetoric will be augmented with hard cash.

Further legislative plans (formalised in the new Green Bill) include a duty on others to clean up their act as well: London Regional Transport, British Rail, river and airport authorities should also be held responsibly for the cleanliness of all the areas they own to which the public have access, as should the owners of private land like car parks, shopping precincts, forecourts and sports grounds. Councils would enforce these responsibilities through the designation of Litter Control Zones and the issuing of Litter Abatement Notices. If offenders took no effective action, the council would have the power to clean up themselves and bill the landowner.

Fast-food premises cause particular problems and the case has been put for making them responsible for the pavements adjoining their premises. The government, however, thinks that this would create an overlap of duty and believes that the threat of designation by the local authority should be sufficient incentive for them to keep their surroundings clean on a voluntary basis.

London's extra difficulties, shared with Paris and other European capitals, come from the daily influx of commuters and the annual invasion of millions of tourists, which all contributes to the rubbish and litter problems. Westminster, one of the capital's richest boroughs, already spends £13 million a year, about one-sixth of its total budget and the highest proportion in any major British city, on its cleaning up operations, yet concedes that it is an uphill struggle to stem the mounting tide of rubbish. The city council argues that it is unfair to ask the local poll tax payer to meet the extra cost of cleaning up after its commuters and visitors. Perhaps the ultimate answer is going to be some sort of tourist tax, levied on hotel and restaurant bills and admission charges, to supplement the cleaning budget.

In the Green Guide section on local boroughs (pp 81-168) we have asked councils about their policies and practices on maintaining and improving the local environment, including rubbish collection and street cleaning, and their individual responses are recorded there, together with a 'league table' on the quality of that response, in which cleaning up is a major factor. The full league table (pp 164-165) gives you a fair indication what your council is doing – or not doing, but it is worth recording here specifically which councils are doing best and which worst.

From our research, we can identify Bromley, Richmond and Sutton as among the very best councils, with Westminster trying very hard but still struggling with its particular problems. At the other end of the scale Haringey, Tower Hamlets, Merton and Camden continue to fail to provide their residents with the minimum standards of cleanliness they deserve. Haringey cut last year's budget by £1.2 million and abandoned weekend street cleaning. While that has now been re-instated and some recent improvements made, much remains to be done. Tower Hamlets, divided into seven semi-autonomous neighbourhoods, is in a chaotic situation with three different organisations responsible for cleaning the borough. Rotten produce from street markets and rubbish from docklands developments continue to strew the streets. Merton has moved to a privatised service, cutting costs, but many parts of the borough continue to be a disgrace. Bottom of the list still comes Camden, where the council, despite a spending of £6 million a year, was quite rightly under constant attack. The new contract for refuse collection and street cleaning was won by an in-house bid, at £4 million a year, a cut of £2 million in the budget with the same people doing the same job. The council claims that a new productivity deal and a publicity campaign are resulting in improvements, but the evidence in the littered streets belies such claims.

## Litter contact addresses:

> Tidy Britain Group
> The Pier
> Wigan
> Greater Manchester WN3 4EX
> (0942) 824620
> National agency for litter abatement, has projects with local authorities, schools, community groups.

## Moving the rubbish mountain

While you may feel you're walking ankle deep in litter in many areas of London, have you ever wondered what happens to your contribution to the problems of our throwaway society? When you are out, you may conscientiously put your litter in the bin and at home, of course, you tie it all carefully in its big black bag, ready for the dustman to take away. But what happens then?

If all the domestic rubbish thrown away in Britain in a day were piled up in Trafalgar Square the top of it would be tickling Nelson's toes. The average household throws away around a tonne of rubbish every year and finding some way and somewhere to get rid of the accumulated millions of tonnes of the stuff is a major – and increasing – headache. Over and above the two and three-quarter million tonnes of household rubbish, there are a further 11 million tonnes of waste from various sources, including commerce and industry, bringing London's annual throwaway total to a colossal 13.75 million tonnes. The usual solution is to bury it in holes in the ground, but the available holes are rapidly filling up and London's rubbish is having to be buried further and further afield. Ninety per cent of it is already being sent to counties outside the Greater London area, nearly 40 per cent to Essex and almost a quarter to Kent. Some of it travels 40 miles to be disposed of.

As the London Waste Regulatory Authority reported recently: 'This dependence on the surrounding counties continues to grow. As pressure on filling space increases and more waste has to be transported over even longer distances, so costs for handling, transport and disposal will inevitably rise.' London and the inner

Home Counties will run out of rubbish-dumping space well before the end of the century and many counties will be hard-pressed to meet their own needs without accepting the additional problem of coping with waste from London.

Our household rubbish causes further problems. You might think that, whatever the difficulties in finding somewhere to get rid of it, once buried it could be quietly forgotten; that the tips, once full, could be landscaped and even built on. But that is by no means the case: full of organic matter, much of our rubbish rots slowly away, producing an explosive gas, methane, which can, and does, blow up. In 1987, for example, methane from a nearby dump caused an explosion on a housing estate at Loscoe in Derbyshire, demolishing one house and causing serious injury.

In addition, noxious chemicals can leak out of the waste, poisoning the surrounding soil and polluting water. So as well as mounting disposal costs, waste authorities are now faced with large and long-term bills to monitor and make safe the escaping methane and the seeping chemicals.

Yet much of our household waste is just that – a waste of resources, a waste of money and a waste of energy.

Much of the packaging in which our everyday products is presented is totally unnecessary in terms of delivering them to us efficiently and safely. Rather the packs and the wrappers are marketing ploys, designed to tempt us to buy and to enhance the products' 'perceived value.'

Often they are made of inappropriate materials which can neither be re-processed nor re-used, but rather sit for ever in the tips and dumps. Even when materials could be re-used, they seldom are. While the latest available figures indicate that it costs us around £720 million a year in Britain to dispose of our rubbish, we're actually throwing away at the same time some £750 million worth of reclaimable material. Paper, glass, aluminium and steel cans – all could be reprocessed and re-used, yet are thrown away with careless abandon.

Britain lags way behind many other countries, both in trying to discourage manufacturers and retailers from producing this plethora of wasteful packaging and in legislation and financial incentive to encourage the recycling of our waste. Not all of it can be recycled. But with the co-operation of central government, local authorities, manufacturers and retailers and with the active participation of the public, there's no real reason why the 18 million tonnes of household refuse we as a country throw away each

# LONDON'S WASTE

## Destinations of waste from London 1989 (%)

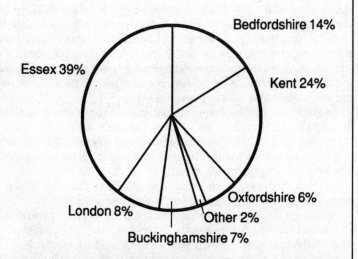

Bedfordshire 14%

Essex 39%

Kent 24%

Oxfordshire 6%

London 8%

Other 2%

Buckinghamshire 7%

## Waste Disposal Methods used by the Public Sector in 1989

|  | Amount ('000 tonnes) | % of Total | Range of Distance Transported (kms) |
|---|---|---|---|
| Incinerated | 400 | 13 |  |
| Transferred to Road Haulage (for landfill) | 1130 | 36 | 10-50 |
| Transferred to River Haulage (for landfill) | 700 | 22 | 20-30 |
| Transferred to Rail Haulage (for landfill) | 650 | 21 | 55-65 |
| Taken Direct to Landfill | 250 | 8 | up to 15 |
| **TOTAL** | **3310** | **100** | 30 (average) |

*Source: London Waste Regulation Authority*

year should not be reduced by half by the year 2000.

## Burying it

The technical term for burying waste in the ground is landfill, and when a landfill site is full the compacted rubbish is covered over with packed topsoil or clay. Unlike chemical waste which might not break down and which could present longer term dangers, household rubbish was considered innocuous: much would rot, the rest was fairly inert and harmless. There was no reason not to build on top of the sites (on concrete 'rafts' for stability) or close around the newly-landscaped open spaces. But the methane menace, with the lighter-than-air gas produced by the rotting processes rising to the surface through holes in the covering or along sewer pipes and telephone ducts, has become an increasing problem in the last twenty years. Deeper dumps and more compacted rubbish mean even more gas is produced and what was at first seen as a relatively cheap and easy way of disposing of waste now turns out to need expensive long-term monitoring and disposal of the gas, which continues to escape for many years after the landfill site is closed. The Inspectorate of Pollution says that leaking gas is now a problem at some 600 tips in England and Wales which are sited near buildings. Methane is an energy source and could be used to heat boilers and generate electricity, but such uses are generally impractical and not economically viable, so the gas from most landfill sites is simply burned off.

A further problem is that some dumps for household waste are also used for hazardous chemicals (both legally and illegally). There would be few problems if the liquid were contained on site, but with rainwater seeping through, run-off of noxious 'leachate' become inevitable. It should be contained before it pollutes streams and underground water courses, but a lack of proper monitoring and inspection, means the danger of accident is ever present, and increasing.

## Burning it

Another solution to the escalating waste problem is to burn the rubbish, but this brings its own problems, in cost and pollution control, and has led to many councils closing their incineration plants in recent years, rather than opening new ones. There are only some 30 municipal incinerators still in operation in Britain and surveys suggest that half of those will close in the 1990s unless they spend a great deal of money in order to meet strict standards on emissions from their chimneys.

This might seem unfortunate, since waste can be regarded as a resource: when incombustible material like metal and concrete is removed, the remaining mixture could be an important source of fuel and also be used to generate electricity. Yet only six per cent of domestic waste is currently disposed of in high-temperature furnaces and only a small proportion of that is used to generate heat or electricity and most authorities which still burn rubbish see it merely as an alternative method of waste disposal. In London at the moment, only Edmonton burns domestic rubbish (and generates electricity), although some other councils are investigating the possibilities of combined heat and power plants.

It is the pollution problems from the smoke stacks, and the costs of overcoming them, which are causing the closure of many of the older incineration plants. The smoke is acid and has to be neutralised and heavy metals must be collected before they go up the chimney. Other toxic chemicals, notably substances called dioxins and furans, are also produced in the furnace when organic materials and plastics, which give off chlorine gas, are burned. While dioxins and furans are created only in very small quantities, there is concern because some of them are extremely toxic: they are known to cause cancer in animals and may also do so in humans. Another cause for concern is that the potential toxicity of only a small proportion of the 200 or so different types has been properly investigated.

High-temperature furnaces (in excess of 1200 degrees C) and efficient recycling of the waste gasses cuts down the discharge of contaminants, as does the removal of chlorine by burning the waste with lime, but all this adds to the capital and running costs.

It now costs some £40 to £50 million to build a new incinerator to conform to current strict pollution control standards, much more than most waste disposal authorities can afford. Even if they could, they would need to be assured that so large an investment would be cost-effective and worth the initial outlay. The figures are unclear, not least because the cost of burying waste seems so much less, although it is unrealistically low and will rise as the costs of transport and methane monitoring increase. At present most councils are not prepared to take the gamble and only two local authorities – in the Isle of Wight and on Merseyside – are at present building plants, although some others are currently investigating the possibilities of local combined heat and power plants, using waste.

## *Waste and rubbish contact addresses:*

Department of the Environment
2 Marsham Street
London SW1P 3EB
(071) 276 3000
Responsible for government policy and legislation on
waste disposal (and recycling). Information packs.

Department of Trade and Industry
Ashdown House
123 Victoria Street
London SW1E 6RB
(071) 215 6081
Brochure, video on 'Watch you Waste'.

Institute of Wastes Management
3 Albion Place
Northampton NN1 1UD
(0604) 20426/7/8.

# RECYCLING: One way ahead

So both burying and burning the growing mountains of rubbish
cause major problems, reflected in growing public concern about
its possible effects on our health and on the environment. How can
we solve them?

There is a clear need for public pressure for change on manufacturers and retailers to reduce the sheer volume of packaging.
We could, for instance, boycott those products excessively pack-
aged, although in today's marketplace it is often very difficult to
find less-packaged alternatives.

But we will only really effectively begin to stem the rising tide
of rubbish, let alone diminish it, if we re-use and recycle a substantial proportion of what we throw away.

Much of our waste could be recycled today, but little of it is; much,
much more could be made of recyclable materials which could be
re-used, with clear economic and environmental advantages. But
while many other countries have introduced the necessary legislation and organisation to make recycling really work in a large-

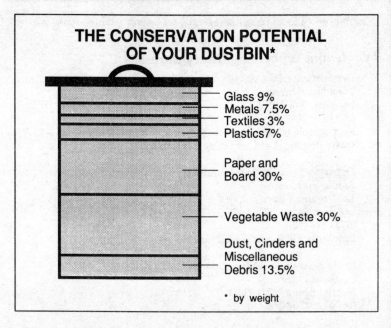

**THE CONSERVATION POTENTIAL OF YOUR DUSTBIN***

Glass 9%
Metals 7.5%
Textiles 3%
Plastics 7%

Paper and Board 30%

Vegetable Waste 30%

Dust, Cinders and Miscellaneous Debris 13.5%

\* by weight

scale and viable way, and provided the motivation for manufacturers and the education for consumers, in Britain many people still seem somehow not to take it seriously. (Although the new Green Bill will now make it a duty for local authorities to recycle their waste.) Unless we have a far more concerted effort, involving central and local government, manufacturers and retailers, and the consumer, many people are going to be face even more difficulties in disposing of our waste.

Nonetheless, there is a growing awareness here of the value of recycling with increasing facilities being made for collecting, particularly, glass and paper. The Green Guide has surveyed recycling activities in all the 33 London boroughs and a comprehensive list of bottle banks, paper collection sites, civic recycling centres and other schemes is provided in The Green Guide to Recycling section, on pages 225-252. Many voluntary groups have found setting up recycling schemes an ideal way both to care for the environment and raise funds and a number of organisations will give help and practical advice on how to do this.

## *Contact addresses: voluntary organisations.*

Friends of the Earth Recycling Information
26-28 Underwood Street
London N1 7JQ
(071) 490 1555
For a recycling Resource List, outlining publications, including guides
for office waste paper collections.

Waste Watch
National Council for Voluntary Organisations
26 Bedford Square
London WC1B 3HU
(071) 636 4066
Support and encouragement for community recycling schemes.
Practical guides for local groups.

Charities Aid Foundation
Pembury Road
Tonbridge
Kent TN9 2JD
(0732) 771333
For national directory of charities collecting recyclable materials.

Shell Better Britain Campaign
Red House,
Red House Park
Hill Lane
Great Barr
West Midlands B43 6LZ
(021) 358 0744
For practical support, small grants, information packages.

## *Contact addresses: official groups*

United Kingdom Reclamation Council
16 High Street
Brampton
Huntingdon
Cambs. PE18 8TU
(0480) 55249
Brings together major organisations concerned with waste reclama-
tion, recycling and waste management.

Local Authorities Recycling Advisory Committee
c/o Jeff Cooper
London Waste Regulation Authority
Room 174 (N)
County Hall
London SE1 7PB
(071) 633 2786

## Problem areas

Thirty-six per cent of our household rubbish is packaging material: plastics, paper, cans and glass. Why do we merely throw it away, instead of re-using it? The answers lie both in the lack of organisation for collecting waste in a way that makes it economic to reprocess its valuable components and in the nature of the materials that are currently used. Below we detail some of the main problem areas and ideas for action:

## PLASTICS

More than two-and-a half million tonnes of plastic materials are used in Britain every year, and packaging accounts for more than a third of the total. Twenty per cent of the contents of our dustbins by volume and seven per cent by weight are plastics, yet virtually none is recycled. There are two main groups of plastics: thermoplastics, found commonly in bottles and wrapping film, and the harder thermosetting plastics, used for electrical plugs and sockets, melamine crockery and so on. While thermosetting plastics cannot be recycled, they tend to be used in more durable products. On the other hand, virtually all of the thermoplastics could be recycled.

One of the biggest difficulties is that there are more than 30 different types in common use and it is difficult and expensive to identify and separate them and costly to transport large enough volumes to make reprocessing worthwhile. Nor can we simply melt down mixed plastics: polyethylene and polypropylene are two of the most common polymers used in packaging, but they cannot be mixed without a loss of strength and flexibility.

One plastics material increasingly being used, notably in the large clear bottles found on supermarket shelves, is PET, polyethylene terephthalate, which can be recycled. In 1987, 1.2 billion PET bottles were sold in the UK, some 60,000 tonnes of plastics costing £1000 a tonne. That means that some £60 million worth of recyclable plastics ended up in the dustbin and the landfill site.

Friends of the Earth and UK2000 have set up a pilot plastics recycling scheme in Sheffield, where house-to-house collections and plastic bottle banks are being tried. The British drinks industry is investing much time and money in projects like this, in an effort to keep ahead of legislation from Europe which will insist on high rates of return or recycling. (There have been other, recent, encouraging signs: Tescos, for instance, has announced a scheme to open plastics banks at supermarkets and a Belfast firm, Boxmore, is well advanced with plans to introduce a recyclable plastic bottle, which can be re-used some 20 times. There still seems, however, to be resistance from drinks manufacturers and supermarkets.)

Other countries faced with similar problems have introduced legislation to encourage recycling. A number of states in the USA, for example, now insist on deposits being charged on the bottles and in California new laws will impose a surcharge on bottles if recycling targets are not met. The West Germans are investigating the re-usable PET bottle, which is heavier and more expensive to make, but which can be washed out at high temperature and re-filled many times.

## Plastics action needed:

* Identify different plastics by code number or initials, to make identification easier;

* Make containers out of just one sort of plastic, to facilitate recycling;

* Introduce returnable deposit schemes, introduce small levy to subsidise collection or a resource tax on raw materials to encourage the industry to reclaim plastics.

## Contact address:

British Plastics Federation
5 Belgrave Square
London SW1X 8PH
(071) 235 9483

## METAL

Seventeen per cent by weight of domestic refuse is metal, much of it made up of discarded food and drink cans. In 1988, we threw away some 5.6 billion drink cans, far more than enough, if placed end to end, to reach the moon. Add in all the food and petfood cans, aerosols and metal cans used for paint and other goods and the number of metal containers thrown away each year doubles. Yet although all cans could be recycled, less than one in fifty is reclaimed, a monster waste of resources.

The cans are made from tinplate (high-quality steel coated with a thin layer of pure tin), from aluminium or from a mixture of both. About half of the drinks cans we use today are made entirely from aluminium. Aluminium and steel cans can be easily separated and with the high price of aluminium collecting these cans can be very worthwhile for charities and other organisations trying to raise funds. But yet again Britain lags well behind many other countries in large-scale recycling: in the USA, for example, 33 billion aluminium cans, more than half the total used, were recycled in 1984 while in The Netherlands more than 40,000 tonnes (43 per cent) of domestic tinplate packaging is recovered each year.

In Britain we have only one plant, in Hartlepool, for the separation of tin and steel from tinplate, and no large-scale facilities at all for the recycling of aluminium (although British Alcan is going to build a plant which will eventually have the capacity to recycle all our aluminium cans).

Nonetheless there have been a number of recycling schemes operating in various parts of the country for some years. In 1979 the Can Makers Federation set up their Save-a-Can scheme, setting up collection skips at sites near supermarkets or in carparks. The cans are taken for de-tinning or aluminium resmelting and donations made to local charities. In addition, the Aluminium Recycling Campaign has collected more than two million cans since 1986, and the Aluminium Federation has launched a nationwide scheme to encourage schoolchildren to collect cans in return for the planting of trees in developing countries. WATCH, the junior wing of the Royal Society for Nature Conservation, has also inaugurated a countrywide scheme among its members.

Producing aluminium is both expensive and energy intensive: it takes the equivalent of 30 barrels of oil to make one tonne of aluminium from bauxite, compared with two barrels from resmelting aluminium, so there is a demand for used cans. Many scrap merchants are happy to take them from voluntary groups, paying around 30 pence for every 50 aluminium cans collected.

Often the only way to identify aluminium cans at the moment is with a magnet, but the Can Makers Federation has promised to move towards a standard symbol on every can identifying the metal type. This already happens in many other countries and would be an invaluable move in encouraging recycling here.

Also of value would be 'reverse vending machines', already in use elsewhere, which would take aluminium cans, crush them and pay out a coin or token in return.

## *Metals action needed:*

* Many more collection sites, new extraction and reprocessing plants;

* Labelling to identify different types of cans;

* Introduce a small levy to encourage collection, or a resource tax on raw materials.

## *Contact addresses:*

Can recycling centres and schemes in London are listed in The Green Guide to Recycling section, pp 225-252.

The Can Makers Recycling Group
36, Grosvenor Gardens
London SW1 0ED
(071) 629 9651

Save-a-Can
Elm House
19 Elmshott Lane
Chippenham
Slough
Berks. SL1 5QS
(0628) 666658

Aluminium Can Recycling Association
Suite 308
I-Mex House
52 Blucher Street
Birmingham B1 1QU
(021) 633 4656

British Steel Tinplate
PO Box 101
Velindre
Swansea SA5 5WW
(0792) 310011

AMG Resources Ltd.
Harborne House
70 High Street
Birmingham B17 9NJ
(021) 427 7272
For information on treatment of used steel cans.

British Scrap Federation
16 High St.
Brampton
Huntingdon
Cambs. PE18 8TU
(0480) 55249

WATCH
22 The Green
Nettleham
Lincoln LN2 2NR
(0522) 752236

## GLASS

Nine per cent by weight of our domestic refuse is glass and each household throws away around seven glass containers every week. We get through some 6,000 million glass bottles and jars every year: all of them could be recycled, but only sixteen per cent of them are.

The classic example of the re-usable glass container is the milk bottle which, on average is cleaned and re-filled about 25 times. Unfortunately few other glass containers are now used in the same way. Some years ago Friends of the Earth and other environmental groups campaigned for legislation to make all bottles returnable, but they were defeated by the commercial interests of the container industry, which increasingly prefers plastics, and the supermarkets, retailers and distributors, for whom returnable bottles are both an inconvenience and an expense.

The emphasis now is on the recycling of glass and its collection in bottle banks. But while there are nearly 4,000 of them around the country, Britain again lags way behind its neighbours in collecting and re-cycling this valuable resource. European countries manage on average to recycle more than 30 per cent of their waste glass, twice the proportion in Britain. Holland heads the league table, with nearly two-thirds of its glass recycled; Austria and Switzerland each recycle nearly half; Italy and Germany, a third; and France, more than a quarter. Nonetheless, 1.5 millions of tonnes of glass has been recycled in Britain in the last ten years and while progress may have been slow, it has certainly been steadily increasing: about 270,000 tonnes are now recycled per year.

Recycling glass makes sound economic and environmental sense. While the raw materials for making glass are cheap, manufacture is high on energy. Every tonne of 'cullet' (broken glass) recycled uses 30 gallons less oil than manufacture from basic ingredients and while we throw away most of our glass, we also import tens of thousands of tonnes of cullet every year from the bottle banks of Europe.

Bottle banks were first introduced here in 1977 by the Glass Manufacturers Federation after the protests of environmental groups on the decline in returnable bottles and there has been a good response from the public when they are made available. Supermarkets, too, are much more sympathetic to the idea of a bottle bank in their carparks than they were to the prospect of having to deal with returnable bottles.

Many local authorities have also seen the bottle bank as a way of demonstrating their positive contribution to the environment. But there are still far too few of them: Holland has one bottle bank for every 1400 people; we share one between every 16,000. The aim is to provide one per 10,000 here by 1991 and to increase to one per 2,000 by 1995, an eightfold increase.

## *Glass action needed:*

* Continued pressure for returnable bottles wherever possible.

* Provision of many more bottle banks.

* Labelling on glass containers emphasising that they are returnable or recyclable.

## Contact addresses:

For locations of bottle banks in London, see The Green Guide to Recycling section.

British Glass Manufacturers Confederation
Northumberland Road
Sheffield S10 2UA
0762 686201
For information and advice on glass recycling.

Glass companies recycling managers:
United Glass: 0727 59261
Rockware Glass: 0604 26391
Redfearn: 0226 710211

# PAPER

Thirty per cent by weight and 50 per cent by volume of our domestic rubbish is paper and cardboard and on average each household throws away three kilogrammes of it every week, most of which ends up in landfill sites. In 1987 we used 8.7 million tonnes of paper and board. Less than half of the paper and board is produced here, the rest is imported.

Newspapers, the quintessential 'here today, gone tomorrow' product, account for a large proportion of our paper waste, of course, and while newsprint is generally simply to recycle, less than 20 per cent of it is recovered from our newspapers and magazines. In fact, we imported 1.2 million tonnes of newsprint in 1987, more than two-thirds of all the newspaper printed in the country. Demand for newspapers and magazines continues to grow and the publications themselves seem to become ever bigger, so unless we grow more trees ourselves, or recycle much more of our wastepaper, imports of raw materials and paper will carry on rising.

Among the biggest problems created by paper production is the contamination caused by the common bleaching processes, which release toxic chlorinated compounds which not only damage the local environment and wildlife (especially fish) but which could also be hazardous to human health.

In total just over a quarter of all our paper waste is recycled, but again, much more could be. While many newspapers use paper with some recycled content (up to 50 per cent), others still use virgin paper or paper with a very small recycled component. Other short-life products, such as toilet rolls and paper tissues are also all too often made wholly from wood pulp, although there can be no environmental arguments for doing so. In our offices and homes, too, we could make much greater use of recycled paper.

In the past recycled paper has been more expensive to buy than virgin paper, which can be produced very cheaply in countries like Sweden where they have vast forests and a plentiful supply of hydro-electricity. But the price is coming down – and will continue to do so as demand rises. That will only happen, however, if we change our attitudes and expectations towards the paper and stationery that we use. Recycled paper is no longer a dull and dreary grey: it can compete with the highest quality virgin paper. As Friends of the Earth point out: 'There is no need to use bright white paper in many situations, such as internal office mail and memos. Many organisations are finding that if they rationalise their stationery needs they can actually save money by using recycled paper'. Among those organisations that have already done this success-fully are the Department of the Environment, Virgin, The Body Shop and the World Wildlife Fund for Nature.

## Paper action needed:

* Encourage the greater use of recycled paper by govern-ment departments, local authorities and businesses.

* Establish collection sites, similar to bottle banks, to reduce collection costs.

* Bring in tougher legislation, such as a resource tax on raw materials, to make recycling more economically viable.

## Contact addresses:

Addresses of paper collection sites and schemes are in the Green Guide to Recycling section, pp 225-252.

British Waste Paper Association
Alexander House Business Centre
Station Road
Aldershot
Hants. GU11 1BQ
(0252) 344454

British Paper and Board Industry Federation
Papermakers House
Rivenhall Road
Westlea
Swindon SN5 7BE
For list of paper mills producing recycled paper and other information.

Independent Waste Paper Producers Ltd.
25 High Street
Daventry
Northants. NN11 4BG
(0372) 703223.

Names of waste paper merchants, who may take paper if more than one tonne is collected at a time, can be found in the Yellow Pages.

## Other materials

Many other materials can be effectively recycled, among them old clothes, waste motor oil, old furniture and so on.

Textiles make up some three per cent by weight of our domestic rubbish and we throw away about £400 million worth every year, or some £20 per household. Little is reclaimed or recycled. Used but wearable clothes are collected and sold in their shops by charities like Oxfam, Save the Children, etc. and a full list of such is to be found in The Green Guide to Shopping and Eating Out section, pp 169-225). Unsold clothing and rags are collected and processed: knitted wools can be unravelled or ripped apart into the original fibre and then spun or mixed with other fibres to make new yarn, while woven woollens are pulled apart and used in the manufacture of dressing gowns, blankets and furnishings. Cottons can be used for paper or industrial wipes while synthetic materials and low grade textiles are used in making 'flock', a filling material for upholstery, bedding and roofing felt.

While three-quarters of the waste oil used in industry is recycled, only about a quarter of that used domestically is. Although it is an offence to throw waste motor oil down the drain (with a fine of up to £2000 or two years in jail), that is what happens to most of it. It pollutes waterways and water supplies and damages the bacteria that break down sewage. Pouring into the ground kills earthworms and bacteria needed for regeneration, while burning it pollutes the atmosphere. Garage and civic amenity centres have facilities for collecting waste oil, which is then converted into fuel

and lubricants. Oil collection sites are detailed in The Green Guide
to Recycling section, pp 225-252.

## Contact addresses: Textiles

British Textile By-Product Association
Thorncliffe
115 Windsor Road
Oldham OL8 1RQ
(061) 624 3611

Oxfam Wastesaver
New Warehouse
Colne Road
Huddersfield
(0484) 539175.
Plant handles 50 tonnes a week of clothing and rags, sorted and baled
for sale to specialist dealers. Turnover £1 million a year, proceeds to
Oxfam.

## Contact address: Oil

The Chemical Recovery Association
5 Coopers Close
The Laurels
Borrowash
Derby D7 3XW
(0332) 677236
For list of merchants who recover oil and other chemical products.

# CAPITAL ISSUES 3:
# AIR POLLUTION AND NOISE

# AIR POLLUTION AND NOISE

## *Foggy days in old London town*

Air pollution has long been one of London's most obvious environmental problems. Here are three reports, the first from an American visitor:

> 'Look down from St. Paul's and see the tiled roofs and steeples, half hid in smoke and mist...all was dirty and foul; the air was chilly and charged with smog and sleet, though it is the genial month of May...the smoke, that you could see streaming in the wind from ten thousand earthen pots, mingled with the vapours and obscured the prospect like a veil ...'

The second is from an analysis of one particular, notorious incident:

> 'The great London smog was a single vast acidic cloud, held down by a mass of warm air above. There was no wind to blow it away. The growing mass of black tarry smoke particles from the home fires and power stations provided the black nuclei on which more fog droplets formed. And the poisonous fumes of sulphur dioxide turned the droplets into a spray of concentrated sulphuric acid... When the smog lifted, it left the mortuaries full, with 4,000 dead ...'

The third, from a research scientist:

> 'While we certainly don't have the obvious deaths caused by the smogs of the past, that doesn't mean to say that air pollution isn't having a detrimental effect on health, particularly for the susceptible groups in the population: the young, the old and those with existing lung conditions and heart problems. We still have serious air pollution problems in the city'.

A century and a half separate those reports. Our American visitor was describing his smoky springtime visit in 1840; the notorious incident was the Great Smog of December 1952; our research scientist's group regularly monitors the noxious gases that still pollute the air of London in 1990.

While the wood fires of earlier centuries undoubtedly gave rise to air pollution, it wasn't until we kept the home fires burning with coal that the problems really began. From the 17th century onwards, fogs and smogs became commonplace, and they were to continue into the 1960s. The diarist John Evelyn recorded in 1671 'the thickest and darkest fog ever known in the memory of man', while the characters in Dickens's novels of the 1840s and '50s roamed streets obscured in swirling fog, through which, later, Sherlock Holmes and Dr Watson struggled in a cautious hansom cab.

Deaths due to fog (or strictly, smog: a mixture of smoke and fog) were also common. During the month of December 1873, for instance, the death rate in London rose 40 per cent above the average, and there were similar increases in 1880 and 1892. And as London grew, so did the extent of the smogs: Croydon was hardly affected in the late 19th century, but in the smog of 1952, there was a sharp increase in mortality in the borough.

Although there had been earlier attempts at regulation, it was that Great Smog of 1952 that led to the legislation that was at last to overcome the smogs that for centuries have not only killed people by the thousand but also strangled transport and ruined the fabric of ancient buildings.

In December of that year, extremely cold weather meant that pollution was trapped in the city: by midday, the capital was as dark as night, the air filled with black particles from domestic chimney and power stations, the fog yellowed with sulphur dioxide fumes. The effects were to kill 4,000 people, at the time the worst disaster from pollution ever recorded anywhere in the world. (Chernobyl is likely, in the long-term, to have caused more deaths, as are the consequences of ozone depletion and global warming, unless we take swift and radical remedial action.)

During a five day period, Deptford had nine times more deaths than usual, Southall seven times, and Finsbury and Chingford five times. It was not just the vulnerable very young or very old who were affected: in fact, most deaths occurred in the 45 to 64 age group. The main factor, scientists now believe was the sulphuric acid in the smog, formed from sulphur dioxide. The smog had a pH of between 1.4 and 1.9, making it more acid than lemon juice.

The Clean Air Act became law in 1956, giving local councils new powers to establish smokeless zones, with government grants for conversion to smokeless fuel. While dealing mainly with smoke, it also insisted on a 'tall chimney' policy to push industrial emissions higher into the atmosphere and that the new generation of power stations were built outside urban areas. The Act proved very effective, though the last killer smog of 1962 still killed 750 people, and, together with the switch from the use of solid fuel to

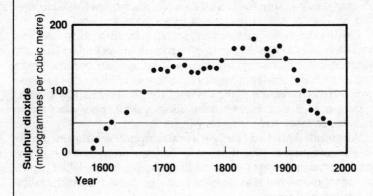

**Estimated sulphur dioxide concentrations averaged over the whole of London**

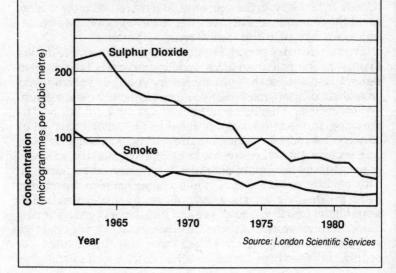

**Sulphur dioxide and smoke concentrations (annual average) in Central London 1962-1983**

*Source: London Scientific Services*

oil and gas, changed the face of the capital. Since 1958 there has been a 50 per cent increase in midwinter sunshine, compared with the previous 30 years.

## London's air today

While the Clean Air Act has undoubtedly been a success story and removed much visible air pollution from the city, London still suffers from serious air pollution problems. The major culprit is no longer the domestic chimney and the power station (although they can still cause some problems in London and have catastrophic wider effects, as outlined below), but the internal combustion engine. Traffic pollution has superseded smoke pollution in the capital. It is more insidious since it is less clearly visible than fog or smog, but its effects, both in the short and long term, can be just as devastating.

The major air pollutants from road traffic are nitrogen oxides, carbon monoxide, hydrocarbons, lead and carbon dioxide. They damage our health, contribute significantly to acid rain and add to global warming.

Lead from petrol is the pollutant that has received the most publicity in recent years and through vigorous campaigns, notably by CLEAR, the Campaign for Lead Free Air, government, industry and the motorist have at last been persuaded to take action to reduce it: the government, through reduced tax to make lead-free petrol cheaper; the industry, through advertising lead-free petrol and providing more outlets and the motorist, through converting existing engines and buying new cars that will run lead-free. An EC directive spurred government action: we were way behind other countries in going lead-free and still only a minority of cars run on unleaded fuel, but at least now an encouraging start has been made. When we were planning this book we had thought to include garages in London that had lead-free pumps; this has proved unnecessary because since then unleaded petrol has become much more widely available throughout the capital.

Important as it is to reduce and ultimately eliminate lead, it is only one of many pollutants that every motorist pours daily into the atmosphere in colossal quantities. In 1987, for instance, British vehicles belched out 4,470,000 tonnes of carbon monoxide, 1,031,000 tonnes of nitrogen oxides and 664,000 tonnes of hydrocarbons.

Dr Duncan Laxen, the scientist quoted at the beginning of this chapter, is the Air Pollution Group Manager for London Scientific Services (LSS), an environmental consultancy whose clients include a number of boroughs. He says: 'The highest air pollution levels in the UK are found in London, particularly nitrogen oxides and other traffic pollutants. Although other cities do have high levels, they are mainly concentrated in small pockets. In London it just goes on and on – you can't escape it.' And London's air pollution problems, have serious health consequences. Carbon monoxide affects the heart, while other pollutants affect the lungs. Some of the hydrocarbons carried by particulates from diesel engines can cause cancers, although there has been little research to try to quantify their effects. Ozone, which we need at high altitudes to protect us from harmful ultraviolet rays, is a pollutant at lower levels, contributing to the greenhouse effect, as well as irritating eyes, throat, nose and lungs.

Some twenty per cent of Londoners fall into the susceptible categories and Dr Laxen says: 'When we have a high air pollution incident, people who are in the sensitive category are better protected indoors rather than outside. They should also try to stay away from busy roads.' He also wants to see publicised 'alerts' to warn people of an impending pollution incident. Following pressure from Friends of the Earth, the Department of the Environment release information about ozone levels, (after the event, not as a warning),but not about other pollutants. Dr Laxen says: 'I would like to see information made available on a regular basis, like a weather forecast'. This is already done in a number of other countries.

Other consequences of air pollution, dirt and smells, are largely attributable to diesel smoke and while car exhaust emissions are to be tackled more vigorously in the 1990s, there is as yet no plan for stricter diesel controls, unlike in the United States, for instance, where stringent new standards are coming into force.

Dr Laxen says that there is evidence to suggest that London's air will get cleaner towards the end of the 1990s, but things may well get worse before they get better, due to increases in traffic volume, particularly in the suburbs. (See Capital Issue: Transport, pp 9-28, for details on traffic volumes in the capital.)

LSS monitors levels of air pollutants at four sites: in a West London residential area near the airport, on a rooftop in Central London, in a residential/industrial area in East London and at a busy roadside in Central London. The first three stations represent where people live and work, the last shows roadside exposure, where most people spend less time.

LSS monitors for carbon monoxide, nitrogen oxide, sulphur dioxide, airborne lead and airborne particulates and, in separate studies, checks ozone levels. The results show that London regularly exceeds the guideline levels laid down by the World Health Organisation for carbon monoxide, sulphur dioxide, nitrogen dioxide and ozone. In 1989 ozone exceeded the guidelines most often, because of the fine summer (sunlight contributes to its formation). Generally, however, the main problem is carbon monoxide, which over the years has exceeded WHO levels most frequently.

Unfortunately these WHO standards, based on world-wide medical research, are merely guidelines, not strict legal standards that have to be met – and the British government is not prepared to accept them as national standards. There are a number of air quality standards, based on European Community requirements, for nitrogen dioxide, sulphur dioxide, smoke and lead, but there are currently none for carbon monoxide, or ozone, although other directives do now control the levels of emission from motor vehicles through the requirements of the test driving cycle, which is designed to mimic urban driving conditions.

# The pollutants: road traffic

## Carbon monoxide

Motor vehicles are responsible for 85 per cent of the carbon monoxide pollution, with peak levels occurring during the morning and evening rush hours. The highest levels are typically found on a winter morning when cold air traps the gas at ground level. While levels do appear to have fallen since the late 1970s, carbon monoxide is still the main pollution problem and WHO guidelines are regularly breached.

At very high levels, carbon monoxide kills, and is frequently used in suicide attempts. Even at lower levels carbon monoxide impairs the ability of the blood to take up oxygen so placing stress on the heart. Perception and thinking are impaired, reflexes slowed and drowsiness sets in. Those most at risk from the effects of carbon monoxide pollution are heart disease sufferers, pregnant women, young children, the elderly (particularly those with heart/lung problems) and people suffering from chronic bronchitis and emphysema. When inhaled by pregnant women, it can retard the unborn child's growth and mental development and long-term exposure is suspected of aggravating hardening of the arteries and heart disease.

While it does not have any direct effects on the environment, carbon monoxide, oxidises to carbon dioxide, the gas most responsible for the greenhouse effect and consequent global warming.

## Nitrogen oxides

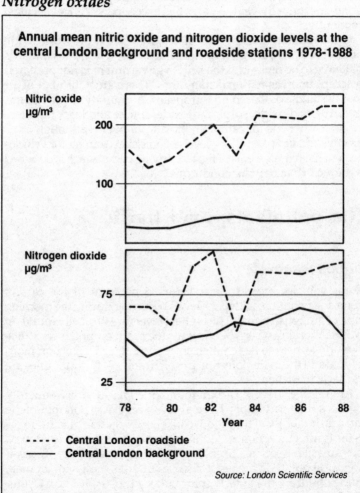

Annual mean nitric oxide and nitrogen dioxide levels at the central London background and roadside stations 1978-1988

Source: London Scientific Services

The principal nitrogen oxides are nitrogen dioxide and nitric oxide. Nitric oxide is not unhealthy in itself, but is converted into nitrogen dioxide in the atmosphere. Motor vehicles are the major source of nitrogen oxides in Britain, contributing overall some 45 per cent (75% in London), with power stations next at 35 per cent. The highest concentrations in Britain are found in London and the highest levels, close to the kerbside during the rush hours. A 1989 Friends of the Earth survey found London roadside levels above European Community limits and LSS monitoring shows that WHO guidelines are often breached. The health risks include increased susceptibility to viral infection, lung irritation and the exacerbation of bronchitis, pneumonia and asthma.

In Europe, nitrogen oxides are major contributors to the acid rain which is damaging soils, plant and water life and eroding buildings. They also react with other pollutants in strong sunlight to produce photochemical smog, a phenomenon which has plagued Los Angeles and which is now occurring, on a smaller scale, in London.

## Ozone

Ozone is a pollutant at ground level. It is a powerful oxidising agent and can react with many other substances, to produce both local and global deleterious effects. It is produced by the reaction of nitrogen oxides and hydrocarbons in strong sunlight and again motor vehicles are the major source, although power stations and industrial processes also contribute.

Ozone levels tend to peak in the afternoon, when the sun's intensity is at its greatest. Interestingly, rural areas can often show a higher ozone count, because of the time taken for the chemical reactions, while in towns high concentrations of nitric oxide effectively destroy it. High levels of ozone are often found in the suburbs and Home Counties (for example, in Teddington and Ascot.)

Dr Laxen says: 'Over the past years ozone levels in London have regularly exceeded recognised air quality standards during the Summer months. Vehicle emissions are going up and all the conditions are there to cause high levels in the future'. In July 1989, LSS recorded ozone levels in central London well above WHO recommendations. (See graph below.)

The government does now monitor, and publish, ozone levels, through a national network set up in 1988, but environmental groups

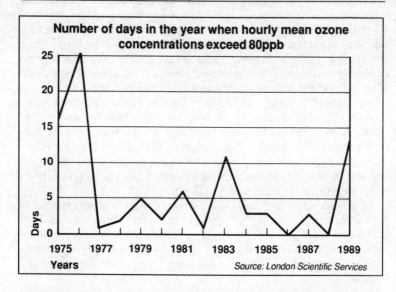

Number of days in the year when hourly mean ozone concentrations exceed 80ppb

Years

*Source: London Scientific Services*

like Friends of the Earth argue that there is a need for forecasts, so that those at greatest risk can have advance warning. In May 1989, for instance, the Dutch government warned of a possible ban on private cars following a week-long smog in eight provinces, and suggested that asthma patients should stay indoors. Fiona Weir, Friends of the Earth Air Pollution Campaigner said: 'People have a right to timely, accurate and easily understandable information to allow them to modify their behaviour to protect themselves'.

Ozone irritates the respiratory system, causing coughing, choking and impaired lung function, particularly during exercise. It aggravates chronic respiratory diseases like asthma and bronchitis and lowers resistance to respiratory infections, from colds and flu to pneumonia.

On the environmental front, ozone is a greenhouse gas contributing to global warming and it has been implicated in the widespread destruction of Europe's forests, seemingly through allowing key nutrients to be leached more easily from the leaves and, in conjunction with other pollutants, making trees less resistant to attack by infections and pests.

## *Hydrocarbons*

Hydrocarbons are a group of pollutants, both gases and solids, which result from the incomplete burning of fossil fuels - gas, coal and oil. Gaseous hydrocarbons react with nitrogen oxides in the formation of ozone (see above). Some of them are carcinogens and are carried by fine particles of soot deep into the lungs. The small particles themselves cause breathing problems, with diesel drivers particularly at risk, along with children, the elderly and those suffering from bronchitis, asthma, allergies and heart complaints.

Diesel engines are the main source of airborne particulates, – tiny black carbon particles. The diesel has traditionally been regarded as 'cleaner' than the petrol engine, because the fuel does not require lead additives and the engine generally pushes out less pollutant gases. But diesel engines produce ten times more particulates than petrol engines and 100 times more than petrol engines fitted with catalytic converters. Our diesel-driven buses, taxis and lorries are also responsible for more than half of all the black smoke found in London, with a highly visible effect on the buildings in the capital (diesel smoke has a soiling capacity three times greater than that of smoke from coal). The cost of cleaning up, at around £8 per square metre of wall, runs into millions. Dartford Tunnel's annual wash and brush up alone costs £370,000, while it is estimated that if all of central London's commercial facades were cleaned once every ten years, the yearly bill would be £24 million.

## Lead

Additives in petrol are the source of 80 per cent of the lead in London's air, but levels have halved since the introduction of low leaded petrol (Jan. 1986) and unleaded petrol. Ten per cent of the cars on London's roads could switch straight away to unleaded fuel without any adjustments, while a further 56 per cent could do so with a minor adjustment. (It is worth remembering, until unleaded petrol becomes universally available, that converted cars can also run on leaded fuel, although cars which are fitted with catalytic converters – see below – must run on lead-free petrol. From October 1990, all new cars have to be capable of running lead free). Despite the recent dramatic increase in unleaded outlets, by 1989 still only a small minority of British cars were running lead-free, compared with, for instance, more than half of those in Germany.

Lead is a poisonous heavy metal which accumulates in the body and even low levels in the environment can lead to problems like anaemia, high blood pressure and damage to the nervous system. Children are particularly at risk, even before they are born, as their mental development can be affected.

All the soil within a six-mile radius of Marble Arch is likely to be contaminated with lead and high levels in playground dusts are frequently recorded. Old lead paint is another important source and many education authorities have repainted all their schools with lead-free paint. Vegetables are also a source, and a survey of twenty London boroughs in 1984 found high-level contamination. The report, from the Association of London Chief Environmental Health Officers and the Institute of Public Analysts, found lettuce and blackberries particularly vulnerable and recommended that they should not be grown in inner London. They also recommended vigorous washing of leafy produce and the peeling of root crops. All new allotments should be screened for heavy metals.

# The pollutants: power stations, industry, traffic

## Sulphur dioxide

Although the levels of sulphur dioxide have been reduced by some 80 per cent in the last 25 years, it continues to be pumped into the atmosphere from power station chimneys. There has been a steady decline in levels since the mid-1960s and they are now well below the European Community limits in the capital, although WHO recommendations have been exceeded on a number of occasions. The closure of the inner city power stations, such as Battersea and Fulham, has been a major contributory factor, but there are still six power stations in the Thames Estuary, at Littlebrook, Northfleet, Kingsnorth, Grain, West Thurrock and Tilbury, pouring out the sulphurous gas. When the climatic conditions are right (or wrong) the station plumes are brought down onto London. In November 1988, for example, sulphur dioxide levels rose to nearly twice that recommended by the World Health Organisation to protect asthmatics and bronchitics. Much of it was borne on an easterly wind from the Thames Estuary stations, added to by sulphur from diesel exhausts.

High concentrations of sulphur dioxide can cause breathing problems and bronchitis and exacerbate asthma, while long-term exposure to lower levels increases both the incidence of heart/lung diseases and the death rates from them. The most serious health effects occur when the sulphur dioxide is present with high levels of airborne particulates. It is absorbed by the tiny particles and breathed deep into the lungs. Once there, the moist conditions lead to the formation of sulphuric acid. It was this deadly combination that is now counted as the major cause of the 4,000 extra deaths during the 1952 smog.

Plants are also seriously affected, either directly or indirectly, through the acidification of the soil. Sulphur dioxide is a major component of acid rain which causes the acidification of lakes and rivers over huge areas of the world and much of Europe, including Britain. (Technically, we should speak of acid deposition rather than acid rain, because both wet and dry deposition causes damage to the environment. The primary pollutant is sulphur dioxide, but nitrogen oxides, hydrocarbons, sulphates, nitrates and ozone all add to the problem.) At present, according to the National Society for Clean Air, Britain is the largest single emitter of sulphur dioxide (27 per cent of the total) in the European Community and probably the second largest emitter of nitrogen oxides.

A Friends of the Earth report, *Air Pollution and Health* in July 1989 noted: 'When acid rain falls in sensitive areas, it cannot be neutralised by the soil and quickly runs into streams and lakes, slowly turning them acidic and destroying aquatic life'. As well as valuable nutrients, toxic metals like aluminium are washed out of the soil and get into water supplies.

With prevailing westerly winds, sulphurous emissions from Britain's power stations generally move eastward across the continent and contribute significantly to the acid rain problems there, but even in Britain the effects can be seen in damage to water and wildlife. Many trees in rural Britain are now sickly because of pollution, while in the city they are even more threatened as their resistance to extremes of heat and cold, to fungi and insect pests, to poor drainage and damage by vandalism is lowered.

Sulphur dioxide has already driven most species of lichen (particularly sensitive to pollution) out of the capital, while the acidification of streams and ponds has reduced the numbers of natterjack toads and further pollution could see the common frog and certain water birds similarly affected.

Sulphur dioxide pollution also accelerates the corrosion of metal, stone and stained-glass windows, damaging London's ancient buildings, – Westminster Abbey, the Palace of Westminster and St. Paul's Cathedral among them. The dome of St Paul's has been dissolved over the past few years at a rate ten times greater than in the previous three centuries. As Friends of the Earth reported:

'Gravestone inscriptions become blurred in less than a decade. Stained glass deteriorates, marble loses its sheen in days of exposure to London air... Even indoor treasures are at risk. Marble sculptures in galleries at the Victoria and Albert Museum must be sealed in glass cases to prevent yellowing due to traffic pollution. Antique leather, textiles and, perhaps worst of all, irreplaceable documents stored in the capital's archives are subject to sulphur dioxide attack. Shakespeare's will, Guy Fawkes' confession, Cook's log, Nelson's last letter to Lady Hamilton .. all pages being slowly eaten out of Britain's history book by acid pollution.'

## Carbon dioxide

Global warming due to the 'greenhouse effect' is one of the greatest problems facing the world we live in. As the Prime Minister said in her famous 'Green' speech in 1988: 'We have unwittingly begun a massive experiment with the system of this planet itself.' Burning fossil fuels, cutting down vast areas of tropical forest and changing agricultural and industrial patterns have all contributed to an increase of 'greenhouse gases', of which carbon dioxide is

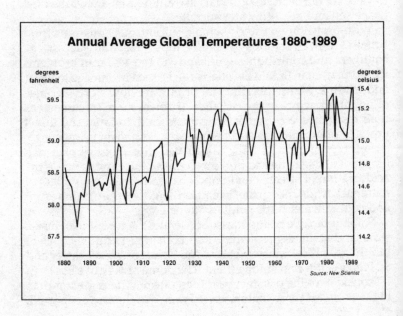

the most important. Another 30 or so, including methane, CFCs, nitrous oxide and ozone, also contribute.

These gases act like the glass in a greenhouse, letting in short-wave radiation from the sun, but blocking the long-wave radiation from the earth, leading to an increase in the temperature of the lower atmosphere. The concentrations of most of the greenhouse gases have been rising steadily for centuries, but particularly since the 1950s the rate has accelerated, notably for carbon dioxide. This is due mainly to the increased burning of fossil fuels like coal and oil and to the cutting down of millions of trees, which normally lower the carbon dioxide levels by converting it to oxygen in the natural process of photosynthesis.

No-one can accurately predict the consequences, but the best analyses suggest that within the next 40 to 60 years, unless we take some dramatic action, the levels of greenhouse gases will rise to an equivalent of double the pre-industrial level of carbon dioxide. That could mean a rise in average global temperatures of anything between 1.5 and 5.5 degrees centigrade, although again there is uncertainty, since we cannot be sure of the effects of 'feedback' – changes in cloud cover, snow and water vapour, for instance – which might alter rates of production and absorption of greenhouse gases. And climatic change does not proceed in a straight line, but rather in a series of undulations. As far as we can tell, the average global temperature has risen by about half a degree centigrade since the middle of the 19th century, although not continuously: there was a cool period between 1940 and 1965, but since the late 1970s there has been a rapid warming, with the five hottest years so far this century occurring since 1980. These changes fall well within the range of past fluctuations and may be mere undulations in the graph, but equally they could be early evidence that the predicted increase in global warming is beginning to be seen.

A global temperature rise to the levels predicted for the next half century would have profound consequences, for the climate, for agriculture and for plant and animal life. We could expect more drought in some areas, perhaps more fertility elsewhere. Some species of plants and animals would be destroyed, unable to cope with major changes in their habitat and the whole delicate inter-relationship between living things in the world would be in jeopardy.

We can also expect sea levels to rise, although again there is uncertainty about the extent. The current 'best estimate' suggests a rise of about twenty centimetres by the year 2030. This would have devastating effects on cities and towns, agriculture and industry in the low-lying areas of the world. In Britain we will need to re-examine our sea defences and the effectiveness of the Thames Barrier has to be re-assessed. Dr Mike Kelly from the Climatic Research Unit at the University of East Anglia reported in October 1989 – 'If those responsible for planning the barrier had had the information concerning the threat posed by global warming that is available today, they would undoubtedly have specified a higher design level. The Thames Water Authority has recognized the problem and is considering its implications. Modifications of the barrier will however take many years. In the interim, it would be advisable to re-examine emergency measures in the event of flooding, considered by many to be redundant since the building of the barrier'.

It is the unceasing demand for energy that makes the biggest contribution to the greenhouse effect. Britain's power stations, burning oil and coal to produce electricity, pump out no fewer than 233 million tonnes of carbon dioxide every year, more than one third of the total production of this gas. Yet often much of the energy produced is wasted. Industry has financial incentives, of course, to be energy-efficient, but in our homes, where one third of the electricity is used, our electrical appliances are often woefully inefficient and our heat insulation systems chillingly inadequate. The most energy-efficient refrigerators, washing machines, cookers and so on use half the electricity to do the same job as the least efficient, saving each owner money as well as making a significant contribution to reducing carbon dioxide emissions from power stations (and sulphur dioxide and nitrogen oxides as well). The technology exists now to reduce electricity demand in Britain by as much as 70 per cent in the next fifteen to twenty years, while maintaining (or even improving) the quality of services.

Yet we have no minimum standards on the efficiency of appliances and no system of 'energy labelling' to enable us to choose between them. In the United States, they have had such energy labelling on a range of appliances for years and new federal laws are now coming into force insisting on minimum efficiency standards. These laws mean that some 70 to 90 per cent of the models in the shops in 1986 would be outlawed. The regulations will come fully into force by 1992 and by the turn of the century they will result in the saving of the output of 22 1000-kilowatt power stations. By 2010, the reduction in carbon dioxide emission should be some 70 million tonnes a year.

Over and above the output from power stations, our cars, vans and lorries make a significant contribution to the greenhouse effects: around fifteen per cent of global carbon dioxide production. One litre of petrol in a car produces 2.5 kilos of carbon dioxide and the total from all vehicles in Britain in 1985 was four and a half million tonnes. It is continuing to rise.

# The pollutants: industry and everyday life

## CFCs and the ozone layer

As we have seen, ozone is a pollutant at ground level and in the lower atmosphere. Yet in the upper atmosphere – some 20 to 30 kilometres high – it is vital to give us protection from the harmful ultraviolet radiation from the sun. Ozone is present only in very small amounts but this absorbs some 99 per cent of the ultraviolet radiation. Now it is thinning at a dangerous rate. Ozone levels have already gone down by three per cent over some of the most densely populated parts of Europe and each year since the 1970s a 'hole' has appeared over Antarctica. It is as big as the United States and recently has been seen to move for a short period over populated areas of Australia. No-one knows why this hole has formed so quickly, but were similar reductions in ozone to occur over Europe, there would be a dramatic rise in exposure to ultraviolet radiation.

The most obvious effects would be a large rise in skin cancer cases: for every one per cent drop in ozone there is likely to be a one to three per cent increase in them. Ultimately, cases could run into millions and deaths into tens of thousands. Other effects include an increase in eye problems such as cataracts, damage to agricultural crops and marine life and an increase in photochemical smog in cities like London and Los Angeles.

All the evidence suggests that the principle culprits in the ozone-depletion process are chlorofluorocarbons, CFCs, gases used in a wide variety of processes, but notably as aerosol propellants, 'blowing agents' in foam packaging and as refrigeration agents.

When CFCs are released into the atmosphere, as hundreds of thousands of tonnes already have been, they can remain there for

100 years or more and they eventually release chlorine, which has a hugely devastating effect on ozone: one molecule of chlorine may wipe out 100,000 ozone molecules. It may be hard to believe that so simple (and convenient) an act as using an aerosol spray could have so fundamental an effect, but when you consider that some 800 million aerosols are used in Britain alone each year, to say nothing of CFCs used in fridges, freezers and in industry, it is easier to envisage the cumulative effect. CFCs are also greenhouse gases, helping to trap heat and prevent its escape.

International action has already been taken. In 1987, 38 countries including the United Kingdom signed an agreement to cut CFC production by 50 per cent by 1999, but many environmentalists say this is both too little and too late and are pressing for drastic action, with the aim of a total phase-out by 1995.

But while current legislation and proposed international action may not be tough enough, the public, alerted to the dangers by campaigns from organisations like Friends of the Earth, has already begun in large measure to take action itself, by refusing to buy aerosols containing CFCs. And manufacturers and retailers, quick to see commercial disadvantage in continuing their production and sale, switched rapidly to aerosols containing other propellants or even to re-presenting their products in non-aerosol forms. (We had planned, as with lead-free petrol, to include lists of CFC-free products and outlets in London, but again their wide availability has now made such listings out-of-date and unnecessary.) Similarly, most fast-food chains have agreed to replace their burger boxes with cartons which do not use CFCs. Many local councils, businesses and industry have also banned the use of CFCs in the products they buy.

Problems still remain, however, notably in refrigeration. CFCs have two uses in fridges and freezers, as the coolant in the sealed refrigeration system and as blowing agents in the foam insulation in walls and doors. There are no alternative refrigerants on the market at the moment for domestic appliances, but new fridges and freezers are now available with a 50 per cent reduction in the CFCs used in the foam walls.

But what about old fridges and freezers, the vast majority of which use CFCs? It is estimated that some 30,000 tonnes of CFC refrigerant is 'trapped' in equipment in Britain, fifteen per cent in the 30 million or so domestic fridges and freezers. When these are dumped and destroyed, the CFCs, from both the sealed refrigeration unit and the foam insulation, escape into the atmosphere.

Companies are increasingly offering to collect old appliances when new ones are bought and to remove the refrigerant safely and recycle it, and a number of local councils (although by no means enough) also now remove CFCs from old fridges at their civic amenity sites. The sites where these facilities are available in London are given in The Green Guide to Recycling section of this book, pp225-252. Unfortunately there is no system in Britain yet for recovering and disposing safely of the CFCs in fridge walls, although research is being undertaken into techniques of crushing the foam to a powder and releasing the CFCs into a gas-tight space.

# Ideas for action

Clearly much needs to be done to reduce and, where possible, to eliminate pollutants in London's air. While they are less visible than the smogs of earlier years, they are still having an adverse effect on our health and even more profound effects on the wider environment. Much can be achieved through tougher legislation and regulation, but much is also in the hands of all of us, as individuals. Some ideas for action are outlined below. Where national or international action is needed, we suggest you write to and lobby your MP and local councillors and join an environmental pressure group. Individual action is something you and your family can take every day.

## *Legislation, regulation and official action:*

The Government should:

*   Adopt World Health Organisation guidelines for air quality as statutory standards and press the European Community to tighten their limits in line with those WHO guidelines.

*   Apply higher standards to sulphur dioxide emissions, particularly from power stations, and insist on 'clean flue technology' to clean up these and other emissions before they leave the chimneys.

*   Set up national monitoring networks for carbon monoxide and hydrocarbons.

*   Issue alerts when air pollution levels could cause significant

problems, especially for the twenty per cent who are particularly vulnerable, and give local authorities powers to reduce levels by closing factories and controlling vehicles during pollution episodes.

* Fund more research into the greenhouse effect and global warming, make a national and international commitment to significant reductions in carbon dioxide production.

* Help Third World countries to invest in energy-efficient technologies and reforestation.

* Tax cars according to their fuel consumption and/or energy efficiency. Remove tax subsidies on company cars. Insist on tough new exhaust emission standards (see below).

* Introduce minimum standards for energy-efficient appliances and a statutory system of energy labelling.

* Invest in an efficient public transport system to reduce the number of cars, especially in London (See Capital Issues: Traffic and Roads, pp 9-28)

* Insist on stricter standards for diesel emissions and police them more effectively with on-the-spot fines.

(The government is already considering some strict new pollution measures and among the ideas under discussion are heavier duties on electricity and gas to encourage energy saving, dearer Road Fund Licences, tied to engine size and fuel consumption, toll payments for the most heavily-used city roads and new regulations on exhaust emissions (see below).)

## Individual action

Thanks to action by the European Parliament, which toughened up proposals from the Commission, new European vehicle emission standards have been drawn up which mean that from 1992 all new cars will have to be fitted with three-way catalytic converters which, incorporated in exhausts, cut carbon monoxide, nitrogen oxides and hydrocarbons. These catalytic converters are currently only available in a limited number of models in Britain, but are likely to become more widespread ahead of the legislation. Manufacturers are also working on 'lean burn' engines which reduce pollutants by burning fuel more efficiently, although at present they cannot meet European standards.

But clean car technology is by no means the complete answer: in the United States, where catalytic converters have been in use since the early 1970s, air quality standards cannot be met in some areas because of the sheer quantity of vehicles. With road traffic continuing to increase over here, and reaching saturation point in much of London (see Capital Issues: traffic and roads, pp 9-28) the benefits of clean car technology and tough regulation could easily be overtaken by the sheer volume of traffic. And at present, although smaller, more efficient and better maintained cars will help a little, there is no technical solution to the carbon dioxide problem, except fewer cars and fewer journeys.

## *What you can do:*

* If you have a car, use it for essential journeys only and use public transport, a bicycle or your feet when you can – and campaign for better public transport.

* Choose a car that runs off unleaded petrol and convert your old one if possible. Buy a new car with a three-way catalytic converter if you can. Make fuel consumption a top priority in your choice of new car.

* Press your council for better air pollution monitoring and controls in your borough (see Borough Guides, pp 81-168, for who's doing what).

* Find out (from the brochures if you can, or the retailer or manufacturer) about the energy efficiency of new electrical appliances you buy. The Consumer Association's magazine Which? now makes comparisons in its surveys. Push for energy labelling.

* Buy CFC-free products wherever possible (and remember that CFC-free aerosols may be labelled 'ozone-friendly', but contain other ozone-depleting chemicals. Also, aerosols cannot be recycled and use a lot of energy in their production  Avoid foamed packaging and insulation materials.

* Insist on manufacturers or retailers agreeing to take back old fridges and freezers and remove CFCs. Alternatively take them to civic amenity sites for safe disposal and recycling. Push for more such sites.

## *Contact addresses*

Department of the Environment
2 Marsham Street
London SW1P 3EB
(071) 276 0990

Department of Transport
2 Marsham Street
London SW1P 3EB
(071) 276 3000

Friends of the Earth
26-28 Underwood Street
London N1 7JQ
(071) 490 1555

Greenpeace
30 Islington Green
London N1 8XE
(071) 354 5100

National Society for Clean Air
136 North Street
Brighton BN1 1RG
(0273) 26313

London Scientific Services
Air Pollution Group
Great Guildford House
30 Great Guildford Street
London SE1 0ES
(081) 962 9884

Campaign for Lead Free Air (CLEAR)
3 Endsleigh Street
London WC1H 0DD
(071) 278 9686

**For pollution complaints, your first port of call should be the Environmental Health Department of your local council.** Addresses and contact telephone numbers are given in the Boroughs section of the guide: pp 81-168.

## Useful publications:

*New Car Fuel Consumption: the official figures. Use of Unleaded Petrol: advisory information*, from the Department of Transport.

Also: *Fuel Saving*, from Department of Transport Publicity Stores, Building No.3, Victoria Road, South Ruislip, Middlesex HA4 0NZ.

Information leaflets on the *Greenhouse Effect, Acid Rain, Motor Vehicle Pollution*, *Air Pollution (Know Your Rights)*, *Lead*, etc., etc. from the National Society for Clean Air.

Information, publications on the greenhouse effect and other global environmental issues from Greenpeace.

London Air Pollution Monitoring Network: annual summaries of results, from London Scientific Services.

*Air Pollution and Health, Particulate Pollution from Diesel Vehicles, Alternatives to CFCs* and numerous other publications on local pollution, motoring and the environment, disposal of fridges/freezers with CFCs, lead etc., from Friends of the Earth.

# Noise pollution

Noise, whether from heavy traffic, motorbikes, pneumatic drills, construction sites, barking dogs or simply noisy neighbours, is always with us. And it is on the increase, especially in cities like London. Indeed, at times in the last year or so it seems that they have been digging up and reconstructing on every other street corner in the centre of the city, with gas, water and electricity authorities excavating the roads and office building continuing apace.

Unwanted noise **is** an environmental pollutant and it certainly adds to the stresses and strains of living in the city. So what can be done to minimise or control it, to make our neighbourhoods more peaceful places in which to live?

The National Society for Clean Air has produced an excellent information leaflet setting out the legal and regulatory frameworks by which national and local government seeks to control noise and the actions which individuals, disturbed by excessive and unreasonable noise, may take under the law. The leaflet is available from the address below. Here are a few salient points from it.

## Noise Abatement Zones:

Under the Control of Pollution Act 1974 a local council may designate all or part of its area as a Noise Abatement Zone (NAZ) for the long-term control of noise in specified premises, which may be factories and commercial premises and, occasionally, domestic buildings. Noise limits are set and monitored by local authority Environmental Health Officers and a register kept for public inspection. You can seek a reduction in those noise levels if it can be shown to be in the public interest and can be achieved at reasonable cost.

### CONSTRUCTION SITES, ROADWORKS:

'Such operations are inherently noisy,' says the NSCA, 'and often take place in areas which are quiet beforehand and which will be expected to be quiet again after the work has ceased.' Again the Control of Pollution Act gives local authorities powers to set noise levels and control times of working. You can still complain about noise nuisance even within these constraints.

### NOISE IN THE NEIGHBOURHOOD:

Loud music, barking dogs, lawnmowers, burglar alarms, noisy parties, domestic appliances, continual family rows – all contribute to noise from neighbours, and they lead to a large number of complaints to Environmental Health Departments every year, more than 55,000 in England and Wales alone. The best approach to noisy neighbours is a quiet word, but if they fail to respond then a complaint can be made to the local Environmental Health Department, who again will try the reasonable argument approach first. Some local authorities run 'noisy party patrols' at weekends, with a 'hotline' number for complainants to ring.

If the nuisance continues, the local authority may issue an Abatement Notice and if an offender fails to comply with that, proceedings can be taken in the Magistrate's Court, or the local authority may seek an injunction in the High Court.

Local authorities also have the power to deal with noise from fixed premises (including places of entertainment, pubs, discos, etc.) if they consider that the noise amounts to a statutory nuisance.

For all neighbourhood noise nuisance, it is also possible for individuals to complain directly to the Magistrates Court (under

Section 59 of the Control of Pollution Act), or you can take civil action under common law if you can show that the noise nuisance substantially affects your health, comfort and convenience. It has to be said that going to law, either through the council or on your own, is a difficult process, not least in gathering satisfactory evidence, and taking civil action can be expensive: you will need proper legal advice. If you win your case, you may obtain an injunction to stop the noise and, possibly, claim damages. Interestingly, civil action differs from magistrates' proceedings in that the judgement is made on how the noise affects other people and for the offender to plead that the 'best practical means' have been taken to reduce the noise is no defence.

As well as the Control of Pollution Act, local authority bye-laws are often used to restrict noise nuisance, for example: noisy conduct at night, noisy animals, loud music, noisy television, radios and record players and noisy street traders.

Many noise difficulties arise not only from the inconsiderate behaviour of others, but because of poor sound insulation, notably in blocks of flats and converted houses. Higher standards of noise regulation are required to lessen these problems. It is encouraging that a number of London local authorities have begun to undertake extra noise insulation in the council flats and houses they own.

## TRAFFIC NOISE

As well as being the most widespread source of noise nuisance, traffic noise is one of the most difficult to control. It does upset a lot of people: one survey found that 23 per cent of people were 'bothered' by it, and eight per cent were 'seriously bothered.' The Motor Vehicle (Construction and Use) Regulations control noise levels, insisting on an efficient exhaust silencer, as well as general requirements for road users not to make excessive noise. Under the Road Traffic Act of 1972, horns may not be sounded in restricted roads between 11pm and 7am and should never be used when the vehicle is stationary, unless there is a danger to another moving vehicle. Offences should be reported to the police. Again, it has to be said that providing the evidence for a satisfactory prosecution is difficult and the best first approach remains the quiet word.

For general traffic noise, it is generally poor planning and the sheer volume of traffic that create the problems and there is no short-term solution. You must press your local authority for road closing, traffic diversion and 'traffic calming' measures. (See also

Capital Issues: Traffic and Roads, pp 9-28).

People living alongside new or improved roads may obtain noise insulation grants, covering double glazing on the roadside facade, if the traffic is causing excessive noise. If your property depreciates in value because of noise from road construction or alterations, you may be entitled to compensation.

## AIRPORTS, AIRCRAFT AND RAILWAYS:

If you live near an airport and are severely affected by noise, you may be eligible for a grant to insulate your home. Noise control at airports is the direct responsibility of the Department of Transport, to whom complaints about take-offs and landings should be addressed. Alternatively you can ring the airport switchboard and they will pass the complaint on.

Railway noise seems to promote few complaints, although many people now have big worries about the noise from the proposed Channel Tunnel rail links. Complaints should be made to the British Railways Board.

## Contact addresses:

Department of the Environment
2 Marsham Street
London SW1P 3EB
(071) 276 0990

Department of Transport
2 Marsham Street
London SW1P 3EB
(071) 276 3000
Airport and aircraft noise: CAP 5 Division. 24 hour answering service for complaints: (071) 7172/3

National Society for Clean Air
136 North Street
Brighton BN1 1RG
(0273) 26313

British Railways Board
Rail House
Euston Square
London NW1 2DZ
(071) 262 3232
Noise complaints to the Director of Public Affairs.

For local noise complaints, first contact your council Environmental Health Department (Council addresses on Boroughs section, pp 81-168); for complaints about individual vehicles, contact the local police.

## Useful publications:

*Noise Pollution,* information leaflet from the National Society for Clean Air.

*Insulation Against Traffic Noise, Land Compensation – Your Right Explained* and *Your Home and Nuisance from Public Development,* all free from the Department of the Environment, or from council offices and Citizens' Advice Bureaux.

# HOW GREEN IS
# YOUR COUNCIL?

# HOW GREEN IS YOUR COUNCIL?

In the first ever comprehensive survey of the attitudes and actions of London boroughs on environmental issues, *The Green Guide to London* asked every council a series of searching questions about their 'green' policies and practices. Every borough replied, many of them taking a great deal of time and care in detailing their response. We would like to record our sincere thanks to all the council officers who took such trouble.

Our survey revealed wide differences in approach, from the councils with well-defined and integrated environmental strategies, who had been pursuing policies to conserve, maintain and improve their areas for a number of years; to those whose policies had been somewhat piecemeal in the past, but who were now formulating new plans and beginning to put them into action; to those who, while undertaking their statutory duties, appeared to give little priority to environmental matters.

The latter half of 1989 saw in local government, as elsewhere, an upsurge in interest in the environment, spurred by public opinion and concern. The publication of Friends of the Earth's *Environmental Charter for Local Government*, with nearly 200 practical recommendations for local authority action, provided a fresh focus for a reappraisal of councils' policies, and the Association of London Authorities also launched an *Environmental Charter for London*, with similar aims of improving the quality of life in the capital and minimising damage to the national and global environment.

In a small way, our own questionnaire proved useful too: several councils used it as a basis for assessing and drawing together the current efforts and future plans of their various departments and directorates.

Later in this chapter we publish the details of the councils' responses, so that you can find out just what your local authority is doing (or not doing) as well as comparing it with the efforts of others, but first there is a general assessment and comparison of the environmental activities of the 33 London boroughs.

# The questions we asked:

We asked nine questions on various aspects of local authority activities:

1.  Does the council have an overall policy on environmental issues?

2.  How is that policy implemented with direct regard to the council's 'in-house' activities? We gave examples of the sort of activities we had in mind: energy-saving in council offices and schools, the use of recycled paper, the purchase of environmentally-sensitive cleaning and other products, control of pesticides in parks, and so on.

3.  In its general planning, how is the council involved in improving the overall environment? We took planning controls, conservation areas, pedestrianisation, traffic-taming and tree-planting as examples.

4.  What is the council policy and practice in the preservation, enhancement and creation of green and open spaces within the borough? We asked if green space was under threat, and for specific examples. We asked about the creation of new open space and work with local voluntary groups.

5.  Is the council able to control or exert influence on air and water pollution in the borough? We asked for examples.

6.  What steps can, and does, the council take on noise pollution and nuisance? We asked about noise nuisance from commercial premises and from individuals, about action on noisy neighbours and whether the council had 'noisy party' patrols.

7.  What are the council policies and practices with regard to waste disposal, rubbish collection, street cleansing and sweeping? We wanted to know about specific waste disposal problems and the council's action to tackle them, about action on litter and street cleanliness, including measures to try to control the mess made by dogs and about the success (or otherwise) in policing and enforcing local bye-laws.

8.  What facilities do the council make available for recycling? We asked about current activities and future plans.

9.  Any other council activities to improve the environment,

worthy of note? We gave as examples educational programmes and support for local groups.

The responses to those questions, we felt, would give a very fair indication about just how seriously a council was taking environmental matters and how much effort and resources it was putting in tackling the problems. We made it very clear that we were aware that boroughs would vary greatly in their intrinsic natural amenities and in the historical legacy of the structure of their society, their buildings and so on. It was not our intention to make subjective comparisons between amenities per se, but rather to assess the council's efforts and activities to improve the environment that they had inherited.

In the assessments and comparisons below, it is effort and resource allocation that count for most, rather than direct success to tackle problems that may be intransigent and long-term. On street cleaning, for example, it is clear that an inner city borough, like Westminster, faces extra problems in trying to keep its streets clean, because of the daily influx of millions of commuters and tourists. And Tower Hamlets faces special problems because of Docklands development. It is clear, too, that many London councils face severe financial difficulties, particularly those that are 'rate-capped', but we wanted to gauge just how much priority they were truly giving to environmental issues, among the many other calls on their limited resources.

# YOUR COUNCIL SURVEYED

## BARKING AND DAGENHAM

*Does the council have an overall policy on environmental issues?*
Barking and Dagenham is adopting a policy on global environmental issues, promoting technologies which cause little or no pollution and are economical in the use of natural resources. The council plans further action on lead-free petrol, CFCs, tropical hardwooods and recycled paper.

*How is that policy implemented with direct regard to the council's 'in-house' activities?*
Energy-saving programmes implemented in public buildings. Recycled paper used for all committee agendas and for printing

and photocopying where possible.

Phased programme introduced for lead-free fuel for vehicles. Use of organophosphate and carbamate pesticides halted, switch to environment-friendly pyrethroids.

*In its general planning, how is the council involved in improving the overall environment?*

Introduced major tree-planting programme; supports 'urban forest fringe' concept to be implemented by the Countryside Commission and Forestry Commission.

Supports and funds development of nature reserve at Eastbrookend, Dagenham.

Plans improvements at all shopping parades: details under consideration.

Plans pedestrianisation at Barking Town Centre, as well as new street furniture and tree-planting. Supports London-wide lorry bans and has introduced local lorry bans, particularly in Becontree and Chadwell Heath areas. Plans borough-wide crackdown on fly-tipping.

*What is the council policy and practice in the preservation, enhancement and creation of green and open spaces?*

Borough well-provided with green space. (Much of area purpose-built in 1930s to include amenity greens, parks etc.) Council resists development or removal of amenity greens, other than environmental improvements through provision of off-street parking space. New open space developed and landscaped at Leys, Dagenham East; country park to be developed at Eastbrookend, Dagenham.

Works closely with London Wildlife Trust, Dagenham Corridor Association, Friends of the Earth.

*Is the council able to control or exert influence on air and water pollution in the borough?*

At forefront in monitoring air pollution. Participates in London Scientific Services air and noise pollution monitoring network with permanent monitoring sites in borough. Health and Consumer Services Department monitors food, air, earth and water pollution. Recently taken action against Thames Water for nuisance from Beckton Sewage Works.

*What steps can, and does, the council take on noise pollution and nuisance?*

No 'party noise' patrol, but noise pollution monitored where possible and strong assistance provided to residents disturbed by new developments etc. Assists with noisy neighbours, asking complainants to keep careful record of noise problems. Produces leaflets and information on noise problems and control.

*What are the council's policies and practices with regard to waste disposal, rubbish collection and street cleaning?*
Council 'fighting a continual battle against minority of residents who drop litter.' New waste collection systems in high-density estates, using Eurobins and other bulk refuse collection systems. New improvements in road sweeping recently introduced: sweeping daily in residential streets, (including weekends) at local shopping parades, and continuously (including evenings) at major shopping areas. Much activity on dog-fouling: bye-laws on footpaths and verges and on parks and open spaces (£100 maximum fine). 'Poop bins' in parks and open spaces. Canine Control Subcommittee plans further action.

*What facilities do the council make available for recycling?*
Bottle banks and paper banks in operation – more to be set up later. Frizlands Lane Waste Disposal Site also includes facilities for waste oil and scrap metal recycling. (For sites, see The Green Guide to Recycling section.)

*Any other council activities to improve the environment?*
Education packs on litter for schools (paid for from bottle bank income).
Barking Reach Riverside Development plans for major new green open space, with wetlands and nature reserve areas.
Grant aid to Wellgate and Thameside community farms.
Renovation of council housing and grants for pre-1919 privately-owned housing to improve basic amenities. (Number of properties lacking these reduced from 1272 in 1979 to 325 by 1986.)

*COUNCIL CONTACTS:*
London Borough of Barking and Dagenham
Civic Centre
Dagenham
Essex RM10 7BN
(081) 592 4500
Public Relations: Ext.2106/8
Cleansing Dept.: Recycling: Mr Mirams

*Green star rating:* ★★★

# BARNET

*Does the council have an overall policy on environmental issues?*
Barnet does not have a specific 'environmental charter' but its various departments, notably Environmental Health, 'respond to numerous day-to-day problems affecting the environment.' The main aim of the Borough Development Plan are to make the area an attractive place in which to live, to improve the quality of life and protect the open views, wildlife habitats and recreational facilities.

*How is that policy implemented with direct regard to the council's 'in-house' activities.*
Energy Saving Unit: rolling programme of updating school heating systems, new heat and power system at main swimming pool complex. New purchasing policy on CFC-free aerosols. Actively supporting use of lead free petrol, considering ways of adapting its own fleet. Seeking to control pesticides in council parks and gardens.

*In its general planning, how is the council involved in improving the overall environment?*
Through general planning controls, with comments and advice from Environmental Health Department. Conservation areas, local nature reserves and countryside management schemes set up. Tree-preservation, landscaping, traffic management policies and schemes.

*What is the council policy and practice in the preservation, enhancement and creation of green and open spaces?*
Green and open spaces are under threat from development in the borough, but the council's policy is to protect open space, especially Metropolitan Open Land and in the Green Belt. Some new open spaces have been created and others made more accessible.

*Is the council able to control or exert influence on air and water pollution in the borough?*
Complaints investigated, air and water monitored, statutory action taken where necessary. No major industrial premises causing air pollution. Close liaison with Thames Water Authority to minimise watercourse pollution.

*What steps can, and does, the council take on noise pollution and nuisance?*
Actively responds to complaints of noise from commercial prem-

ises, construction sites, noisy neighbours, open-air pop concerts and discotheques. Takes statutory action where necessary. No 'noisy party' patrol but has 'positive procedure' on acid house parties. Recent successful action in obtaining an ex parte injunction to prevent and stop such events.

*What are the council's policies and practices with regard to waste disposal, rubbish collection and street cleaning?*
Strives to deal with ever-present problem of fly-tipping.

*What facilities do the council make available for recycling?*
Two civic amenity sites at Brent Cross and Finchley. Bottle banks around the borough.

*Any other council activities to improve the environment?*
Number of educational initiatives, including investigation into CFCs, lead in soil, leptospirosis and water sports. Dump campaign for safe disposal of medicines.

> COUNCIL CONTACTS:
> London Borough of Barnet
> Town Hall
> The Borroughs
> London NW4 4BG
> (081) 202 8282
> Technical services: (081) 446 8511

**Green star rating: ★★**

## BEXLEY

*Does the council have an overall policy on environmental issues?*
Bexley has **no** specific overall environmental policy. However, a working party has been set up. In the meantime guidelines are given in a series of policy documents relating to specific service areas.

*How is that policy implemented with direct regard to the council's 'in-house' activities?*
The working party will be examining Bexley's purchasing policies over a wide range of environmentally sensitive goods. Some energy saving takes place in council buildings and there are moves to convert vehicles to lead-free petrol.

*In its general planning, how is the council involved in improving the*

*overall environment?*
Environmental consideration forms a key part of the development control process. Conservation areas have been designated and plans made to pedestrianise the main shopping area. A major tree-planting programme is underway and Bexley operates a 'free trees' scheme for local residents.

*What is the council policy and practice in the preservation, enhancement and creation of green and open spaces within the borough?*
Planning is underway to establish nature reserves in parks, more playing fields and a Country Park. In conjunction with local businesses and communities, the council is using £250,000 per annum to improve and enhance both open spaces and shopping/commercial areas.

*Is the council able to control or exert influence on air and water pollution in the borough?*
Pollution levels are monitored in industrial areas of the Borough. Both statutory powers and voluntary agreements are used. Council works closely with residents in Belvedere to monitor air pollution.

*What steps can, and does, the council take on noise pollution and nuisance?*
Statutory powers and voluntary agreements are used to combat major noise problems in industrial/commercial premises. Advice and support is given to residents to combat domestic noise problems.

*What are the council policies and practices with regard to waste disposal, rubbish collection, street cleaning?*
Waste is 'land-filled' in Kent. All waste disposal plans are under review. Concerted efforts are being made in street cleaning, particularly in shopping areas. A 'litter line' provides a prompt response to complaints about litter and fly-tipping.

*What facilities do the council make available for recycling?*
Two civic amenity sites take glass, paper, oil and rags. Co-operation with voluntary groups to promote recycling activities. (See The Green Guide to Recycling section.)

*Any other council activities to improve the environment?*
Support given to voluntary groups in several initiatives to collect and recycle materials. A special litter patrol was run in the main shopping area in conjunction with local police, school children

and a fast food shop. A free graffiti-removal service is be launched early 1990.

COUNCIL CONTACTS:
London Borough of Bexley
Bexley Civic Offices
Broadway
Bexleyheath
Kent DA6 7LB
(081) 303 7777

**Green star rating: ★**

# BRENT

*Does the council have an overall policy on environmental issues?*
Brent has drawn up a new Environmental Strategy, including an Environment Review for all council committees on current state of local environment, and launched Environment Action Plan for comprehensive improvements and protection. Council seeking active partnership with community, businesses, voluntary groups. Current Planning Policy statements also take environmental and conservation improvements into consideration.

*How is that policy implemented with direct regard to the council's 'in-house' activities?*
Energy Conservation Section's rolling programme saves council some £2 million a year. Includes combined heat and power schemes at Vale Farm and Willesden Sports Centre and, shortly, at Brent Town Hall. Electricity generated from waste heat. Waste incineration and heat recovery unit being installed at Chalk Hill.
Energy management systems developed for many council buildings, including Mahatma Ghandi Houses and schools, to optimise efficiency. Energy monitoring systems in 40 council buildings. Converting all 300 council vehicles to lead-free petrol.
Not purchasing CFC aerosols and other products unless absolutely necessary. Low-energy light bulbs and street light bulbs being tried in certain areas. All paper towels made from recycled paper. Other recycled products used wherever feasible.
London Ecology Unit advising on suitable pesticides for parks and gardens.

*In its general planning, how is the council involved in improving the*

*overall environment?*
Ten conservation areas designated, 157 listed buildings. Other buildings and groups identified on Local List and subject to stricter planning controls. Built-up environmental quality influenced and controlled through Town and Country Planning Acts and through grants in Commercial and Industrial Improvement areas.

*What is the council policy and practice in the preservation, enhancement and creation of green and open spaces?*
Few large areas of open land. Those remaining, including public open space, under redevelopment threat. Some significant areas (Welsh Harp, Fryent Country Park, Riverside Open Space at Tokyngton, and Northwick Park) designated Metropolitan Open Land.
Riverside open space system links open spaces along River Brent and landscape and enhancement schemes inaugurated along Grand Union Canal.
Several new open spaces created, though generally less than an acre in size.
Council works with local environmental groups, notably at and around Welsh Harp reservoir (170 acres) and Fryent Country Park (250 acres).
Major tree-planting programme in hand following 1987 hurricane.
Tree Preservation Order surveys under way.

*Is the council able to control or exert influence on air and water pollution in the borough?*
Entire borough covered by Smoke Control Orders. Smoke and sulphur dioxide levels monitored at various sites to check air quality. Levels of 32 heavy metals monitored at four further sites. Council led field nationally in campaign against lead in petrol, surveying blood lead levels in almost entire school population.
Nitrogen dioxide, from vehicle exhausts, monitored, and council participates in London-wide monitoring programme of other air pollutants.
Council has responsibility to 'ensure wholesomeness and sufficiency' of water supplies: liaises with water and river authorities. Investigates pollution incidents in River Brent and Wealdstone Brook.
Comprehensive asbestos removal programme for council properties.

*What steps can, and does, the council take on noise pollution and nuisance?*

Late night 'noise patrol' on Saturday nights. Traffic and railway noise cause considerable disturbance: all planning applications for housing near busy roads and railways monitored, conditions imposed to minimise impact and improve insulation.

Wembley Stadium and Arena cause considerable noise for nearby residents: noise monitored and control measures introduced.

Complaints of noise investigated and statutory action taken where necessary.

*What are the council's policies and practices with regard to waste disposal, rubbish collection and street cleaning?*

Brent suffers widespread rubbish and litter problems. In shopping areas, many other streets and open spaces, rubbish, dog-fouling, fly-tipping and abandoned cars are all too evident. Lack of resources hampers council action.

Reorganised refuse collection and street cleaning services suffered teething troubles and significant improvements expected soon. Special, charged, collection service for bulky items like cookers, beds, garden refuse. Sponsored litter bin and clean-up campaign launched.

Illegal large lorry-tipping prosecuted, where possible, through London Waste Regulatory Authority. Domestic tipping and unauthorised trade refuse dumping to be tackled by six temporary Enforcement Officers.

Pavement notices on dog fouling but insufficient resources to mount campaign.

Education and publicity anti-litter campaigns launched.

*What facilities do the council make available for recycling?*

Civic amenity and recycling centre for cans, bottles, paper, cardboard, oil, silver foil and waste metals at Alperton Depot. Paper-saving igloos re-cycling and aluminium foil collection schemes in operation. (See The Green Guide to Recycling).

*Any other council activities to improve the environment?*

Wide range of projects carried out as part of Inner Areas Programme: new open space and play area at Dudden Hill Lane, Willesden. Paddington Cemetery opened up for greater community use, works carried out by London Wildlife Trust to promote conservation use. Dog-free play area in South Kilburn. Activity Centre and 'Commando Course' for older children in Chalk Hill.

Schools environment projects.

Working with London Wildlife Trust to provide and improve new habitats and open spaces: e.g. Neasden Grange Wildlife Garden.

Working with community groups, e.g. Streatley Gardens project in Kilburn.

*COUNCIL CONTACTS:*
London Borough of Brent
Town Hall
Forty Lane
Wembley
Middlesex HA9 9HX
(081) 904 1244
Head of Environmental Design: Mike Manuel (081) 900 5104
Park Rangers: (081) 900 5449
Recycling Officer: (081) 998 3747 Betty Morton

*Green star rating:* ★★★★★

# BROMLEY

*Does the council have an overall policy on environmental issues?*
Bromley is now drawing up an overall strategy on environmental issues. Up till now individual departments have taken their own initiatives. Working party of senior managers will co-ordinate action and consider new moves.

*How is that policy implemented with direct regard to the council's 'in-house' activities?*
Only ozone-friendly aerosols purchased. Council vehicles converted to lead-free petrol where possible. Energy Management Officer appointed with target of cutting council energy spending by fifteen per cent in five years. Pesticide use strictly controlled in public parks and open spaces.

*In its general planning, how is the council involved in improving the overall environment?*
More than 300 listed buildings in borough, 40 conservation areas (almost doubled since 1987), 700 tree preservation orders. Early conservation interest in villages, like Cudham and Downe, but much focus now on Victorian/Edwardian suburban housing areas. Environment team vets planning applications for design, landscaping, effects on trees, choice of materials etc. Applications within conservation areas also vetted by advisory panel of local representatives and independent architects and planners. Special budget for town centre works to improve paving and co-ordinate street

furniture, new designs for railings, bollards. Bromley High Street has just been pedestrianised; Maple Street, Penge, to be pedestrianised. Town Centre Management Scheme under way to improve shopping environment.

'Clean and Green' campaign for environmental improvement ran 1985-87: 100 eyesore sites landscaped and improved; 30,000 shrubs and 2,500 trees planted. Other projects included creation of minipark from derelict glasshouse area in West Street, Bromley and creation of park and play area on allotment site at St Mary Cray. Works with voluntary groups on tidy-up, graffiti control and landscape schemes (e.g. in Farnborough Village and Barnmead Road).

Two large estates upgraded: sub-divided into smaller neighbourhoods, more off-street parking, trees, fences and walls provided.

*What is the council policy and practice in the preservation, enhancement and creation of green and open spaces?*
Borough open space policy seeks to protect Green Belt, protect, enhance and expand existing open space, preserve good quality agricultural, forestry and horticultural land. Green spaces under threat from developers. Strong resistance from council: e.g., over plans to develop Co-op sports ground in Beckenham as superstore. Some new open space created, but mainly small corner sites or potential development sites landscaped for interim use (e.g., on Beckenham Lane and College Road).

Countryside Management Service launched in May 1989, to protect and enhance landscape features, wildlife habitats, historical and archaeological sites, increase public understanding and access. Tries to create active dialogue between landowners, community groups, local authority and public and resolve any conflicts of interest.

Countryside Consultative Panel brings together council departments, local amenity groups and Government bodies.

Two nature centres established, at High Elms and Scadbury, run by borough ecologist and rangers.

Works jointly with ENBRO – Environment Bromley – on clearance work, producing guides, walks and trails.

*Is the council able to control or exert influence on air and water pollution in the borough?*
Almost all borough subject of smoke control orders. Sulphur dioxide permanently monitored. Equipment available to monitor effects of nitric oxide and radiation. All new industrial installations must comply with Clean Air Act.

Domestic and commercial water supplies regularly sampled. Guidelines recently issued on combating threat of legionella from water coolers and air conditioning systems. Rivers in borough recently surveyed.

*What steps can, and does, the council take on noise pollution and nuisance?*
1,000 complaints a year received from residents, investigated, solved where possible. Construction sites subject to Control of Pollution Act. Limited 'out of hours' service.
Monitoring and controls on aircraft noise at Biggin Hill Airport, owned by council. Investigations on new highway schemes and proposed British Rail Channel Tunnel link.

*What are the council's policies and practices with regard to waste disposal, rubbish collection and street cleaning?*
Collections for domestic and commercial premises, minimum once a week, more frequently as required. Charged collection of bulky items and garden rubbish. Disposal at landfill sites.
Street cleansing once or twice daily in High Streets; fortnightly in less-used residential roads. Fly-tipped waste quickly removed from council land.
Litter Abatement Officer appointed 1987 to co-ordinate 'Clean and Tidy' campaign: education, encouragement of local voluntary groups, prosecution where necessary (e.g. littering, fly-tipping, abandoned supermarket trolleys, dog-fouling).
Free 'Amenity Collection' of bulky items, to augment charged service: two-thirds of borough now covered. Skips provided free for community groups. Removal of graffiti from public and private property.

*What facilities do the council make available for recycling?*
Recycling facilities for glass, waste oil and rags at two civic amenity/transfer station sites, plus newspapers and magazines only. Many bottle banks, more planned, CFCs removed from fridges/freezers at amenity sites. Sealed skip for deposit of cement-bonded asbestos. Abandoned vehicles recycled through scrap metal merchants. (See The Green Guide to Recycling section.)
A-Z recycling guide produced (updated annually). Friends of Earth aluminium can collection scheme supported. Local schools have can collection schemes, phone Litter Abatement Officer for details.

*Any other council activities to improve the environment?*

Large-scale exhibitions, videos to promote 'Clean and Green', 'Clean and Tidy' borough.

*COUNCIL CONTACTS:*
London Borough of Bromley
Civic Centre
Rochester Avenue
Bromley
Kent BR1 3UH
(081) 464 3333
Litter Abatement Officer (including recycling) and litter hotlines: (081) 313 4510
Countryside Management Service: Ext.4290
Environmental Services Division: Ext.5257/5270
Planning Section: Ext.5738

*Green star rating:* ★★★★★

# CAMDEN

*Does the council have an overall policy on environmental issues?*
Camden's Borough Plan lays down policy objectives to protect and improve the physical and natural environment and local character in Camden.
Environmental Working Party (formerly Ecology Working Party) set up 1983, with council and voluntary members.
LGAAPS – Local Government Audits and Action Plans – being introduced to monitor environment in specific areas and outline plans for action.

*How is that policy implemented with direct regard to the council's 'in-house' activities?*
Corporate purchasing policy includes moratorium on purchase of chlorine-bleached and environmentally-unfriendly products.
Council policy of buying only lead-free vehicles since 1983, others converted, phased out.
Use of re-cycled paper for council business being re-examined.
Combined heat and power, district heating scheme using waste refuse investigated by consultants, now being considered by council.

*In its general planning, how is the council involved in improving the overall environment?*
Annual capital programmes in tree-planting, environmental improvements, ecology sites, grants for building improvements,

cycle and pedestrian routes and facilities, traffic-calming measures, campaigns for public transport improvements.

Camden Healthy Cities Project and local health directory, jointly funded with health authorities.

Campaigns for new legislation and controls; publicity and encouragement to communities and individuals on green matters.

Assessment and introduction of Local Government Audit and Action plans.

Planning protection in conservation areas and for listed buildings, plus plans to retain other buildings and areas 'of some character, worthy of retention and rehabilitation'.

All new developments will require high standards of landscaping.

*What is the council policy and practice in the preservation, enhancement and creation of green and open spaces?*

Removal of trees resisted, tree planting encouraged. Various open spaces created, some with local groups, some as part of developments. Ecological 'corridors' and sites identified and protected. Ecological survey of borough, identification of deficient areas and creation of new habitats, e.g. Camley Street Natural Park.

Particular protection for areas of special character, e.g. Regent's Park, Primrose Hill and surroundings; Royal Courts of Justice and Inns of Court; Bloomsbury and University of London precinct; Hampstead/Highgate Ridge.

Improvements to ponds, e.g. in Waterlow Park and to Regent's Canal (e.g. booms to create still water for plant life, duck ramps, wild flower planting.)

Meadow areas in Camley Street Natural Park, Adelaide Nature Reserve, Hampstead Heath, Hampstead Cemetery; woodland areas in Kenwood and Mortimer Terrace (council helps local groups license sites from private landowners.) Belsize Wood being developed as part nature reserve, part leisure woodland.

Temporary community gardens developed in Acton Street and Seaford Street.

Threats to undeveloped land owned by public bodies like British Rail and Thames Water.

*Is the council able to control or exert influence on air and water pollution in the borough?*

Investigations and inspections, statutory action taken where necessary. Controls on new developments to ensure minimising of emissions of grit, dust, ash, soot, smoke, fumes, smells, par-

ticularly in residential areas. Pollution from traffic controlled by
traffic-calming measures and encouragement of use of public
transport and of lead-free vehicles.

*What steps can, and does, the council take on noise pollution and nui-
sance?*
Complaints investigated, statutory notices served as necessary.
Sound-proofing installed where necessary. New developments,
conversions subject to noise abatement standards, construction
site noise monitored and controlled.

*What are the council's policies and practices with regard to waste dis-
posal, rubbish collection and street cleaning?*
New measures to improve refuse collection and street cleaning,
but still many problems with litter, refuse dumping etc. £500,000
'environmental package' announced October 1989 for cleaning
services, repairing pavements, improving street lighting and traffic
safety. New Direct Services department investing £140,000 in street
vacuum-sweepers, mechanised street-sweepers, trucks etc; £85,000
on 1000 extra litter bins plus plans for further sponsored bins;
£200,000 on repairing pavements in north and south of borough
and on Regents Park Estate; £75,000 on upgraded street lighting
in Somers Town.
Voluntary groups on litter supported, and publicity campaign
launched on litter and dog-fouling (including 'good doggie' cards,
to be handed to recalcitrant owners.

*What facilities do the council make available for recycling?*
Jamestown Recycling Centre one of most advanced in country:
paper, cans, glass, oil, metal, rags, CFCs, soft plastics. 60,000 people
a year use site.
Bottle bank scheme, plans to replace existing bottle banks (badly
affected by fly-posting) and acquire more.
Plans for paper-collection igloos being considered. (For sites, see
The Green Guide to Recycling section.)
Five community-based recycling schemes in neighbourhood
centres, contact Michael Newport for details.

*Any other council activities to improve the environment?*
Council considering creation of non-executive environmental sub-
committee, made up of individuals and community representatives to advise in the development of green and health issues.

*COUNCIL CONTACTS:*
London Borough of Camden
The Town Hall
Euston Road
London NW1 2RU
(071) 278 4444
Recycling officer: (071) 485 4111, Ext.276

Jamestown Recycling Centre,
28 Jamestown Road, NW1
(071) 485 1553 Contact: Michael Newport.

*Green star rating:* ★★

# CITY OF LONDON

*Does the council have an overall policy on environmental issues?*
The City is run by the Corporation of London, which is currently
drawing together its 'numerous policies which affect environmental
issues' into a single document. At the same time practices and
policies are being reviewed 'to see whether we can make any
improvements'. The City's Local Plan outlines policies on environmental quality, particularly in the control on high building
developments, the preservation of ancient buildings and the
protection and creation of open space.

*How is that policy implemented with direct regard to the council's 'in-
house' activities?*
Energy management team and energy committee to review energy
use. Purchasing Officer 'pursues environmentally-friendly policies where it is practical to do so'. Open spaces are managed 'in
an environmentally-friendly manner'.

*In its general planning, how is the council involved in improving the
overall environment?*
Two local plans, The City of London Local Plan and the Smithfield District Plan set out policies which try to improve the quality of the physical environment. Development of high buildings
resisted in appropriate areas, 'significant' views protected. Streets,
lanes, alleys and courts protected where possible. Shopfront designs
and advertising controlled. 21 conservation areas, with strict
development controls, designated. Listed buildings protected.
Special controls on riverside developments (trying to complete

the Riverside Walk, a series of linked landscaped areas, along the river bank). Special controls, especially on building heights, around St Paul's Cathedral and The Monument. Particular attention to wind turbulence and daylight blocking from new buildings. Smithfield District Plan seeks to preserve and enhance the character of the area around the market and St Bartholemew's Hospital. New pedestrian zones being introduced. Elevated walkway system being introduced to segregate traffic from pedestrians.

*What is the council policy and practice in the preservation, enhancement and creation of green and open spaces?*
The Corporation owns, funds and manages more than 8,500 acres of open space, including Epping Forest, Burnham Beeches, West Ham Park, Queen's Park, Highgate Wood and six commons in Kent and Surrey. Last year it took over responsibility for Hampstead Heath. There are more than 190 small parks and gardens in the City itself. In the last two years a further 650 acres of land have been acquired or are in the process of acquisition. Many open spaces are designated Sites of Special Scientific Interest. Corporation opposes development that threatens its land and buys 'buffer land' to protect open spaces.
Recent projects include extending horse rides in Epping Forest, new walks in Surrey commons.

*Is the council able to control or exert influence on air and water pollution in the borough?*
Corporation of London pioneered Clean Air Acts and created first smoke free zone in the country. Combined heat and power scheme for City centre being investigated. Thames water quality tested annually through investigations of types of fish caught.

*What steps can, and does, the council take on noise pollution and nuisance?*
Introduced the first Considerate Contractor scheme. General noise levels controlled by environmental health officer; complaints investigated and statutory action taken as necessary.

*What are the council's policies and practices with regard to waste disposal, rubbish collection, and street cleaning ?*
Waste and rubbish taken by barge to landfill in Rainham, Essex. All streets cleansed daily, swept at least twice per day. 1,000 litter bins provided.

*What facilities do the council make available for recycling?*
None at present, being investigated.

*Any other council activities to improve the environment?*
Sheep being introduced on Riddlesdown Common to encourage wild flowers, butterflies etc. Encouragement of local conservation groups, grants to organisations like London Wildlife Trust. Recent conference promoted on energy conservation and the greenhouse effect.

COUNCIL CONTACTS:
City of London
Guildhall
London EC2
(071) 606 3030

**Green star rating:** ★★★

# CROYDON

*Does the council have an overall policy on environmental issues?*
Croydon's policy is 'to properly maintain and, where appropriate, to progressively update, the local environment.' The District Plan also calls for conservation and improvement of the local environment. Each council department or service also has its own strategy in helping towards 'enhancing Croydon as a place in which to live and work.' Major programmes of environmental improvement are incorporated in council's 'Keep Croydon the Natural Choice' (KCNC) and 'Caring for Croydon' initiatives.

*How is that policy implemented with direct regard to the council's 'in-house' activities?*
No use of aerosols containing CFCs. New controls over use of pesticides introduced. Council transport being converted to lead-free petrol. Environmentally-sensitive cleaning materials used. Some recycled paper used in council correspondence, Environmental Health department investigating further use. Energy-saving exercises have produced progressive £200,000 cost savings.

*In its general planning, how is the council involved in improving the overall environment?*
Ten conservation areas designated in borough, agreed in consultation with London Ecology Unit. Measures to protect overall environment include road improvement, traffic management and calming schemes, upgraded street lighting, improved vandal-resistance in public conveniences, street furniture and tree-plant-

ing. Experimental pedestrianisation of North End shopping area.
Small-scale environment improvement schemes include tree
planting/brick paving in Addington Village; restoration work/
tree-planting/paving in The Waldrons and paving/planting in
George Street.

*What is the council policy and practice in the preservation, enhance-
ment and creation of green and open spaces?*
Policy is to plan public open spaces rather than sell off. Council
endorses recommendations for provision of recreational open space,
but present financial constraints mean efforts limited to low-cost
improvements of existing facilities. Green Belt land within the
borough maintained and protected. Four areas designated Metropolitan Open Land: near Croydon Cemetery, Purley Way playing fields and surroundings, Bethlem Royal Hospital and series
of open spaces between Elmers End and Shirley. Particular attention to be paid to Broad Green, Thornton Heath, South Norwood
and western part of Addiscombe, where local residents are short
of open space and sports and leisure facilities.
Despite fall in demand, council resists loss of allotments and seeks
alternative recreational use for poorly-used allotments.
South Norwood Country Park, with wild flower meadows, wetland
areas, created, covering 120 acres. Open space and recreational
facilities being considered for South Norwood Farm; similar facilities
should be provided in developments at Woodside Brickworks;
planned expansion of public park at Crystal Palace to become 150
acre Metropolitan Park. 'Green chain' walks being developed.

*Is the council able to control or exert influence on air and water pollution
in the borough?*
Investigations carried out and statutory action taken as required.
Road-side monitoring of nitrogen dioxide and daily monitoring
for other air pollutants. Water supplies sampled and monitored.
Specialist pollution team within Environmental Health Department. Unleaded petrol campaign and campaign against lead in
fruit and vegetables has heightened public awareness.

*What steps can, and does, the council take on noise pollution and nui-
sance?*
All noise complaints investigated and monitored by Pollution
Control Team in Environmental Health Department. Noise
Abatement Zone being considered.
Stand-by party patrol operates in summer months. Tape record-
ers used to monitor noise in people's homes.

*What are the council's policies and practices with regard to waste disposal, rubbish collection and street cleaning?*
Extensive new activities to improve waste disposal and street cleaning, e.g., street cleaning frequencies recently doubled. All waste (130,000 tonnes per year) containerised before transport, to reduce nuisance. New trade waste services introduced. Three civic amenity sites and free skip/mobile civic amenity service at weekends. 'Care for Croydon' programme aims at improving cleanliness, reducing fly-tipping, litter, graffiti and vandalism by direct measures and through involvement of local householders, businesses and schools. Dog litter notices installed, direct contact with offending owners. High profile prosecutions for litter, graffiti and vandalism have had significant deterrent effect.

*What facilities do the council make available for recycling?*
Croydon probably recycles a wider range of materials than most other London boroughs, including metals, paper, glass, oils and timber, producing some £24,000 annual income. Further extensions planned. Three recycling centres at civic amenity sites in Factory Lane, Purley Oaks and Fishers Farm. Bottle banks, with further recycling arrangements with local restaurants, caterers etc. Can and paper banks being planned.

*Any other council activities to improve the environment?*
Environmental projects encouraged in schools, particularly primary. Financial support for voluntary groups for clean-up campaigns. Awards to residents willing to provide evidence on litter, graffiti and vandalism. Free weekend skips to residents' groups for clean-ups; mobile civic amenity facilities for residents' associations. Extensive publicity on litter, graffiti and vandalism. Litter bin sponsorship schemes.

> *COUNCIL CONTACTS:*
> London Borough of Croydon
> Taberner House
> Park Lane
> Croydon
> Surrey CR9 3JS
> (081) 686 4433
> Highways and Public Works, recycling: (081) 681 5928
> Parks and Recreation: (081) 760 5584
> Waste Disposal Manager: Mr Scott (081) 681 5928

*Green star rating:* ★★★

## EALING

*Does the council have an overall policy on environmental issues?*
Ealing is committed to increase recycling facilities, use bio-degradable sacks; improve canals; conserve energy; ensure a rolling programme of planting trees; and alleviate the damaging effect of traffic fumes.

*How is that policy implemented with direct regard to the council's 'in-house' activities?*
Energy conservation is achieved through more efficient use of fuel, and reduction of wastage in heating and lighting, primarily due to a complete modernisation and better control of the systems. Technical Services Department controls 466 vehicles, 311 run on either diesel or 2 star unleaded petrol. Remaining 155 will be replaced by 1992. Council operates a loan system to enable officers to buy cars, by 1991/92 this is expected to go only to cars using unleaded petrol. Catalytic convertors are being considered.
No aerosols containing CFCs are now purchased under contract, and by early 1990, by individuals. Further research continues into the use of insulation, paint and plastic, as building materials. Packaging of goods and the use of biodegradable sacks will be looked into. New Line Services Department (Parks) uses the Food and Environment Protection Act 1985, the Control of Pesticides Regulations 1986 and COSHH Regulations when using pesticides in parks and open spaces. Only three out of the fifteen sizes of manilla envelope used by the council are not made of recycled paper.

*In its general planning, how is the council involved in improving the overall environment?*
Council is committed to retaining existing tree stocks and to increase numbers. Between 1500 and 2000 trees have been planted each winter for the last four years, additionally many thousands of smaller transplants are moved annually into parks and open spaces.
Attempts are made to avoid areas containing rare and endangered species when development is taking place. Efforts are made to lessen traffic intrusion and pedestrianisation schemes, footpaths and cycle routes are considered as part of any development plan.

*What is the council policy and practice in the preservation, enhancement and creation of green and open spaces within the borough?*
Sites gained as open spaces have been landscaped and include some canal-side land. Tree preservation orders have been made

since 1986. Tree sponsorship scheme – members of the public can contribute twenty pounds towards the cost of planting a tree; 150 out of 1500 street trees have been sponsored during 1988/89.

*Is the council able to control or exert influence on air and water pollution in the borough?*
Ealing carried out a major seven year pollution tracking survey which ended in 1981 and resulted in 97 sites of pollution being identified and cured. Fish are now in the River Brent and Yeading Brook. Council is seeking to get Thames Water Authority to raise the water Quality Objective to improve appearance, wildlife value, etc of the Brent River Park. Study requested to achieve this aim. Environmental Health Division deals with enforcement of Clean Air Acts and monitors smoke emissions for sulphur dioxide, nitrous oxide and lead. Records emissions from cooling towers to prevent legionella.

*What steps can, and does, the council take on noise pollution and nuisance?*
Environmental Health Division serves notices and prosecutes builders and commercial concerns under the Control of Pollution Act, also monitors aircraft and railway noise and undertakes sound insulation testing at premises. 'Party Patrol' operates between 23.00 - 04.00 Friday and Saturday nights.

*What are the council policies and practices with regard to waste disposal, rubbish collection and street cleaning?*
Waste disposed of by West London Waste Authority. Household, commercial, clinical and special collections of bulky items available. Five hundred kms of highway cleaned, 1200 litter bins emptied and 3000 cubic metres of fly-tipping removed each year. Voluntary 'dog-free' zones in parks.

*What facilities do the council make available for recycling?*
Three council civic amenity sites accept glass, scrap metal, while one additionally takes textiles, paper, cardboard and sump oil. Bottle and paper banks. (see Recycling section)

*Any other council activities to improve the environment?*
Council aims to see that school children are better prepared to ensure the welfare of future generations in their own locality and worldwide.
Grant of £1000 given to Ealing Friends of the Earth to print a recycling guide.
Nature Conservation section manages Horsenden Hill and Brent

River Park, each with a Ranger giving walks and study days, together with river trips. Ealing Countryside Day (annual event), Ecology Day (biennial). Play leaders trained in environmental play activities. Development of Litten Nature Reserve (Greenford), Brent River Park Environmental Centre.

Production of booklets and information packs. Other projects include: species lists; land use information; the West London Waterways Walk,in conjunction with Brent, Hounslow, Hillingdon and Richmond; the Green Patchwork Project with schools, which will form the central theme of the 1990 Ealing Ecology Week. Substantial grants given to London Wildlife Trust, Selborne Society (Perivale Wood Local Nature Reserve).

*COUNCIL CONTACTS:*
London Borough of Ealing
Town Hall
New Broadway
London W5 2BY
(081) 579 2424
Head of Administrative Services: Amanda Venning
Recycling: Civic Amenity Site Supervisors (081) 578 5674

*Green star rating:* ★★★★

## ENFIELD

*Does the council have an overall policy on environmental issues?*
Enfield council is involved in shaping the overall environment through the policies laid down in its Borough Development Plan, adopted in 1983. The council's stated aim is to 'ensure the provision and maintenance of a pleasant and healthy physical environment in which residents, workers, shoppers and other persons in the borough can enjoy to the maximum their homes, surroundings and the facilities available to them.' Particular stress is laid on minimising the impact of roads and traffic and in reducing environmental pollution.

*How is that policy implemented with direct regard to the council's 'in-house' activities?*
Wherever possible environmentally-sensitive products purchased; CFC aerosols not used unless no alternative available. Minimum possible use of pesticides; only government approved chemicals used, by trained operators. Energy Management Unit co-ordinates

energy efficiency schemes in all public buildings, including schools, through better insulation, more sensitive heating controls etc. Secondary schools also encouraged to save energy through cash awards for using less energy than the Borough Architect's target figures.

*In its general planning, how is the council involved in improving the overall environment?*
Borough Plan policies impose strict standards on development, including high design standards, landscaping and tree-planting where appropriate, adequate amenity space in all residential developments, promotion of improvements in untidy private and public sites, protection of historic buildings and conservation areas, control advertising displays, improve footpaths, etc.

*What is the council policy and practice in the preservation, enhancement and creation of green and open spaces?*
Fourteen conservation areas designated in borough, five ancient monuments, numerous listed buildings, plus others on council Local List. Some 2,000 acres of open space land in borough. Landscape plan for areas of Green Belt, including controls on nearby development, tree-planting and conservation of wildlife habitats. Greatest pressure on open space comes from proposed development of private playing fields: council tries to resist such loss. Council open land (some 50 acres of allotments and school playing fields) has been released in recent years because of financial requirements on local authorities. Private developer recently restored ten acre area of derelict mineral workings as part of housing scheme: to be handed over to council for use as public open space. Other agreements with private developers for provision and layout of open space. Two sites (six acres) of new parkland being developed. Maintenance and enhancement of extensive trees and woodlands undertaken: 2,000 trees planted 1988/89. Private owners also assisted in tree-planting and conservation. Major road building of north/south route, easing traffic in commercial and residential areas, currently under way, costing council £45 million, of which £1.77 million devoted to landscaping.

More than 30 projects in rolling environmental improvements scheme, to remove eyesores, enhance conservation areas and improve open spaces, particularly along A10. Local amenity, conservation groups consulted and voluntary participation encouraged and supported.

Capel Manor Environmental Centre advises schools and teachers; schools encouraged to developed habitat areas in grounds.

*Is the council able to control or exert influence on air and water pollution in the borough?*
Complaints investigated and statutory action taken where necessary. Council works with Inspectorate of Pollution in investigating air pollution incidents: as a result, emissions from a number of industries in eastern part of borough improved or reduced.
Periodic water pollution surveys undertaken, funded by Thames Water Authority.
Planning approval for roadstone coating plant recently refused on environmental pollution grounds.

*What steps can, and does, the council take on noise pollution and nuisance?*
Noise conditions imposed on planning applications. Noise nuisance complaints investigated and followed by statutory action when satisfactory evidence obtained. No regular 'party patrol' but preplanned out-of-hours visits to deal with persistent nuisance.

*What are the council's policies and practices with regard to waste disposal, rubbish collection and street cleaning?*
Policy on these services is to get best value for money: waste collected in all categories, but charges made for prescribed domestic, commercial and industrial wastes. Road-sweeping frequencies raised in last three years and mechanical sweeping machines introduced in shopping areas to improve litter control. Extra £100,000 a year allocated for street cleaning, including raising minimum frequency in residential areas to once a week, and double rate of litter bin emptying.
Free clinical waste collection service.
New bye-laws planned for more control on dogs; recent successful dog-fouling prosecution.

*What facilities do the council make available for recycling?*
Two civic amenity sites, at Carterhatch Lane, Enfield and Barrowell Green, Winchmore Hill, recycling paper, card, scrap metals, bottles and oil (plus wood at Barrowell Green). Bottle banks; wastepaper bank scheme being set up.
Aluminium can recycling scheme being considered.

*Any other council activities to improve the environment?*
Support of residents and amenity groups clean-up projects, e.g. free skips, bags, disposal. Considering appointment of Waste Reduction Officer for anti-litter education, enforcement, recycling

etc.

Lead in paint danger to schoolchildren reduced through extensive school redecoration programme.

> COUNCIL CONTACTS:
> London Borough of Enfield
> Civic Centre
> Silver Street
> Enfield
> Middlesex EN1 3XB
> (081) 366 6565
> Environmental Health Department: Ext.3600
> Borough Architect: Ext.3019
> Public Cleansing, recycling: (081) 807 0918, Mr Dean.

**Green star rating: ★★**


# GREENWICH

*Does the council have an overall policy on environmental issues?*
Greenwich has numerous policies which address environmental issues, notably an energy policy and an ecology and conservation policy.
Council now developing an environmentally sensitive strategy to ensure all existing and future council policy and practice 'is subject to a consideration of their environmental impact.'
Council procurement strategy being developed to ensure all products bought by council are 'environmentally sound.'
Five year plan on 'Greening Greenwich' being drawn up.

*How is that policy implemented with direct regard to the council's 'in-house' activities?*
Energy Conservation Policy now being implemented in council buildings, to be extended to schools, colleges next year. Energy Policy on council homes, with better insulation, more energy-efficient heating, boiler surveys, low energy light bulbs. Only ozone-friendly aerosols used. Biodegradable products used where practical. CFCs being phased out in cooling systems. Hardwood use restricted.
Recycled paper used where possible. Computer paper, print department off-cuts recycled. Plans for recycling all office waste paper.
Pesticide use restricted to government-approved chemicals.

Healthy eating policy in food purchases for schools, council canteens.

*In its general planning, how is the council involved in improving the overall environment?*

Borough Plan contains many references to environmental matters, including open, space, heritage, trees, design, control of development, control and pollution. Development controls, building controls and enforcement all concerned with protection and enhancement of borough, controlling appearance, traffic nuisance etc. Advertisement controls to try to maintain satisfactory appearance in shopping areas. Major impacts expected in transport field, with proposals for Channel Tunnel links, East London River Crossing, South Circular Assessment studies. Council opposed to two latter. Traffic management priority areas designated in Greenwich Town Centre, East Greenwich, Plumstead and Deptford. New traffic management schemes begun in association with Rochester Way relief road. Traffic calming measures, overnight lorry parking ban. Condition of highways, footpaths, street furniture, dumping, all difficult to control due to lack of resources.

*What is the council policy and practice in the preservation, enhancement and creation of green and open spaces?*

Part of designated Green Chain, virtually continuous arc of public and private open space through boroughs of Bexley, Bromley, Greenwich and Lewisham, to be safeguarded from development and habitats, walks developed. Bostall Woods, Shooters Hill, Avery Hill, Eltham Palace form backbone of chain in Greenwich, together with links to other open space, e.g. Plumstead and Woolwich Commons and Charlton and Maryon Parks. Borough plan also protects open space.

Conservation areas and listed buildings protected. New and replacement tree-planting programme in operation; joint tree-planting schemes with voluntary groups being considered. Woolwich Polytechnic commissioned to prepare guided walk leaflets for open space in deprived areas. Charlton Sand Pits in Maryon Wilson Park and Oxleas Wood designated Sites of Special Scientific Interest. (Oxleas Wood at present under threat from East London River Crossing).

Open space management plans and wildlife areas currently being developed, particularly in Oxleas Wood, Blackheath, Dothill Nature Reserve, Harmony Woods.

Support given to local groups, e.g. Greenwich Environment Forum,

Friends of the Earth.

*Is the council able to control or exert influence on air and water pollution in the borough?*
Investigations and inspections, statutory action taken where necessary. Water and air quality monitored, for smoke, sulphur dioxide, nitrogen oxides, ozone and smell, as part of London-wide scheme.

*What steps can, and does, the council take on noise pollution and nuisance?*
Monitoring of noise nuisance, including railway noise/vibration. Statutory controls as necessary. Negotiating with river authorities and ferries to ensure off-loading of noisy passengers from late-night disco boats is away from residential areas.
Operates 'noise patrol'.

*What are the council's policies and practices with regard to waste disposal, rubbish collection and street cleaning?*
Waste disposal by landfill, but combined heat and power scheme under discussion. Domestic waste collected weekly in plastic sacks. Bulk bins and 'Eurobins' emptied five times a week, trade refuse, up to six times per week. Bulky household refuse removed free. Considering providing skips for bulky items and local clean-up campaigns. Prosecution of litter-droppers considered under new laws, and of those who leave refuse on streets outside collection times. Fly-tipping causing major problems in borough: removed at great cost. 'Hotline' available for urgent removal of fly-tipping and other litter.
Current resources insufficient to cope with litter problems and keep up high street cleansing standards: dirty streets in some areas and particular problems in tourist areas. Residential streets swept once a fortnight (aiming for higher frequency), busy side roads, up to three times per week, major shopping centres up to three times per day and continuously in Woolwich Town Centre. Education and publicity campaigns have been mounted.

*What facilities do the council make available for recycling?*
Civic amenity and recycling centre in Nathan Way for glass, metal, cans, oil and paper. Receiving centre for discarded electrical appliances, especially fridges and cookers. Bottle banks, paper banks, can banks, more planned, (for sites, see The Green Guide to Recycling section).

*Any other council activities to improve the environment?*

Further educational and publicity drives planned.

> COUNCIL CONTACTS:
> London Borough of Greenwich
> Riverside House
> Woolwich High Street
> London SE18 6PW
> (071) 854 8888
> Lead Officer on Green Issues: Chris Shurety, Ext.2059
> Recycling: Mr K. Tristram.

**Green star rating:** ★★

# HACKNEY

*Does the council have an overall policy on environmental issues?*
Hackney council agreed the development of a comprehensive environmental policy in May 1988. Following extensive public consultation in Spring 1989, including questionnaire to all households, policy statement being drawn up: implementation by April 1990.

*How is that policy implemented with direct regard to the council's 'in-house' activities?*
Council use of CFC aerosols banned. Leaded petrol use being phased out.

*In its general planning, how is the council involved in improving the overall environment?*
Wide range of policies set out in Local Plan, which lays down criteria for design, landscaping etc. Fourteen conservation areas have been designated in the borough, including Victoria Park, Clissold Park and Stoke Newington reservoirs, and areas of architectural importance, like Albion Square, De Beauvoir, Hoxton Street and Queensbridge Road. Hackney Marshes and their surroundings have been designated an 'area of special landscape character'. Many fine local buildings were left off the statutory list of listed buildings, so council has drawn up local list. Further, nineteen London squares have been identified for protection and, in conjunction with the Museum of London, two 'areas of archaeological importance' have also been designated. Nature conservation areas have been created along the railway line to the West of Stamford Hill and along Hackney Marshes rivers. Environmental

improvements made through projects funded by council Environmental Urban Programme, including work on housing estates and derelict land as well as in conservation areas, public open spaces and waterside developments. Landscape strategy, being drawn as part of environmental strategy, will 'appraise and develop opportunities for co-ordinating and strengthening improvements to the overall physical environment.

*What is the council policy and practice in the preservation, enhancement and creation of green and open spaces?*
Environmental improvements and new green and open spaces developed by Inner City Partnership Environment Programme. Borough's Landscape Department works closely with local groups. Recent examples include creation of Butterfield Green, a major new park in Stoke Newington and Mark Street Park, a small oasis in Shoreditch. Also plans to improve existing parks, such as Hackney Marshes and Shoreditch Park, but hampered by shortage of funds.
Council notes: 'Threats to open space include not only development pressure, but also a scarcity of resources to maintain green space to an adequate standard.'
Council supports proposals put forward by Lee Valley Regional Park Authority to increase recreational facilities, improve landscape and conserve areas of ecological interest.

*Is the council able to control or exert influence on air and water pollution in the borough?*
Smoke control over entire borough. Smoke and sulphur dioxide levels monitored daily. Investigations of smoke, emissions etc. made and statutory powers used as necessary.
Concern over quality of supplies of drinking water from Thames Water Authority: council 'influences, lobbies and advises' authority. Water supply quality tested for council tenants. Extensive Drinking Water Quality survey recently completed in borough after two-year sampling period.

*What steps can, and does, the council take on noise pollution and nuisance?*
Complaints investigated and statutory action taken as necessary. More than 55 complaints of noisy parties received last year: council runs 'noisy party service' on Saturday nights and Sunday mornings, generally reducing noise through persuasion: few prosecutions necessary.

*What are the council's policies and practices with regard to waste disposal, rubbish collection and street cleaning?*
Contract to provide refuse and street cleaning service until 1995 won by council in-house team. £5 million a year spending on refuse collection and £2 million on street cleaning in 1989/90, a reduction of £1 million on previous year. Features of service include late night cleaning of main road and market areas, free collection of bulky household and garden waste. Plans to increase 1000-plus litter bins by 30 per cent. Problems include lack of civic amenity site or recycling centre (several planned); dumping of refuse by businesses, only a third of which contract with the council for their rubbish collection; parked cars, which impede street cleaning (council pushing for alternate day/alternate side parking, but needs extra resources to enforce it).
Dog fouling a problem: council considering 'pooper scooper' use to be compelled by law.

*What facilities do the council make available for recycling?*
Recycling programme 'in formative' phase. Feasibility study completed autumn 1989. Bottle banks in use with further planned, together with igloos for waste paper collection. (For sites, see Recycling section)
Plans for can banks in schools. Two supermarket/shopping centre car park owners being asked to install recycling containers. Council hopes to establish several civic amenity sites with recycling facilities. Recycling Officer may be appointed, targets set for waste reclamation.

*Any other council activities to improve the environment?*
Other projects financed by the council include Hackney Environmental Education programme with two full time workers developing urban studies in primary schools; Hackney Urban Studies Centre, working with local community, schools and colleges; Hackney Environmental Action Resource, offering free advisory service, including feasibility studies, on environmental improvement schemes, external landscaping works etc.
Freeform Community Design and Technical Aid Service offers free technical and design advice on building works, housing estates grounds and on playgrounds for disabled children.

*COUNCIL CONTACTS:*
London Borough of Hackney
Town Hall
London E8 1EA
(081) 986 3123
Rubbish, street cleaning, recycling:
Civic Amenities
Joseph Priestley House
73 Morning Lane
London E9 6ND
(081) 986 3123 Ext.4390/1 and 4278

**Green star rating: ★★★**

# HAMMERSMITH AND FULHAM

*Does the council have an overall policy on environmental issues?*
Hammersmith and Fulham has a working group now, bringing
together individual departments' long-standing initiatives into
overall strategy on environmental issues aiming at and enhancing pride in the borough.

*How is that policy implemented with direct regard to the council's 'in-
house' activities?*
Recycled paper used for some time, use being increased. Contracts,
e.g. for cleaning materials, stipulate environmentally-safe products. All chemicals used by council being examined. Insulation,
heating and lighting improvements have brought ten to fifteen
per cent saving in energy consumption in council offices. Use of
solar power for public buildings being examined. Alternatives to
hardwoods used on council premises; developers encouraged to
do likewise. No aerosols containing CFC's are purchased.

*In its general planning, how is the council involved in improving the
overall environment?*
Fighting against government road plans (e.g. Western Environmental Improvement Route). Installed several miles of cycle lanes:
you can now cycle from one end of the borough to the other by
using these. Planning applications carefully studied for potential
effects on environment. Tree-planting and re-location after public consultation followed 1987 hurricane. Hanging flower baskets
installed in streets; flower and garden competitions sponsored.

*What is the council policy and practice in the preservation, enhance-*

*ment and creation of green and open spaces?*
Negotiates for public open space to be included in major planning developments (e.g. BBC agreed to temporary public open space, Greyhound Park, during building of their new White City Centre, environmental improvements in proposed development of Hammersmith Broadway Island Site.) Wildlife habitats being created in public open spaces.

*Is the council able to control or exert influence on air and water pollution in the borough?*
Involved in local and London-wide monitoring of air and water pollution. Investigates complaints and problems and takes statutory action where necessary.

*What steps can, and does, the council take on noise pollution and nuisance?*
Operates 'noisy party patrol' service. Noise nuisance considered in all planning applications.

*What are the council's policies and practices with regard to waste disposal, rubbish collection and street cleaning?*
Street cleansing schedules periodically revised. Skips available for rubbish clearance. Owners of commercial premises encouraged to increase frequency of collections. Special refuse collection for frail elderly residents. Frequent campaigns on litter and dog-fouling: dog-free zones in parks, 'pooper scooter' to clean streets.

*What facilities do the council make available for recycling?*
Sixteen bottle banks. Nine paper banks, others to be added soon. Planning a fridge collection service; CFC's will be dipsosed of safely. Civic amenity skips sited at the weekends for disposal of household rubbish.

*Any other council activities to improve the environment?*
'CFC-free' exhibitions in schools and shopping centres. Grant-aid to voluntary groups and businesses involved with environmentally-friendly goods or services. Borough Health Fair publicising council and other services.

COUNCIL CONTACTS:
London Borough of Hammersmith and Fulham
Town Hall
King Street
Hammersmith
London W6 9JU

(081) 748 3020
Recycling officer: Tony Talman (071) 736 2529

*Green star rating:* ★★

## HARINGEY

*Does the council have an overall policy on environmental issues?*
Haringey developed a Corporate Environment Policy in June 1985
and was the first local authority in the UK to set up an environmental committee – a full strategic committee of the council. An
Environmental Policy Unit was established in April 1986.

*How is that policy implemented with direct regard to the council's 'in-
house' activities?*
Council has a Cross-service Environment Officers Working Party
to implement its policies. Energy Management Unit promotes
energy saving, including checklists for caretakers, porters, office
managers, head teachers and other council employees. Special
working party, involving trades unions, local environmental groups.
Regulated pesticides use in parks and public open spaces.

*In its general planning, how is the council involved in improving the
overall environment?*
Seventeen conservation areas created in borough.
Numerous traffic calming schemes.
Specialist planning posts created, e.g. Women's Issues Planner,
Conservation Officers, Disability Access Workers, Transport
Planners, Parks Service Tree Officer and Conservation Officer.

*What is the council policy and practice in the preservation, enhance-
ment and creation of green and open spaces?*
New parks created, old ones improved. 115-acre Finsbury Park
taken over by council on GLC abolition in 1986. Improvements
and additions made to playground in Priory Park. New landscaping work at Bruce Castle Park. But Parkland Walk, following old
railway line from Finsbury Park station to Alexandra Palace, under
threat from new road developments projected in London traffic
assessment study. (See traffic chapter for more general details.)

*Is the council able to control or exert influence on air and water pollution
in the borough?*
Air regularly monitored for dust, sulphur dioxide, lead, other heavy
metals and asbestos. Smoke emissions from bonfire and chimneys

investigated and controlled. (bonfire guidelines issued.) Boiler installations and chimney heights controlled. Health problems from air-conditioning and heating systems investigated.
Water supplies monitored for nitrates.
Advice given, statutory action taken as necessary.
Council funds Environmental Monitoring Unit at Tottenham College of Technology.

*What steps can, and does, the council take on noise pollution and nuisance?*
'Noisy party' patrols in operation. Noise complaints on problems from neighbours, industry, road traffic investigated and controlled where necessary. Guidelines on industrial noise levels issued. Health and Safety inspections include noise monitoring.

*What are the council's policies and practices with regard to waste disposal, rubbish collection and street cleaning?*
Council resources for street cleaning and rubbish collection severely overstretched. Severe problems with litter in the borough. As well as standard services, council operates free special collection for bulky household and garden rubbish. Has special squads for anti-litter and clean-up drives. Runs anti-litter campaigns. Byelaws on litter and dog-fouling being revised.

*What facilities do the council make available for recycling?*
Haringey has highest number of bottle banks per head of population in London: one for every 8,000 people. Paper 'igloos' are being introduced. Waste paper collected and recycled at Jamestown Recycling Centre in Jamestown Road (owned by Camden council), where waste oil and scrap metal also recycled.
One can bank, more planned.
(See The Green Guide to Recycling section)

*Any other council activities to improve the environment?*
Environmental Education Co-ordinator appointed. Team of three teachers staffs Campsbourne Environmental Education Centre. Community groups on environment, recycling supported. Publications now printed on recycled paper.

*COUNCIL CONTACTS:*
London Borough of Haringey
Civic Centre
High Road
London N22 4LE

(081) 975 9700
Environment Unit, recycling: Mike Malina, Ext.2318
Environmental Health Service: (01) 808 1066

*Green star rating:* ★★★

# HARROW

*Does the council have an overall policy on environmental issues?*
Harrow has, as yet, no specific overall environmental policy, but
the 1986 Borough Plan aims to protect and enhance special areas,
improve design and landscaping of new development and improve
access to public and private open spaces. Environmental and
Ecology Panel set up 1989 to prepare guidelines and information,
produce educational material and develop awareness of environmental issues.

*How is that policy implemented with direct regard to the council's 'in-
house' activities?*
Each department responsible for deciding on its own initiatives.
Department of Architecture and Planning has energy saving group
overseeing design of all buildings. Policy is that no CFC aerosols
should be bought or used by council.

*In its general planning, how is the council involved in improving the
overall environment?*
Twenty-four conservation areas in borough, with detailed policy
guidance for each. Further areas to be designated.
Main shopping area around St Ann's Road and Station Road,
Harrow is pedestrianised, due to be extended to include College
Road and north of St Ann's Road. High Street, Wealdstone also
to be pedestrianised once town centre relief road completed.
Traffic-taming measures in Harrow Town Centre Plan; width
restrictions in some residential streets to prevent excessive through
traffic.
Existing trees in borough protected, tree-planting ensured in new
developments. Tree Planting Strategy to replace 1987 hurricane
losses and increase numbers in borough.

*What is the council policy and practice in the preservation, enhance-
ment and creation of green and open spaces?*
Green Belt Management Strategy to promote recreational use of
Green Belt, which follows Harrow Weald Ridge along the north

of the borough, while also protecting environment. Circular walks being designated in Green Belt and open space areas, eventually to be linked up as part of inter-borough network.

Areas of Metropolitan Open Land, with limitations on acceptable use, designated at Stanmore Golf Course and Harrow-on-the-Hill. New or enhanced green and open spaces include: the City Cottages, woodlands; Newton Park, wetland, flowering meadow and woodlands to be introduced later.

*Is the council able to control or exert influence on air and water pollution in the borough?*
Informal action taken as appropriate. Enforcement powers used as necessary.

*What steps can, and does, the council take on noise pollution and nuisance?*
Informal advice given; notices served under Control of Pollution Act, as necessary.
No 'call out' service but complaints of noisy parties investigated.

*What are the council's policies and practices with regard to waste disposal, rubbish collection and street cleaning?*
Refuse collection being changed to cleaner wheeled-bin method. Disposed of at landfill site.
Street cleaning 'high priority': improvements currently being considered. No enforcement work on litterers at present.

*What facilities do the council make available for recycling?*
Glass recycling centres and paper banks. School paper banks encouraged. (See The Green Guide to Recycling section)

*Any other council activities to improve the environment?*
Various environmental projects in schools; links between schools and cleansing service to create awareness; standardisation of refuse storage arrangements for domestic and commercial users, to ensure all refuse in properly constructed containers. Graffiti removal in partnership with local voluntary groups. Future action planned on fridge/freezer disposal and use of tropical hardwoods.

COUNCIL CONTACTS:
London Borough of Harrow
Civic Centre
Harrow
Middlesex HA1 2UY
(081) 863 5611

Recycling: Andrew Baker: (081) 427 1779

*Green star rating:* ★

# HAVERING

*Does the council have an overall policy on environmental issues?*
Havering has long been a 'green' borough, as more than half of the area is open countryside or green belt. There is **no** overall environmental policy. However, the green belt is strongly defended.

*How is that policy implemented with direct regard to the council's 'in-house' activities?*
Full-time Energy Officer with a borough-wide policy of energy conservation in both schools and public buildings. Major reductions have been achieved in consumption of fossil fuels. Publicity given to the benefits of insulation and the dangers of using CFC aerosols and damaging cleansing materials.

*In its general planning, how is the council involved in improving the overall environment?*
A number of conservation areas have been established. Pedestrianisation of shopping areas with a Park & Ride scheme, where possible, over the pre-Christmas period. Several thousand trees are planted each year in streets and parkland. Subscription tree scheme for residents and also an agreement with a local estate agent to ensure that a tree is planted outside every home they sell, giving 500 extra trees each year.

*What is the council policy and practice in the preservation, enhancement and creation of green and open spaces within the borough?*
A wide range of parks and open spaces are preserved. Two country parks have been created at Havering atte Bower and Hornchurch, the latter being reclaimed from a former RAF airfield. Local residents and schoolchildren are involved in tree-planting.

*Is the council able to control or exert influence on air and water pollution in the borough?*
Inspections and investigations; statutory action taken as necessary.

*What steps can, and does, the council take on noise pollution and nuisance?*
Inspections and investigations; statutory action taken as neces-

sary.

*What are the council policies and practices with regard to waste disposal, rubbish collection, street cleansing and sweeping?*
Efficient rubbish collection and disposal system. Mechanical street sweeping. 'Litterline' established for residents to report rubbish problems. Ongoing litter and dog fouling campaigns. Disposal facilities made available for dog excrement in the parks. Green sacks on sale to residents for garden rubbish, which the council will then dispose of to prevent 'dumping'.

*What facilities do the council make available for recycling?*
Waste paper and cardboard collections, monthly from residents. Paper sorted and baled. Bottle banks throughout borough. (see The Green Guide to Recycling section).

*Any other council activities to improve the environment worthy of note?*
Countryside Management Services established to help improve and preserve the countryside, working with local groups on footpaths, and managing woodland. Talks are given to groups. Leaflets produced detailing walks.
Annual Environmental Award Scheme is run to encourage builders, developers, residents etc. to look at environmental aspects of both restoration projects and new developments.

> *COUNCIL CONTACTS:*
> London Borough of Havering
> Town Hall
> Romford
> Essex RM1 3BD
> (0708) 46040
> Head of Public Relations and Information Services:
> Martin Hawkins

> *Green star rating:* ★★★

# HILLINGDON

*Does the council have an overall policy on environmental issues?*
Hillingdon has **no** overall policy, but is responding to pressure by the public and council members. Individual policies for hardwoods, lead-free petrol and CFCs.

*How is that policy implemented with direct regard to the council's 'in-*

*house' activities?*
CFC aerosols have been phased out. Energy conservation is encouraged in council buildings, also posters and leaflets sent to residents. Promotion campaign for lead-free petrol. Poisonous chemicals are not used in any department. A review is being carried out as to whether chemicals are necessary at all, and it is likely to reduce the amounts and types used.

*In its general planning, how is the council involved in improving the overall environment?*
Central Hillingdon Local Plan and Borough Planning Strategy aim to maintain and enhance the natural assets of the area. There are fifteen conservation areas in the Borough, with plans for improved pedestrianisation of local centres. A tree-planting programme is underway. Uncut areas of grass are left in non-sensitive areas.

*What is the council policy and practice in the preservation, enhancement and creation of green and open spaces within the borough?*
Hillingdon has 3,000 acres of parks and open spaces. New open space has been created at Stockley Park from a derelict infill site – a golf course has been built. Close working relationships exist between the borough and local environmental groups, mainly through the Ecology Forum. Local residents, London Wildlife Trust and Herts & Middlesex Trust have carried out river and wood clearing together with the creation of new bridleways.

*Is the council able to control or exert influence on air and water pollution in the borough?*
Hillingdon is 100% smoke controlled. Action is taken on individual bonfires under the Clean Air Acts. Legal action taken when required on other air pollutants. Close liaison occurs with Thames Water Authority on rivers and drainage.

*What steps can, and does, the council take on noise pollution and nuisance?*
Particular action is taken on construction sites. Inspection and investigations; statutory action taken as necessary. No party patrols.

*What are the council policies and practices with regard to waste disposal, rubbish collection, street cleansing and sweeping?*
A working party has been set up to look at the initiatives proposed in the 'New Look for London', with regard to waste disposal. Dog fouling, 'pooper scooper', and 'kerb your dog' schemes are under consideration, as are dog wardens. Bye-law enforcement is proving difficult with regard to the removal of waste in connection

with rats.

*What facilities do the council make available for recycling?*
Three civic amenity sites and bottle banks are around the borough.
Resource Recovery and Recycling working party recently set up
to study further projects (see The Green Guide to Recycling section).

*Any other council activities to improve the environment worthy of note?*
Support of CLEAR, grants and support for local voluntary groups.
An 'Environment' week is held every year. *Conservation News* issued
annually. Two nature reserves have been designated – Yeading
Brook Meadows and Yeading Woods.

> COUNCIL CONTACTS:
> London Borough of Hillingdon
> Civic Centre
> UXBRIDGE
> Middlesex UB8 1UW
> (0895) 50111
> Recycling Officer: Bob Summers Ext.5590.

**Green star rating:** ★★

# HOUNSLOW

*Does the council have an overall policy on environmental issues?*
Hounslow is 'moving towards' an overall policy statement on
environmental issues.

*How is that policy implemented with direct regard to the council's 'in-
house' activities?*
Energy efficiency of council buildings monitored, and computerised temperature remote controls used to maximise energy saving. Energy Conservation Officer being appointed. Policy to transfer as many council documents and publications as possible to
recycled paper. Pesticide use currently being reviewed by Hounslow Ecology Forum. Policy to minimise the use of hardwoods.

*In its general planning, how is the council involved in improving the
overall environment?*
Ecology Strategy incorporated into planning decisions. Landscaping and open space provision sought in all new developments.
Draft Green Belt Management Plan. Urban forestry scheme being

investigated.

*What is the council policy and practice in the preservation, enhancement and creation of green and open spaces?*
Acquisition programme to stop development on key sites in Green Belt .
Council works closely with London Wildlife Trust. Hounslow Ecology Forum set up to co-ordinate council and voluntary sector efforts. Urban farm shortly to be set up. Ecology and conservation 'key elements' in parks policy. Borough-wide 'green strategy' developed. Ecology Advisor appointed: helps planners, local groups and schools. West London Waterways Walk, joint project with neighbouring boroughs, completed late 1989.

*Is the council able to control or exert influence on air and water pollution in the borough?*
All air and water pollution complaints investigated, statutory action taken as necessary. Sulphur dioxide, smoke, nitrogen oxide and lead levels in air monitored. Heathrow Airport monitored for ozone, carbon monoxide and hydrocarbons.

*What steps can, and does, the council take on noise pollution and nuisance?*
Out-of-hours noise patrol on Friday and Saturday nights. Enforcement of statutory powers on individual and commercial noise nuisance.

*What are the council's policies and practices with regard to waste disposal, rubbish collection and street cleaning?*
Borough part of West London Waste Authority, responsible for waste disposal. Plastic sack backdoor collection service and commercial waste collection service operated. Fly tipping cleared as necessary. Routine and regular street cleansing according to location: main roads once a day, on minor roads, litter picked up once a week. Tidy Town Service: charged special collection of household rubbish, subsidised for pensioners.
'Pooper scooter' scheme to dispose of dog mess in many parks.

*What facilities do the council make available for recycling?*
Bottle banks and paper banks. Space Waye Recycling Centre in Feltham recycles range of products, including cardboard, textiles, tins, metal and motor oil. (For sites, see The Green Guide to Recycling section).

*Any other council activities to improve the environment?*

Funding in part officer from British Trust for Conservation Volunteers, working with council to set up local group.

COUNCIL CONTACTS:
London Borough of Hounslow
Civic Centre
Lampton Road
Hounslow
Middlesex TW3 3DN
(081) 570 7728
Recycling officers: Andrea Davies, Leslie St. James.

**Green star rating: ★**

## ISLINGTON

*Does the council have an overall policy on environmental issues?*
Islington has a policy for the environment which intends to 'promote the quality of life for people living in the inner city' and work towards a 'greener, cleaner Borough'.

*How is that policy implemented with direct regard to the council's 'in-house' activities?*
Recycled paper is used extensively throughout the council. Council has an energy centre for public information and a programme to insulate 4000 council houses a year. Pesticides are only used when absolutely necessary and then only from a selected range. Only vehicles that run on diesel are now purchased for council use. The assisted car purchase scheme for employees is only available for cars that run on unleaded petrol or those that can be converted. Products using CFCs and halons are only used where absolutely necessary and alternatives are being sought.

*In its general planning, how is the council involved in improving the overall environment?*
Neighbourhood offices manage the BINSEI (Brighter Islington Neighbourhood Security and Environmental Improvement) schemes, which include: measures to improve security; to improve appearances by cleaning, painting etc; to improve recreational and play opportunities with new and improved playgrounds; to improve safety using ramps, rails, road humps and reduce traffic problems; to improve cleanliness.
Larger schemes cover major traffic programmes and landscap-

ing of areas. Street, park and open space 'furniture' will be reviewed to get a more co-ordinated approach. Active and positive tree-planting programme, including a 'tree for a tree' scheme, (residents donate a tree, the council matches this and plants both trees). Creation of a chain of 'green' walks through the borough. Council now has a Tree Preservation Officer, Nature Conservation Officer and three Nature Conservation Wardens.

*What is the council policy and practice in the preservation, enhancement and creation of green and open spaces within the borough?*
Islington has the least green space of any London borough. Gillespie Park is under threat of development, but hopefully the area can be retained. The New River Walk and the Parkland Walk are examples of 'green corridors' that have been created from old river and railway routes.

*Is the council able to control or exert influence on air and water pollution in the borough?*
The Scientific Services Team monitor air and water and assess pollution related matters including, asbestos, noise, atmosphere, soil and radiation, and in addition they offer a Scientific Testing Facility to the general public.

*What steps can, and does, the council take on noise pollution and nuisance?*
Statutory notices are served on offenders in the industrial sector and action is taken if conditions are breached by tenants of council property. Insulation advice is given to householders to reduce noise levels.

*What are the council policies and practices with regard to waste disposal, rubbish collection and street cleaning?*
Domestic waste is collected weekly, from council provided dustbins, trade refuse is collected up to six times a week. Streets swept two to three times a week with main shopping roads swept twice a day on shopping days. Skips provided for residents at weekends for bulky objects. 'Hotline' provided to report fly-tipping and dumping. Waste is landfilled by the North London Waste Authority some distance from the City. Islington is looking at pre-treatment of its waste before landfill, i.e. incineration, in order to reduce the amount transported away.
Islington intends to introduce a bye-law that requires owners to clear up after their dogs. Also to introduce larger dog-free zones in parks, and some parks to be dog-free. Dog exercise areas will

be provided.

*What facilities do the council make available for recycling?*
Islington has bottle banks in the borough, and in early 1990 a recycling centre taking, glass, paper, oil, cans, white metal and wood, will be opening (see The Green Guide to Recycling section). Early 1990 will see the setting-up of some paper banks. Fridges/ freezers delivered to the recycling centre will have their CFCs removed before scrapping. Computer paper from the council offices is already recycled. Existing hardwood timber found during refurbishing or demolition work will be reused, and the public encouraged to bring, buy and re-use timber.

*Any other council activities to improve the environment worthy of note?*
Liaison and joint councillor level meetings with the Islington Ecology Forum – the umbrella group for voluntary wildlife and environmental groups.
Animal Charter adopted in 1983 – to use non-animal tested products, to give information to the public on such products, to discourage local trade in ivory, furs and reptile skins. To encourage owners to have their animals speyed/neutered. To promote animal welfare.

> *COUNCIL CONTACTS:*
> London Borough of Islington
> Town Hall
> Upper Street
> London N1 2UD
> (071) 226 1234
> Recycling information: Mr. Lapsley (071) 354 7239

> *Green star rating:* ★★★

## KENSINGTON AND CHELSEA

*Does the council have an overall policy on environmental issues?*
Kensington and Chelsea have **no** overall policy on environmental issues. However, the Environmental Health Department as part of its statutory duties deals with various environmental issues such as noise, and atmospheric pollutants.

*How is that policy implemented with direct regard to the council's 'in-house' activities?*
Pesticides, weed killer and other toxics are restricted in general

but may be applied under supervision, as a last resort. No paraquat based products are permitted on any council site.

*In its general planning, how is the council involved in improving the overall environment?*
Policy is to keep as much greenery in the borough as possible. Over the past five years, extensive tree and shrub planting has taken place and this is extended to cover the next five years. District Plan policies give great emphasis to protection of the borough's historic environment and to the preservation of open and garden spaces.

*What is the council policy and practice in the preservation, enhancement and creation of green and open spaces within the borough?*
Green areas are not under threat. Policy is to maintain all current areas and to create more where possible. On the Silchester Estate, an underground garage was demolished and turned into a semisunken garden. Swinbrook Estate has been redeveloped from older, terraced properties to modern housing with a large landscaped area.

*Is the council able to control or exert influence on air and water pollution in the borough?*
Road traffic is the only major local source of air pollution in the borough. Three monitoring stations measure smoke and sulphur dioxide in the atmosphere. Bonfires, building sites etc. are monitored and statutory action taken. Drinking water is regularly tested.

*What steps can, and does, the council take on noise pollution and nuisance?*
Noise pollution is a major cause for concern. Statutory enforcement procedures are taken in all cases of established nuisance. There is a 24-hour 'out-of-hours' service for complaints.

*What are the council policies and practices with regard to waste disposal, rubbish collection and street cleaning?*
Domestic collections twice a week. Free bulky collection service for small quantities at ground level. Charges made for larger amounts or higher levels.
Trade collections seven nights and seven days each week, every day except Christmas Day. Street cleansing in high-profile shopping areas, seven nights and seven days every day. Residential areas swept three or five times a week, with mews once a week. 24-hour sweeping at Earls Court.
Statutory notices sent out to rubbish/litter offenders. Publicity

given to areas with dog-fouling and cleansing problems.

*What facilities do the council make available for recycling?*
Bottle and paper recycling facilities. Four civic amenity sites (see The Green Guide to Recycling section). Western Riverside Waste Authority deals with CFC disposal.

*Any other council activities to improve the environment?*
Energy saving policy adopted in 1987 to try and reduce energy consumption by twenty per cent. Project still being monitored. The Thames Conservation area designated in 1980 and extending along the whole of the Royal Borough's river frontage. Many other conservation areas set up, 26 in all.

> COUNCIL CONTACTS:
> Royal Borough of Kensington and Chelsea
> The Town Hall
> Hornton Street
> London W8 7NX
> (071) 937 5464
> Recycling: (071) 352 9402
> Recycling Officer: Sharon Deane (071) 373 6099

*Green star rating:* ★★★

## KINGSTON

*Does the council have an overall policy on environmental issues?*
Kingston has no specific environmental policy document, but 'by decisions and actions has actively promoted environmental issues.' An Environmental Advisory Steering Group has been appointed and an Environmental Centre, with a staff of two, recently set up.

*How is that policy implemented with direct regard to the council's 'in-house' activities?*
Council has banned the use and purchase of products containing CFCs; started converting vehicle fleet to unleaded petrol; banned a range of suspect preservatives and of some specified hardwoods.

*In its general planning, how is the council involved in improving the overall environment?*
Environmental needs taken into account in planning procedures and size of developments considered for effects on street scene, adjoining residents and visual impact. Conservation areas pro-

tected and enhanced. Pedestrianisation schemes implemented: latest and largest is the Clarence Street Project.

Numerous traffic-calming measures (road closures, sleeping policemen etc.) introduced. Extensive tree-planting, maintenance and preservation policy.

*What is the council policy and practice in the preservation, enhancement and creation of green and open spaces?*
Virtual embargo on development in Green Belt and Metropolitan Open Land in borough. Local plan identifies areas deficient in green and playground spaces, requires developers to include such space in their plans. Areas for nature conservation identified and protected.

*Is the council able to control or exert influence on air and water pollution in the borough?*
Regular sampling programme on rivers and for water quality. Action taken and statutory powers used as necessary.

Participates in London-wide nitrogen dioxide and lead level monitoring and in gathering data for air pollution atlas. Environmental Health Department carries out further sampling for pollutants 'as required.'

*What steps can, and does, the council take on noise pollution and nuisance?*
No 'party patrols' provided, as these are not considered necessary, but council investigates all complaints thoroughly and takes action and serves statutory notices under the Control of Pollution Act where necessary.

*What are the council's policies and practices with regard to waste disposal, rubbish collection and street cleaning?*
Council considers waste disposal, rubbish collection and street cleansing services to be adequate and well-managed. Statutory action taken against dumpers.

Dog warden service being considered, but little success so far in enforcing bye-laws relating to dog-fouling and litter.

*What facilities do the council make available for recycling?*
Glass recycling collection points, more planned. Wastepaper collection point, also more planned. Recycling by voluntary groups encouraged through council, paying them extra eight pounds a tonne on top of money from waste contractors, resulting in an extra ten voluntary schemes, with six more at planning stage. (See The Green Guide to Recycling section).

*Any other council activities to improve the environment?*
Environmental Co-ordinator appointed, to encourage and support voluntary groups and provide educational material etc.
Diary of Environmental Events delivered to every household in borough, listing at least one event per week. Runs 'Business Management of the Environment' and 'Forget-Me-Not Plot' schemes and gives Environmental Awards.

> *COUNCIL CONTACTS:*
> The Royal Borough of Kingston upon Thames
> Guildhall
> Kingston upon Thames
> Surrey KT1 1EU
> (081) 546 2121.
> Environmental Co-ordinator: Sylvia Angel (081) 549 7065
> Althestan Road Civic Amenity Site: (081) 549 6373 - refuse disposal enquiries
> Special Collection Enquiries: (081) 546 2121 Ext.4210

**Green star rating: ★★★**

# LAMBETH

*Does the council have an overall policy on environmental issues?*
Lambeth has **no** overall policy.

*How is that policy implemented with direct regard to the council's 'in-house' activities?*
'Environmentally-friendly' purchases, including herbicides and pesticides for parks etc., made on a directorate/departmental basis. Council employs an Energy Efficiency Officer.

*In its general planning, how is the council involved in improving the overall environment?*
Lambeth has a Local Plan, which includes sections on Urban Landscape and Environment and on Ecology and Nature Conservation. More than 40 conservation areas have been established and there is an environmental improvements programme for projects north of the South Circular Road.

*What is the council policy and practice in the preservation, enhancement and creation of green and open spaces?*
Lambeth is one of most intensely built-up boroughs with great pressures on vacant land outside parks and open spaces. Council

seeks to preserve open space wherever possible, against great pressure from developers. Survey identified 25 sites of some ecological interest, nine of which designated 'key sites': Eardley Road Sidings, Streatham Vale, Shakespeare Road Sidings (first order sites); Palace Road, Sunnyhill Road temporary open space, York Hill Wood (second order); Archbishop Sumner Primary School Nature Garden, Reedworth Street, Elmwood Primary School Nature Garden, Carnac Street, Tulse Hill Nature Garden (Third order). But Eardley Road Sidings now earmarked for council housing, York Hill Wood lost to housing development and Shakespeare Road's ecological interest obliterated by current owner. Palace Road currently being developed as public open space by council.

*Is the council able to control or exert influence on air and water pollution in the borough?*
Council takes statutory action against individual polluters but main problems come from car and lorry exhausts. Monitors pollutants (notably lead from motor vehicle engines). Also has programme for removal of asbestos from public buildings, including public housing.

*What steps can, and does, the council take on noise pollution and nuisance?*
No 'noise patrol' at present, but new service to be set up at weekends. Commercial, domestic and industrial complaints investigated and statutory notices served as necessary.

*What are the council's policies and practices with regard to waste disposal, rubbish collection and street cleaning?*
Causes major problems in borough: hampered by lack of resources. Some 400 manual staff employed, half in street cleaning and market cleaning; provides twelve skips, moved in rotation among 70 sites, in effort to combat 'fly-tipping.'

*What facilities are made available for recycling?*
Bottle banks in the borough, with plans for further sites in the future. Paper recycling facilities at civic amenity site in Vale Street, more paper banks planned. Plans for more council wastepaper banks, can recycling being investigated. (See The Green Guide to Guide to Recycling section.)

*Any other council activities to improve the environment?*
Council has an Environmental Education Team, in the Directorate of Environmental Health. Has also prepared a series of pam-

phlets on local environmental issues. Lambeth Analytical Service provides analysis/consultation on air, water, soil, dust, food contamination.

COUNCIL CONTACTS:
Lambeth Council
Town Hall
Brixton Hill
London SW2 1RW
(071) 622 6655
Public Relations: Ext.271
Recycling: Bob King: (071) 720 2177 Ext.266

*Green star rating:* ★

# LEWISHAM

*Does the council have an overall policy on environmental issues?*
Lewisham has **no** overall policy on the environment, but has taken a large number of one-off initiatives. An Environmental Charter has been drawn up, targeting policies for a healthier environment and the monitoring and control of environmental risks and hazards. The policy was drawn together at a 'Caring for our Environment' conference in Autumn 1989. A 'green' officer is to be appointed to co-ordinate policy.

*How is that policy implemented with direct regard to the council's 'in-house' activities?*
Council vehicles and cars leased by the council are all lead-free. Vehicle oil is recycled.
Energy saving schemes in operation in council buildings.
Paper (including computer paper) and glass recycled in council offices.
Cleaners use water-based products and no aerosols.
Building trades not using tropical hardwoods.

*In its general planning, how is the council involved in improving the overall environment?*
Priority given to residents needs; business and residential areas segregated; traffic calming and other measures to keep through traffic out of residential streets; roads closed and controlled parking zone introduced in 1988.
Deptford High Street and Limes Grove, Lewisham pedestrian-

ised. Plans for whole of Lewisham High Street to be pedestrianised, starting in 1992.

On top of normal annual planting of some 700 trees, a further 1,000
plus to be planted 1989/90 as part of a 'clean-up' initiative.

'Lewisham 2000', High Street shop with detailed plans of new
developments within the borough, open six days a week.

*What is the council policy and practice in the preservation, enhance-
ment and creation of green and open spaces?*

Conservation areas and green spaces maintained throughout the
borough, although British Rail plans to put ventilation shafts for
Channel Tunnel rail link in some of them. More green spaces being
opened, e.g. Elmira Street Public Open Space.

Major works by Thames Water have proceeded only after detailed
work by council, water authority and London Wildlife Trust to
ensure maximum number of trees etc. preserved.

*Is the council able to control or exert influence on air and water pollution
in the borough?*

Complaints investigates, statutory powers used where necessary.
Recent sampling of water following contamination of supply:
prosecution being considered.

Lewisham is a smokeless zone.

*What steps can, and does, the council take on noise pollution and nui-
sance?*

'Noisy party' patrol in operation in residential area. Statutory action
taken on residential and commercial noise nuisance as necessary.

*What are the council's policies and practices with regard to waste dis-
posal, rubbish collection and street cleaning?*

Street washing being carried out and areas of borough 'blitzed' in
one-off clean-up as part of 'Clean up/Green up' campaign. Frequency of street sweeping being increased.

First borough to introduce wheeled bins. Free collection of household 'lumber'. Long term plans for combined heat and power waste
plant.

Two thousand additional litter bins provided. Campaign to stop
businesses dumping in streets. High-profile prosecutions of
persistent offenders planned.

Lewisham MP Joan Ruddock successfully introduced parliamentary bill to give councils increased powers over fly-tippers.

'Pooper scooter' for dog mess under trial. 'Pooper scoopers' handed
out. Dog sand pits located on streets. High-profile prosecutions

of persistent offenders being considered as way of raising public awareness.

*What facilities do the council make available for recycling?*
Major recycling and waste transfer facility opened at Creekside, Deptford in June 1989: glass, cans, paper, oil, rags all recycled. Bottle banks and paper banks. (for sites, see The Green Guide to Recycling section). Future plans for mini-recycling centres for glass, paper and cans. Computer paper and other paper waste collections being established.

*Any other council activities to improve the environment?*
Monthly council newsletter on environmental issues. Environmental Services directory published. Surveys of public concerns carried out. Assistance and support given to wide range of voluntary groups, including Friends of the Earth.

COUNCIL CONTACTS:
London Borough of Lewisham
Depford Town Hall
New Cross Road
London SE14 6AE
(081) 695 6000
Recycling: Malcolm Kendall, Ext.5116
Environmental Services Directorate: (081) 690 4366. Philip Walker, Policy Officer.

**Green star rating: ★★★**


# MERTON

*Does the council have an overall policy on environmental issues?*
Merton has a Corporate Policy Plan putting important priority on environmental issues, many of which are raised in the the revised Borough Plan, at present the subject of public consultation. Plan seeks to enhance and protect identified high-quality environmental areas and open space from unsympathetic development.
Traffic nuisance a particular problem: council seeks to reduce traffic nuisance in environmental areas and reduce traffic in residential areas.

*How is that policy implemented with direct regard to the council's 'in-house' activities?*
Continuing programme of energy conservation; energy saving

measures introduced in council offices and schools. At main offices in Crown House, has lighting control scheme which automatically switches off when natural lighting good enough, and at set times of day, to prevent lights burning in empty offices. Computerised heating controls to regulate heat in schools efficiently.

Purchases only ozone-friendly aerosols and has reduced volume and toxicity of pesticides used. Fertiliser use also reduced and fertilisers not used when nitrates and phosphates could find their way into water courses.

Most council vehicles now run on unleaded fuel.

Low energy light bulbs gradually replacing conventional ones.

*In its general planning, how is the council involved in improving the overall environment?*
Fourteen conservation areas designated, with additional planning controls in some. Tree preservation orders made to protect trees and woodland areas.

Traffic calming introduced in a number of residential areas to reduce 'rat running'. Part of Mitcham town centre pedestrianised, extended to most of town centre in next few years and including major landscaping project.

*What is the council policy and practice in the preservation, enhancement and creation of green and open spaces?*
Tries to retain and enhance existing private and public open space. In some cases, where private sports grounds have been developed, significant areas of public open space have been secured (e.g. ten acres provided at Kings College/Chelsea College play fields).

Eight areas of Metropolitan Open Land protected; plans to extend this over another twenty acres from Morden Hall Park to Watermeads.

Snuff Mill Environmental Centre established with National Trust in 1988: related to exploring Morden Hall Park with unfertilised meadow and woodland areas. Management agreements with London Wildlife Trust for three areas in borough. Council funds and acts as agent for Mitcham Common Board of Conservators.

*Is the council able to control or exert influence on air and water pollution in the borough?*
Statutory action taken against polluters.

*What steps can, and does, the council take on noise pollution and nuisance?*
All complaints responded to and statutory action taken as neces-

sary. Council assessing 'bad neighbour' problems in north-west Mitcham to cut down on noise, pollution and traffic nuisance.

*What are the council's policies and practices with regard to waste disposal, rubbish collection and street cleaning?*
Joined with four neighbouring authorities to form co-ordinating South London Waste Disposal Group: household waste collected by independent contractor; groups sends waste to landfill sites in Kent.
Refuse collection and street cleaning privatised in 1982. Domestic rubbish collected weekly, trade rubbish by private agreement. Street cleaning carried out daily in town centre areas, weekly or fortnightly elsewhere.
Litter bins throughout borough (some sponsored), emptied two or three times a week, or daily, depending on location and use.
Council looking for further powers to control dog-fouling, including exclusion of dogs from sports areas and playgrounds and from 50 per cent of public open space.
Voluntary litter clearing schemes supported.

*What facilities do the council make available for recycling?*
Two civic amenity/recycling centres, where paper, metal, glass, cans, rags, waste oil and asbestos can be disposed of separately. Contract with local scrap metal merchant to maximise metal reclamation.
Bottle banks in the borough. Schools provided with skips for waste paper collections; special collections of large quantities of waste paper arranged. (For recycling sites see The Green Guide to Recycling section)

*Any other council activities to improve the environment?*
Schools encouraged to establish ecological areas in grounds; support for voluntary groups, including City Farm and Keep Merton Tidy Group. Allotment holders encouraged to reduce use of pesticides.

*COUNCIL CONTACTS:*
London Borough of Merton
Crown House
London Road
Merton
Surrey SM4 5DX
(081) 543 2222
Recycling: Development Department

*Green star rating:* ★★★

# NEWHAM

*Does the council have an overall policy on environmental issues?*
Newham has no overall policy at present, but an Environmental Strategy is being prepared.

*How is that policy implemented with direct regard to the council's 'in-house' activities?*
Recent policy to ensure all aerosol purchases and insulating foams for buildings are CFC free. All scrapped refrigeration units to be sent for CFC recovery.
Only Government-approved pesticides used; staff sent on spraying courses and require certificate of competence.
Building Energy Management Systems being incorporated into new and refurbished premises heating schemes, for more efficient energy use.

*In its general planning, how is the council involved in improving the overall environment?*
Encouragement for relocation of, or in situ improvements to, firms which cause environmental nuisance in residential areas.
Four conservation areas within borough, with present particular activity in Stratford (St John's) area: St. John's Church refurbished, adjacent area pedestrianised, landscaping churchyard planned.
Major environmental improvements, including pedestrianisation, planned for other major shopping area, East Ham Town Centre.
Traffic improvements, including redesign of road junctions, traffic light installation and adjustment, planned and implemented to draw fast and heavy traffic from residential streets.

*What is the council policy and practice in the preservation, enhancement and creation of green and open spaces?*
Dense residential development in borough and shortage of open space. Council aims to rectify this: e.g. major new area of open space (36 hectares) created at Beckton District Park. Efforts to incorporate open space in new developments: e.g. three hectares of open space programmed for Upton Park Goods Yard housing and school development; 1.9 and two hectares planned with housing development on Forest Gate Maternity Hospital and Stratford Market sites; 9.5 hectares planned for Thames Barrier site.
Housing development resisted on Metropolitan Open Land in Roding Valley (Burgess Road).
Council works with British Trust for Conservation Volunteers on scheme for long-term care of newly-planted trees.

*Is the council able to control or exert influence on air and water pollution in the borough?*
Statutory action taken under Public Health, Clean Air and Control of Pollution Acts. Recent prosecutions against firms causing dark smoke emissions.

*What steps can, and does, the council take on noise pollution and nuisance?*
Statutory action taken under Control of Pollution Act. Team investigates out-of-hours noise complaints.
Noisy dogs controlled under bye-laws.

*What are the council's policies and practices with regard to waste disposal, rubbish collection and street cleaning?*
Council has 'commitment to a clean, tidy and safe environment. Seeks to educate public and induce sense of civic pride. Recycling encouraged where appropriate.
Cleansing Policy Statement prepared as first stage of service specification for street cleaning.

*What facilities do the council make available for recycling?*
Only bottle banks at present in borough (see The Green Guide to Recycling section). Plans for recycled paper use and in-house recycling of paper and aluminium cans being prepared.

*Any other council activities to improve the environment?*
Nature reserve and centre planned for Cuckold Haven in Roding Valley.
Winsor Terrace residents fighting for creation of wildlife area next to proposed Docklands Light Railway extension; council supporting them in negotiations with London Docklands Development Corporation.
Policy on use of lead-free petrol in council and contractors fleets being ratified.

COUNCIL CONTACTS:
London Borough of Newham
Town Hall
East Ham
London E6 2RP
(081) 472 1430
John Samuel, Chief Executive: Ext.23049
Recycling: (081) 472 1450 Isobel Stacey

*Green star rating:* ★

# REDBRIDGE

*Does the council have an overall policy on environmental issues?*
Redbridge has no specific overall policy, but 'for many years has actively encouraged the enhancement and improvement of the environment', through planning, purchasing, recycling and energy conservation policies.

*How is that policy implemented with direct regard to the council's 'in-house' activities?*
Council has long-standing energy policy, with energy conservation measures and new technology, including combined heat and power installations to generate electricity and reclaim waste heat. Loft insulation in all council houses and flats and cavity wall insulation in most.
CFC-free aerosols purchased for general use; all cleansing materials CFC-free and biodegradable. Recycled paper used in toilet rolls and paper towels; recycled photocopying paper being investigated.
Use of hardwoods discontinued in replacement windows and doors, UPVC used instead. Extension of this use to soffit boards, fencing, canopies, etc, being investigated. Lead-free petrol used wherever possible: all new vehicles lead-free, old ones converted where possible.
Use of pesticides in parks and gardens carefully controlled and used as sparingly as possible.

*In its general planning, how is the council involved in improving the overall environment?*
Ten conservation areas created within borough, together with five 'residential precincts' and six 'general improvement areas'. Main shopping street in Ilford Town Centre pedestrianised. Local list of buildings worthy of protection in addition to Dept. of Environment statutory list. Redbridge Merit Awards scheme to encourage good design. Traffic-calming measures, including road closures, chicanes, mini-roundabouts, introduced in residential areas near town centre.
Local residents' tree-planting schemes encouraged and co-ordinated.

*What is the council policy and practice in the preservation, enhancement and creation of green and open spaces?*
Several new open spaces created, including Fairlop Country Park, on former gravel workings; Roding Valley Park, following M11

construction; new park in Chadwell Heath, formerly part of industrial site. New creations more than outweigh losses of green space. Further green spaces created in development of Ilford Town Centre. Ecological survey of former hospital site commissioned to facilitate sensitive development.

*Is the council able to control or exert influence on air and water pollution in the borough?*
Borough has been smoke free zone for many years, reducing air pollution. Energy policy also helps by ensuring most efficient burning of fuel. Air conditioning units in public buildings regularly checked and treated for legionella bacteria.
New water bye-laws reduce water pollution. Environmental Health Officers continuously check connection of household appliances and toilets to reduce pollution to water courses through wrong connections to sewerage system.

*What steps can, and does, the council take on noise pollution and nuisance?*
Environmental Health Officers 'extremely active' in controlling noise from industry, redevelopment work and parties.

*What are the council's policies and practices with regard to waste disposal, rubbish collection and street cleaning?*
Waste disposal through East London Waste Authority. Refuse collection from households and commercial premises at least once a week. District roads swept every eighth working day; areas with much litter, such as the shopping precinct, swept daily or throughout the day.
Prosecutions for dropping litter difficult because of reluctance of witnesses to give evidence. New bye-laws being introduced to control dog fouling in parks, recreation grounds and highways, which give rise to a large number of complaints.

*What facilities do the council make available for recycling?*
Many glass recycling collection sites in borough. Paper, oil and metal recycled after collection at Civic Amenity Site in Chigwell Road. Increase of glass- and paper-collection sites and possibility of door-to-door paper collection being investigated. Can recycling scheme being considered. (for sites, see The Green Guide to Recycling section).

*Any other council activities to improve the environment?*
Publicity campaigns to encourage residents to protect the environment.

Very successful tree replacement scheme and fund to replace trees lost in October 1987 hurricane: borough won Silver Jubilee Tree Trophy in 1989 and Residential Areas Trophy in London in Bloom competition.

*COUNCIL CONTACTS:*
London Borough of Redbridge
Town Hall
Ilford
Essex IG1 1DD
(081) 478 3020
Cleansing/recycling: Mr P.Beck

**Green star rating: ★★★★**

# RICHMOND UPON THAMES

*Does the council have an overall policy on environmental issues?*
Richmond has adopted a 'Charter for the Environment' which aims to 'protect, monitor and improve the quality of the environment in the borough. It has specific policies on the use of lead-free petrol and the elimination of CFCs and also monitors specific pollutants, notably contamination of the Thames and aircraft noise.

*How is that policy implemented with direct regard to the council's 'in-house' activities?*
Council has long-standing energy-saving programme, increasingly uses recycled paper for stationery and photocopying and collects office paper for recycling. Purchases environmentally sensitive cleaning products, recycles cooking oil in welfare kitchens and has established two wildlife gardens. Healthy eating and exercise programmes supported through all services, such as Day Centres and Welfare Catering.

*In its general planning, how is the council involved in improving the overall environment?*
Planning controls for conservation areas, listed buildings, environmental improvements, etc. contained in Local Plan adopted in 1985. Fifty five conservation areas have been designated and a register of 'buildings of townscape merit' is kept. New conservation award scheme and environmental improvement schemes, including shopfront grants and grants for repair of historic buildings.

*What is the council policy and practice in the preservation, enhancement and creation of green and open spaces?*
Ecology and Nature Conservation Officer appointed, drawing up management plans for some open spaces. Nature conservation strategy being produced by London Ecology Unit. Local Conservation Volunteers group has been formed.

*Is the council able to control or exert influence on air and water pollution in the borough?*
Environmental Health Division investigates complaints of air pollution from industrial and commercial premises. Routine monitoring carried out by London Scientific Services, as part of London-wide programme.
Environmental Health Division monitors Thames regularly for sewage and contamination by toxic chemicals.

*What steps can, and does, the council take on noise pollution and nuisance?*
No noise patrol: few complaints received about organised parties. Environmental Health Division investigates all noise complaints and issues abatement orders where necessary. In its own premises, like public halls and some residential units, has improved noise insulation and other noise mitigation measures.

*What are the council's policies and practices with regard to waste disposal, rubbish collection and street cleaning?*
Domestic refuse collections once a week, free of charge. Commercial collections, as requested, up to seven times a week, charged. Little industrial waste. Costs high, due to rear/alleyway collections. Dumped builders waste causes problems, as no-one takes responsibility: collected on ad hoc basis. Council wants Enforcement Officer. Council funds community-based Tidy Group and has won National Keep Britain Tidy award twice (1985 and 1987). Introducing Tidy Code of Practice for Traders, anti-dog-fouling campaign.

*What facilities do the council make available for recycling?*
Council has Recycling Officer, salary funded from recycling schemes. An additional £30,000 of this income went in grants for environmental improvement schemes. Recycling centres at Townmead Road civic amenity site, plus mini recycling centres (paper, bottles, cans, rags) in borough, more small paper banks and bottle banks (see The Green Guide to Recycling section). More purpose-built mini recycling centres planned, plus easily-acces-

sible paper and can banks, such as in schools and work places. Council organises commercial cullet (glass) and office waste paper collections from businesses.
Investigating CFC recycling scheme for CFC recovery from fridges and freezers.

*Any other council activities to improve the environment?*
Gives grants to and works with voluntary groups; education through Nature Conservation Officer.

COUNCIL CONTACTS:
London Borough of Richmond upon Thames
York House
Richmond Road
Twickenham TW1 3AA
(081) 891 1411

The Recycling Officer
Technical Services Department
London Borough of Richmond upon Thames
Regal House
London Road
Twickenham TW1 3QB
(081) 891 7329
Recycling Officer: Rosana Scholes

Keep Richmond upon Thames Tidy Group
Craneford Way Depot
Craneford Way
Twickenham TW2 7SG
(081) 891 6878/6880 – Sue Duckworth

*Green star rating:* ★★★★

# SOUTHWARK

*Does the council have an overall policy on environmental issues?*
Southwark approved a Green Issues policy in September 1989, calling on all council departments to prepare 'green audits'. It is also supporting the setting up of an Environmental Forum by local groups like Friends of the Earth.

*How is that policy implemented with direct regard to the council's 'in-house' activities?*

Recycled paper in use for several purposes within council, including committee agendas and press cuttings. Only non-bleached paper used.

Most council cars and vans are being converted to lead-free petrol. Purchase of tropical hardwoods banned.

*In its general planning, how is the council involved in improving the overall environment?*

Thirty two conservation areas designated: e.g. Camberwell, Dulwich, Sydenham Hill Wood.

Ecologist appointed to assist in all planning matters. First inner London council to launch handbook of nature conservation sites. Heavily involved in local campaigns against Channel Tunnel (£40,000 donated recently to pressure groups for publicity.)

*What is the council policy and practice in the preservation, enhancement and creation of green and open spaces?*

Largest London borough project to create new public open space: Burgess Park, 135 acres when complete. Russia Dock woodland being managed with particular emphasis on planting native woodland species. Many smaller landscape schemes, including model school nature garden. Local Nature Reserve designated in agreement with Nature Conservancy Council. Support for environmental improvements by local groups.

*Is the council able to control or exert influence on air and water pollution in the borough?*

Whole of borough is smoke-free zone. Regular monitoring carried out, as well as investigations and inspections. Statutory action taken as necessary.

*What steps can, and does, the council take on noise pollution and nuisance?*

Complaints investigated and legal action taken as necessary. Continuous night and weekend complaints service. Building sites watched and monitored.

*What are the council's policies and practices with regard to waste disposal, rubbish collection and street cleaning?*

'A Greener Southwark' initiative started April 1989, including anti-litter poster campaign in schools, major anti dog-fouling campaign. Major expansion in provision of litter bins throughout the borough.

*What facilities do the council make available for recycling?*

Bottle banks, plus a paper recycling unit.
(For sites, see The Green Guide to Recycling section.)
Public consultation now in progress on new sites and more facilities.

*Any other council activities to improve the environment?*
Establishing, with other boroughs, new combined heat and power scheme burning waste and reducing landfill requirements. Grants to local amenity and environmental groups, support for independent urban studies centre. Environmental education policy being drafted.

> *COUNCIL CONTACTS:*
> London Borough of Southwark
> Town Hall
> Peckham Road
> London SE5 8UB
> (071) 703 6311
> Green Audit: Stephen Morris (071) 403 3322 Ext.2136
> Recycling: Peter Jones (071) 703 5464
> Ecology: David Solman (071) 403 3322 Ext.2136
> Pollution Control: (071) 237 4551 Ext.2149

> *Green star rating:* ★★

# SUTTON

*Does the council have an overall policy on environmental issues?*
Sutton has an 'Environmental Statement', adopted in 1986, which lays down a series of policies to protect and enhance the local environment and to conserve resources: 'These policies also establish a proper balance between short term economic requirements and the longer term ecological need of our community.'

*How is that policy implemented with direct regard to the council's 'in-house' activities?*
Recycled paper used in council offices, use being extended. Pilot project under way to recycle office paper waste. Energy Management team appointed to improve energy conservation in council buildings and elsewhere. Two council developments, New Highview School, Sheen Way and Mollinson Road housing site, being designed as model energy-conscious developments. Action taken to stop/minimise use of CFC aerosols. Council vehicles being

converted to run on lead free petrol. Bonfires discouraged in parks: wood chippings machines installed, chippings used as mulch. Use of chemicals, especially in parks, monitored and reveiwed. Healthy eating promoted through food buying policies and catering in schools, Meals on Wheels etc. Use of tropical hardwoods reviewed. Landscaping of council capital schemes for housing, major road works and utilities now being carried out.

*In its general planning, how is the council involved in improving the overall environment?*
Council works to protect Green Belt, Metropolitan Open Land, playing fields and other open space. Tries to protect back gardens from development. Makes environmental improvements to shopping and residential areas, including traffic calming. Pedestrianisation in Sutton Town Centre. Has tree-planting target of 10,000 per year and promotes large-scale community involvement in the environment.

*What is the council policy and practice in the preservation, enhancement and creation of green and open spaces?*
Protection via Local Plan policies and acquisition. Enhancement through introduction of nature conservation management regimes (e.g. meadow areas in Rosehill Park East and Roundshaw Park; Anton Crescent flood alleviation scheme partly designed as wetland nature reserve). New woodland planting with local environmental groups (e.g. Revesby Wood and Anton Crescent).
Private open space under threat: London Regional Transport Sports Ground being developed, but five-acre park created due to council policy. Water-based leisure park planned at Beddington Sewage works, under threat from road and commercial development proposals.
Extensive hedge planting around both council land (parks and schools) and privately-owned land.

*Is the council able to control or exert influence on air and water pollution in the borough?*
Monitors air and water pollution as part of London-wide scheme. Working towards lead-free fuel in council transport fleet. Discourages bonfires in public open spaces and sites: wood chipping machines (for mulch) reduce need for burning. CFC aerosol use reduced or eliminated.

*What steps can, and does, the council take on noise pollution and nuisance?*
Statutory offences vigorously investigated and notices served as

necessary. Planning applications examined for potential noise problems. Helicopter noise attracting increasing amount of public complaint: report of noise mapping to be produced.

*What are the council's policies and practices with regard to waste disposal, rubbish collection and street cleaning?*
Routine street cleaning augmented by thorough cleaning of each road (Scour-Clean) three times a year, including providing skips free of charge for householders to dispose of rubbish. System in operation to keep collection/disposal chemical rubbish away from domestic refuse system. Plastic sack system to be introduced throughout borough.
Greener Cleaner Borough Campaign to change attitudes to litter in schools and community and encouragement of recycling, adopt-a-plot. Experimental 'pooper scooper' scheme for dog fouling in parks and on estates. Dog free areas in some parks. Animal Warden employed, in mainly educational role.
Recycling to reduce waste actively encouraged.

*What facilities do the council make available for recycling?*
Bottle banks running with more planned. Can bank at Rosehill car park and collection projects at various schools; new can banks being considered. CFCs from old fridges/freezers recycled at Oldfield Road Transfer Station. Thirty neighbourhood recycling centres planned, in first instance for glass, paper and, hopefully, rags. Composting being examined, to divert vegetable material from waste stream. (See The Green Guide to Recycling section for sites).

*Any other council activities to improve the environment?*
Large scale community involvement central to council's policies. Sutton Conservation Group is umbrella organisation for voluntary involvement. Adopt-a-bank schemes to look after recycling facilities; Adopt-a-plot, for improving neglected corners. All recycling profits returned to community for environmental initiatives. Council has set up The Ecology Centre, first of its kind, at the Old Rectory, Festival Walk, Carshalton.

*COUNCIL CONTACTS:*
London Borough of Sutton
Civic Offices
St Nicholas Way
Sutton
Surrey SM1 1EA

(081) 661 5000
Recycling officer: Duncan Bell (081) 770 5000

Environmental officers, etc., at
Planning Division, Technical Services
24 Denmark Road
Carshalton
Surrey SM5 2JG
(081) 661 5619

Community ecologist, etc., at
The Ecology Centre
The Old Rectory
Festival Walk
Carshalton
Surrey SM5 3NX
(081) 773 4018

*Green star rating:* ★★★★★

## TOWER HAMLETS

Tower Hamlets council has divided itself into seven 'neighbour-hoods', to provide more local, and locally-accountable, services to its residents.

The local Borough Plan outlines policies on the urban landscape and conservation, including development (large and small), planning controls, protection and enhancement of environment, landscaping, conservation (21 conservation areas, 1500 statutory listed buildings, 700 more on local list). Particular attention is paid to areas of special character, like Thames-side, London squares. Each neighbourhood was asked about specific activities in its area and the work they considered to be of importance is detailed below.

*Does the council have an overall policy on environmental issues?*
Bow Neighbourhood: No overall policy, but being investigated at the moment.
Bethnal Green Neighbourhood: Green monitoring group has prepared a 'Charter for the Environment'.
Globe Town Neighbourhood: Has prepared a 'Green Strategy' for action on environmental issues.
Isle of Dogs Neighbourhood: Newly established Green Working Party developing Charter for Environmental Action.
Poplar Neighbourhood: Poplar has no overall policy.

Stepney Neighbourhood: Works within guidelines of Urban Landscape and Conservation section of Tower Hamlets' Borough Plan.

Wapping Neighbourhood: Works within policy guidelines in Borough Plan.

*How is that policy implemented with direct regard to the council's 'in-house' activities?*

Bow: Banned use of CFC aerosols. Council vehicles converted to lead-free petrol. Use low-energy light bulbs.

Bethnal Green: Use of recycled paper. Lead-free petrol in all leased cars. Questionnaire drawn up on 'smoking in the neighbourhood's offices'. Aims to review its own purchasing policy – instigate an energy conservation programme and promote a healthy eating and nutrition policy for the neighbourhood's catering activities.

Globe Town: Organising purchase of environmentally sensitive materials, including recycled paper and cleaning materials. Pesticides not used in parks and open spaces. Neighbourhood vehicles and lease cars are in process of conversion to lead-free fuel. Pool cover to save energy in swimming baths.

Isle of Dogs: Green Working Party focusing on 'in-house' action on purchasing strategies, recycling opportunities and Green Office Guide. Recycled paper already used.

Poplar: Neighbourhood newsletter is printed on recylced paper.

Wapping: Energy saving initiatives. CFC-free products purchased. Use of pesticides carefully controlled.

*In its general planning, how is the council involved in improving the overall environment?*

Bow: Seven conservation areas, to preserve buildings of historical interest. New trees planted along market place in Roman Road.

Bethnal Green: Protects and improves areas of good townscape quality and buildings of architectural or historic interest. Has a target of reducing the use of pesticides, herbicides and chemical fertilisers and to move towards organic horticulture.

Globe Town: Two new conservation areas agreed; extensions to existing four. Several traffic management schemes introduced, new traffic calming measures planned. Cycle routes being investigated. Major street planting programme begun Autumn 1989.

Isle of Dogs: Within London Dockland Development Corporation area for planning: neighbourhood consulted, but no planning powers. But mini-local plans being drawn up for activity such as housing estate improvements.

Stepney: Four conservation areas, one designated 1989 (Commercial Road), one extended (York Square). New area proposed around London Hospital. Shop front improvement grants for listed buildings along Mile End Road. Improvement and refurbishment of buildings along Commercial Road. Old Town Hall in Whitehorse Road refurbished for Half Moon youth theatre.

Wapping: Policy to create open spaces wherever possible. Planning applications to build on green and open space opposed.

*What is the council policy and practice in the preservation, enhancement and creation of green and open spaces?*

Bow: £10 million being spent in next ten years on Victoria Park, largest park in East London. Historic buildings in park to be restored and preserved.

Bethnal Green: £1m to be spent this financial year on open space improvements. Seek to increase the amount of green and open spaces. Promote and encourage tree planting.

Globe Town: Two major open spaces: Bethnal Green Gardens and Meath Gardens, possibility of nature park. Feasibility study on better use of leisure facilities in Meath Gardens being undertaken by Tower Hamlets Environment Trust.

Isle of Dogs: Works within Borough Local Plan. Rolling programme of preserving and enhancing open space, including tree-planting. Parks User Group set up for consultation and participation in improvements. Open space being reduced as development continues. A 30-acre site in centre of Isle of Dogs, Mudchute Park Farm, is leased by council and has largest area of natural/wildlife in area. Leisure, recreational, educational activities, further developments planned.

Poplar: Policy to discourage development on open land; improve parks.

Stepney: Policy to extend and improve open space. Four major projects in hand with local people and groups: St Mary's Gardens, Stepney Green Open Space, Trafalgar Gardens and Sidney Street Library. Neighbourhood Open Space Strategy for improving and utilising open space and playgrounds.

Wapping: Tree planting in Wapping Woods. Numerous schemes to preserve and enhance open space, e.g. King Edward Memorial Park. Public consultations on creation of open space and improvement to open space in Wellclose Square, Shadwell.

*Is the council able to control or exert influence on air and water pollution in the borough?*

Generally, inspections, investigations and monitoring; statutory action taken as necessary.

Wapping: commissioned investigation by London Scientific Services into New International plant, given clean bill of health.

*What steps can, and does, the council take on noise pollution and nuisance?*

Bow: Noise patrol from Environmental Health Service

Bethnal Green: Seeks to control noise from all sources.

Globe Town: Much work by Environmental Health Section. Offenders prosecuted when necessary. New equipment purchased to measure sound levels.

Isle of Dogs: Many complaints arising from Docklands construction sites and print works. Notices served where appropriate. Emergency 24-hour call-out service.

Poplar: Noise patrol at weekends.

Wapping: No noise patrols, but respond to complaints on noisy neighbours and parties. Publicity material urging complaints about excessive noise from building sites (major problem in development area). One prosecution so far.

*What are the council's policies and practices with regard to waste disposal, rubbish collection and street cleaning?*

Bow: Streets 'regularly cleaned and washed.' Problems with fly-tipping. Anti dog-fouling campaign launched.

Bethnal Green: Regular reviews of effectiveness of refuse collection and street cleansing operations. Works in conjunction with the Tidy Group. Encourage traders etc. to reduce packaging and use bio-degradable sources. Anti dog fouling campaign to be launched. Removes graffiti in public places. All action taken to prevent fly-tipping.

Globe Town: New cleansing contract started August 1989, being closely monitored. Animal Working Party set up on problems of dog nuisance and bye-laws. Animal Warden proposed, education programmes under way.

Isle of Dogs: Street cleaning and sweeping out to private tender. Dog faeces to be removed as part of specification. New Environmental Protection Inspectors posts established to enforce bye-laws, pollution and litter acts.

Stepney: Waste disposal and civic amenity site at Northumberland Wharf which is used by all of the Neighbourhoods and other local Authorities. Cleansing contractor commenced in August 1989, high standards of street cleaning expected and insisted upon. Bin/

sack and bulk container collection of rubbish, also bulk refuse collection. Trade refuse – nominal charge. Furniture etc. – free removal. Legal action against fly-tipping.

Wapping: In-house service contract for rubbish; service improved and streamlined. Supports borough-wide implementation of bye-laws in parks, open spaces, housing amenity areas. Encourages identification of 'dog free' areas. Publicity on dog control.

*What facilities do the council make available for recycling?*
Borough-wide working party set up to look at recycling possibilities. Neighbourhood offices collecting paper for recycling. Recycling facilities for metals, oil, cans, paper at Northumberland Wharf.
Bow: Bottle banks.

Bethnal Green: Centrally run bottle bank scheme.

Globe Town: Bottle bank in Roman Road. Paper skip in Market Square. Once a month collections.

Isle of Dogs: Green Working Party investigating paper recycling scheme for neighbourhood offices and surrounding businesses. There is glass collection, more planned. Plans for collection of more materials.

Poplar: Paper, textiles, scrap metal, waste oil and glass can be left at the municipal rubbish tip, Yabsley Street, for recycling. Bottle bank in Chrisp Street.

Stepney: Bottle banks. Future plans for recycling paper, cardboard and aluminium. Schools asking for bulk containers for paper collection.

Wapping: Bottle banks are in operation with plans for more in the future. (For sites, see The Green Guide to Recycling section)

*Any other council activities to improve the environment?*
Bethnal Green: Touring exhibition in 1990 in order to give publicity to the Charter for the Environment.

Globe Town: Work with local community groups. Priority given to expanding environmental work and education.

Wapping: Projects planned through Inner Area Programme. Wapping Healthy City Project in operation.

*NEIGHBOURHOOD CONTACTS:*
Bow:
Neighbourhood Centre, 159 Bow Road E3 2SE.
 (081) 980 1812. Chief Executive: Keith Ivory.
Bethnal Green:
Neighbourhood Centre, 255/279 Cambridge Heath Road, E2 0HQ.
(071) 739 4344. Chief Executive: J.R.A. Ward

Health and Consumer Services Officer: Philip Machen,
(071) 729 5684
Globe Town:
Neighbourhood Centre, 62 Roman Road E2 0PG
(081) 980 8067. Chief Executive: Tony de Sautoy
Environmental Development Officer: Peter Brooker, Ext.2210
Isle of Dogs:
Neighbourhood Centre, Great Eastern Enterprise, Millharbour
E14 9TE
(071) 538 4571. Chief Executive: Tony James.
Green Worker: Bridget Prentice.
Poplar:
Neighbourhood Centre, Bow House, 147/159 Bow Road, E3
(081) 980 4414. Chief Executive: Bill Tomlinson
Stepney:
Neighbourhood Centre, 217/223 Commercial Road, E1 2BU.
(071) 790 1818. Chief Executive: Sean Baine.
Wapping:
Neighbourhood Centre, 646 Commercial Road E14 7HA
(071) 987 9200. Chief Executive: Ian Orton.

*Green star rating:* ★★★

## WALTHAM FOREST

*Does the council have an overall policy on environmental issues?*
Waltham Forest has for many years been implementing policies
and programmes to improve the environment. These policies have
now been drawn together into 'The Waltham Forest Green Charter'.

*How is that policy implemented with direct regard to the council's 'in-
house' activities?*
Council intends to adopt a detailed chemicals policy providing
guidance on the use of safer alternatives and on the limited circumstances in which chemicals may be used. Proper training and
supervision of operatives, including contractors. An energy audit
of all the council buildings will be carried out, with a view to energy
conservation. Products that contain CFC's will no longer be
purchased and all new vehicles will use lead free petrol. Existing
vehicles will be converted (if possible). Also looking into the possible
use of catalytic convertors. Biodegradable washing and cleaning
materials only will be used. No tropical hardwoods will be bought
or used unless they come from a sustainable forest. Healthy eating

policy will be introduced.

*In its general planning, how is the council involved in improving the overall environment?*
Waltham Forest is promoting 'Good Design' by holding meetings between architects, developers, and council officers. Recently reviewed its planning standards and controls. Five conservation areas, and one area of special character have been designated. Town centre shopping improvement programme underway. Traffic management measures include cycle routes, speed humps, and road chicanes.

*What is the council policy and practice in the preservation, enhancement and creation of green and open spaces within the borough?*
Council is committed to the retention and upgrading of open space. A new Park at Wingfield Road and Stoneydown in Walthamstow is to be provided. Two further planned at Drysdale Avenue in Chingford and Cann Hall in Leytonstone. Ecology garden for the disabled in Walthamstow. Waltham Forest now has a new Nature conservation strategy after working with the London Ecology Unit and a nature conservation handbook is to be published. Local groups work in Ainslie Wood and woodland area by Green Way Avenue.

*Is the council able to control or exert influence on air and water pollution in the borough?*
Borough is 100% smoke controlled. Twenty-four hour continuous air monitoring at Chingford, Leyton and Walthamstow. There is a lead sampling programme covering school playgrounds in conjunction with Health Authority Staff. Regular samples taken of all drinking and swimming pool water.

*What steps can, and does, the council take on noise pollution and nuisance?*
A weekend Noise Complaints Investigating Team has been established to monitor parties. Statutory action taken against noise from industrial, commercial and entertainment premises.

*What are the council policies and practices with regard to waste disposal, rubbish collection, street cleansing and sweeping?*
Waltham Forest gives its waste, as collected, to the Waste Authority. Streets are swept daily if necessary. Bye-laws are to be introduced to deal with dogs fouling footways.

*What facilities do the council make available for recycling?*

At two civic amenity sites the council recycles glass, paper, oils, metals and rags. Bottle banks throughout the Borough. Recycling activities are to be expanded (see The Green Guide to Recycling section).

*Any other council activities to improve the environment?*
Waltham Forest is particularly involved with the Disability Resource Centre to try and improve the environment for disabled people. Planning Department has recently published a document called 'Access for All'. Wide range of Ecology and Environmental education programmes and projects through two Field Study Centres, (Suntrap for primary schools, Hawkwood Lodge for Secondary). Plans under discussion for the establishment of a parallel Urban Studies Centre.

> *COUNCIL CONTACTS:*
> London Borough of Waltham Forest
> Town Hall
> Forest Road
> Walthamstow
> London E17 4JF
> (081) 527 5544
> Chief Executive: L.G. Knox
> Group Manager of the Committee Secretariat: Ken Kilby
> Recycling: Low Hall Depot – (081) 520 6782

> *Green star rating:* ★★★

# WANDSWORTH

*Does the council have an overall policy on environmental issues?*
Wandsworth has recently brought together its various environmental policies into a comprehensive policy statement.

*How is that policy implemented with direct regard to the council's 'in-house' activities?*
Spray paints are banned for road marking and the council has asked the public utilities to do the same.
Mechanical methods are used for weed control instead of chemicals.
Wandsworth was the first authority in London to convert its fleet of vehicles to lead-free petrol. Council staff are encouraged to do

the same and all new leased vehicles are only supplied as 'unleaded' cars. Existing leased vehicles can be converted at the council's expense. A borough-wide sticker and poster campaign is being organised to promote lead-free petrol.

Recycled paper products are used wherever it is viable. All dry toner photocopiers will now use recycled paper. Any waste paper from the offices is recycled.

Energy Management Unit has a target of reducing energy consumption in the public buildings and group-heated properties by fifteen per cent within five years from August 1988.

*In its general planning, how is the council involved in improving the overall environment?*

Borough Plan includes policies for development control, protecting: areas of local or special character, the riverside and sites of special architectural and historic interest. Sixty-eight tree preservation orders covering 1600 trees made since 1984. Brighter shops scheme gives grants to encourage improvements to the appearance of business premises in targetted areas.

Grants and enhancement programme for conservation areas – 28 areas have been declared since 1984.

Tree-planting programme which also incorporates mature trees into new developments.

Work going on to complete the Riverside Walk, which follows the borough's five-mile Thames boundary.

Cycle routes will be extended across the Borough and plans are being considered to improve public transport and to examine the scope for increased use of the river for transportation.

*What is the council policy and practice in the preservation, enhancement and creation of green and open spaces within the borough?*

Wandsworth has developed management plans for all its parks and open spaces to provide an ecological balance and protect the environment. Regular observation and record keeping of animals, plants, habitats, etc. will build up knowledge. Council intends to improve the access and facilities and to encourage volunteer help.

*Is the council able to control or exert influence on air and water pollution in the borough?*

Environmental Health Officers monitor: lead levels; quality of drinking water; toxicity of pools, fountains; quality of swimming pool water; nitrogen dioxide; sulphur dioxide; smoke; ozone levels. Action taken where necessary.

*What steps can, and does, the council take on noise pollution and nuisance?*
Regular monitoring of noise and vibration levels. Noise patrol for parties. Leaflet sent to all residents to encourage them to be more considerate to their neighbours.

*What are the council policies and practices with regard to waste disposal, rubbish collection and street cleaning?*
Litter picking both in parks, open spaces and in the street is considered vital and the council ensures that this service is effective.
Fast-response graffitti removal service.

*What facilities do the council make available for recycling?*
Civic amenity site for public use at Smugglers Way, SW18. Bottle banks in and around the Borough, paper banks due to arrive in early 1990.
Fridges/freezers collected free-of-charge. CFCs removed before scrapping (see The Green Guide to Recycling section.)

*Any other council activities to improve the environment worthy of note?*
Financial support given to the following voluntary sector schemes:
'Heatwise' – advises and undertakes insulation works;
'Wandsworth Works and Play Project' – collects materials for use in school activities;
'Wandsworth Recycling Centre' – repairs furniture and electrical equipment.

*COUNCIL CONTACTS:*
London Borough of Wandsworth
The Town Hall
Wandsworth High Street
London SW18 2PU
(081) 871 6000
Chief Executive and Director of Administration: Gerald Jones
Senior Policy Analyst: Nicola Slawski
Recycling Services – Principal Services Officer : (081) 871 6381

*Green star rating:* ★★★★

# WESTMINSTER

*Does the council have an overall policy on environmental issues?*
Westminster has launched The Westminster Initiative, the council's most ambitious attempt yet to improve the quality of the environment in the city. It augments specific environmental policies in the council's District Plan and other projects.

The Westminster Initiative has 13 themes: greening the city; war on litter; brighter buildings; attractive streets; improved parking; filling potholes; protecting pavements; cleaner air; reducing noise; considerate builders; curbing graffiti; stopping fly-posting; recycling waste.

*How is that policy implemented with direct regard to the council's 'in-house' activities?*
Ozone-friendly products used wherever possible. Bans on CFC aerosols and phosphate-based detergents being considered. Investigating use of hardwoods only from well-managed sources. Only approved pesticides used.

Green Charter being drawn up detailing council action, as employer, on environmental issues.

Recycled paper used for all committee documents, use to be extended to internal memoranda, reports, photocopying and, possibly, letter-headed paper.

Pilot study on collection and sale of all waste paper carried out; contractor being sought.

*In its general planning, how is the council involved in improving the overall environment?*
Major problems in Westminster because of intensive commercial, business, tourist etc. activity, creating real threat to residential amenity: council views 'the maintenance of the quality of the residential environment in its widest sense as a priority'.

Strict planning controls on development, particularly extensive developments and those seen from parks and River Thames and in historic views. Control over building heights and high standards of design in alterations and extensions, notably in Queen's Park Conservation Area, Sussex Gardens, Pimlico, Westbourne Conservation Area, Wilton Row and Old Barrack Yard Mews, Renton Mews, Ennismore Gardens Mews.

Thirty-four conservation areas designated, more than 12,000 buildings of special architectural or historic interest listed and protected.

Council strives to ensure high standards of townscape detail and tree-planting, through controls on signs and advertisements, blinds, awnings and flags; design of street furniture, railings, walls, paving etc.

Five hundred trees a year being planted.

Commuting by private vehicles controlled by number and use of parking spaces. Traffic-taming measures: pedestrianisation and street re-designing to improve access to shopping areas and divert traffic away from residential areas. Conditions for pedestrians and cyclists improved through better road crossings, pavement widening, cycle tracks and safer cycle routes.

Mass of environmental improvement projects completed in recent years. Projects for 1989/90 include: Soho: Rupert Street/Berwick Street/Peter Street, market improvements, pedestrianisation etc., on-site rubbish compactors; Romilly Street/Moor Street, pavement widening, tree planting, new street furniture, etc.; Great Marlborough Street/Noel Street, pavement build-outs, tree-planting. Covent Garden: St Martin's Court, Cecil Court, Mays Court, Brydges Place, repaving and improved lighting. Elsewhere: Leicester Square refurbishment and work on approach routes; Strutton Ground, market improvements; Villiers Street/Embankment Place, repaving, new lighting, co-ordinated street furniture.

*What is the council policy and practice in the preservation, enhancement and creation of green and open spaces?*

Green spaces not under threat. Existing open spaces maintained, protected, e.g. Christchurch Gardens, Victoria Street, where development resisted to preserve public open space in area short of it. More open spaces created in conjunction with developers as 'planning advantage' and through wider use of private open space. Riverside Walk being developed and plans to complete Canalside Walk.

*Is the council able to control or exert influence on air and water pollution in the borough?*

Regular inspections and investigations carried out, statutory powers used as necessary. Advice to residents on CFCs and other atmospheric pollutants. No smoking policies in restaurants and commercial premises.

Random tests etc. on swimming pool water. Following outbreak of legionnaire's disease, council pushing for conversion of air-conditioning systems with evaporative cooling towers to dry systems.

*What steps can, and does, the council take on noise pollution and nuisance?*

More than 3,000 complaints a year, more than 2,000 related to building activities. Considerate Builders' Inspectorate and Noise Inspectorate launched with Code of Practice and telephone hotline for complaints.

Weekend Noisy Party Patrol set up 1987, statutory notices served if necessary.

*What are the council's policies and practices with regard to waste disposal, rubbish collection and street cleaning?*

Westminster in voluntary group with City of London and Tower Hamlets for waste disposal: transported by barges to landfill site in Essex.

Major problems with rubbish collection and street cleaning due to: large concentration of shops, offices and entertainment (daytime population of one million); inadequate storage for rubbish in buildings, so remains too long at kerbside; refuse dumping, particularly where houses converted to flats; evening dumping of rubbish by cleaners etc., not collected until morning; mass of fast food outlets, leading to increased litter. Action includes: Cleaner City Campaign, targeted at litter blackspots, involving businesses, residents and volunteers. Sponsored Litter Bin scheme: more than 300.

Despite 8000 litter bins in total (500 in Oxford Street), litter still major problem. City of Westminster Litter Act, 1988, allows for fixed penalty fines, enforced by Street Watch Inspectorate and Zone Improvement Patrol.

Liaison with fast food industry to reduce packaging and improve litter collection etc. Refuse compactors for business encouraged. Large green Eurobins provided for residents to take rubbish outside collection times. Plans for multi-purpose Cleansing Task Force, to enforce laws, advise on refuse storage and collection etc.

*What facilities do the council make available for recycling?*

Bottle banks in City with more being purchased. Bottle bus, started 1985, collects glass from restaurants, cafes, bars and hotels.

Paper collection lorry in West End, five days a week, for computer and mixed paper, cardboard. Planned extension, including residential areas.

One-stop recycling facility being investigated, with possible CFC recycling point. (For recycling sites, see The Green Guide to Recycling section.)

*Any other council activities to improve the environment?*
Numerous practical measures introduced since 1980, including anti-litter education and projects in schools, improved refuse service; Cleaner City Campaign and sex industry clampdown; anti dog-fouling initiatives.

COUNCIL CONTACTS:
City of Westminster
City Hall
Victoria Street
London SW1E 6QP
(071) 828 8070
Cleansing service enquiries, recycling: (071) 798 2774/2782 andJim Hyatt (071) 798 2412.
Noise Control: commercial (071) 798 1094; residential: (071) 798 1145

*Green star rating:* ★★★★★

# Your council: a general assessment

The responses to our questionnaire highlight great differences in the approaches of the 33 London boroughs to environmental issues. Many of them are still doing little more than undertaking the duties which various Acts of Parliament have put upon them over the years, in the protection of ancient buildings and open spaces, for example, or in the investigation and prosecution of offenders who threaten the quality of the air and water.

Others, in response no doubt to increasing public concern about the environment, have begun to formulate overall strategies to 'clean up their act' and try to improve their areas from often depressingly low standards.

A notable few have been working hard for years with wide-ranging initiatives to make their boroughs better places in which to live and to ensure that their own activities, in building, energy consumption, waste disposal and reclamation and in the maintenance of their public parks and open space, do as little damage as possible to the global environment.

Following a detailed assessment of all the council's policies and practises, we have given each council a 'Green Star Rating', denoting the extent and the success of their activities. It should be emphasised again that these ratings are not directly related to the 'look and feel' of the areas, since many councils have inherited major historical problems or are operating in particularly difficult circumstances, but rather reflect commitments to, and the practical actions taken on, local and global environmental issues. In our analyses, we have taken care to 'reward' positive initiatives, rather than to 'punish' lack of activity.

Our analyses easily distinguished four borough councils who were doing the most on green issues – Sutton, Brent, Bromley and Westminster – and we awarded all of them the top rating of five stars. We identified another four councils – Ealing, Redbridge, Richmond and Wandsworth – who were doing very well, although not quite enough at the moment to justify the highest rating.

---

## THE GREEN GUIDE TO LONDON
# Boroughs of the Year

### THE BEST ★★★★★

SUTTON   (Green Borough of the Year)

Runners up *(in alphabetical order)*

BRENT
BROMLEY
WESTMINSTER

### DOING VERY WELL ★★★★

EALING
REDBRIDGE
RICHMOND
WANDSWORTH

## MAKING PROGRESS ★★★

BARKING
CITY OF LONDON
CROYDON
HACKNEY
HARINGEY
HAVERING
ISLINGTON
KENSINGTON and CHELSEA
KINGSTON
LEWISHAM
MERTON
TOWER HAMLETS*
WALTHAM FOREST

## MUCH STILL TO DO ★★

BARNET
CAMDEN
ENFIELD
GREENWICH
HAMMERSMITH
HILLINGDON
SOUTHWARK

## A LONG WAY TO GO ★

BEXLEY
HARROW
HOUNSLOW
LAMBETH
NEWHAM

*difficult to assess due to differences in
the seven neighbourhoods*

At the other end of the scale, we found that five councils – Bexley, Harrow, Hounslow, Lambeth and Newham – fell far short of giving care for the environment the emphasis and commitment it now requires. Indeed, some of them seemed to be doing little more than paying lip service to such issues. We gave them our lowest rating, of one star.

The bulk of councils fell into the three and two star categories, some 'making progress', others with 'much still to do'. In most of these councils there were the first stirrings of co-ordinated policies and positive commitment, but in many, translating ideas into action still has some way to go.

The full 'league table' appears on the previous pages.

## *The best and the worst*

We had no hesitation in designating **Sutton** as our Green Borough of the Year, since its environmental record is almost universally excellent. Sutton adopted its Environmental Statement in 1986 and its 'in-house' energy-saving, recycling and environmental practices are very good indeed. Planning policies, including the protection of back gardens against developers, traffic-calming and tree-planting and the council's record in protecting and enhancing open space are all highly commendable. The council has set up an ecology centre, the first of its kind, in Carshalton. Rubbish and litter are well-controlled, augmented by a three times a year 'Scour Clean' of every road. Recycling facilities are well above average, with many more neighbourhood recycling centres in the pipeline. Large-scale community involvement is encouraged and fostered.

The fact that **Brent** is one or our runners up may well surprise many people and there is no doubt that the borough continues to suffer from litter and rubbish problems which are still not being successfully tackled, although further improvements are promised. But we were impressed by the council's new Environment Action Plan, as well as its record on energy conservation and its work in protecting, enhancing and creating green and open spaces. Pollution and noise monitoring and control are also of a high standard.

**Westminster**, too, has its litter problems, despite high council spending and clean-up campaigns, due to large influxes of visitors and commuters. On the positive side, we applaud the Westminster Initiative, an ambitious attempt to improve the quality of life in the City. In its 'in-house' activities and its general planning, the council has a very good record, particularly in trying to protect residential areas from intense commercial. business and tourist pressures. Traffic-taming, pedestrianisation, street redesigning and cycle routes have all been introduced. Numerous environmental projects have been completed in recent years and more are planned for this year.

**Bromley** has an excellent record in most environmental areas, although it is only now drawing up an overall strategy. Its planning activities, notably in shopping centre improvements, major tree- and shrub-planting and action on open spaces, have been very good. Apart form the occasional hiccough when new services were introduced, street cleaning and rubbish collection has been of a high standard and there are good facilities for recycling.

At the other end of the scale, **Bexley** seems to be doing little more than its statutory duty. Street cleansing remains a major problem, despite what the council calls 'concerted efforts'. A working party has been set up to produce an environmental policy, but much of the council's work in this field still seems to be at the planning, rather than the action stage.

**Harrow**, again, has no specific environmental strategy, although a panel was set up last year to work towards one. While it does strive to protect and enhance its open space, notably in the Green Belt, the council still has a long way to go in introducing wide-ranging environmental protection measures. The same is true of **Hounslow**, which is still 'moving towards' an overall environmental policy, although it too is striving to stop developments in key sites in the Green Belt. In **Newham** dense residential building means pressure on open space and although attempts have been made to create more in new developments, most environmental improvements still seem to be at the planning stage.

At the bottom of the list, **Lambeth**, one of the most intensely built-up boroughs in the capital, seems almost bowed down with its problems. There is great pressure from developers on open space and although key sites have been identified, some of them are already lost, notably York Hill Wood to housing development and Shakespeare Road Sidings, where ecological interest has been completely obliterated by the current owner. A lack of resources is blamed for rubbish and litter which remain major problems in the area.

# THE GREEN GUIDE TO SHOPPING AND EATING OUT

# SHOPPING AND EATING OUT

To make this guide more practical for everyday use we have divided
Greater London into fifteen geographical and 'cultural' areas, in which
local people are most likely to do their shopping and enjoy their eating
out, rather than using the more artificial borough boundaries. The map
below outlines the areas and in each section that follows we detail the
postal districts covered in each area.

Many people and organisations have given unstinting help in the
preparation of the guide and we would particularly like to acknowledge
the help of the Vegetarian Society, the Vegan Society, the Henry Doubleday Research Association, Friends of the Earth headquarters (for good
wood outlets), the London Cycling Campaign (for bike shops) and a large
number of charitable organisations (for charity shops). Two wholefood
wholesalers, The Wholesome Trucking Company of South-east London
and Infinity Foods of Portslade also gave us helpful advice and information.

But most of all, we would like to pay tribute and give heartfelt thanks
to the volunteers from local Friends of the Earth groups all over the capital

who, using their local expertise, have researched and produced lists for us of 'green' shops, restaurants and businesses in their areas. Their help has been invaluable.

Despite our comprehensive research, we have undoubtedly missed one or two 'green' shops and businesses: to them, we apologise. Nomination forms for inclusion in the next *Green Guide to London* can be found at the back of the book. We will investigate all nominations for inclusion in the next edition.

## Criteria for inclusion

The basic criteria for entry into the *Green Guide to London* are shops, eating places and businesses which offer a good choice of products which:

- ✔ are not tested on animals,
- ✔ do not contain materials or substances, nor are manufactured by processes, which cause serious damage to the environment,
- ✔ can be disposed of with as little environmental damage as possible, or can be recycled,
- ✔ do not threaten endangered species of animals or plants, and
- ✔ do not exploit cheap labour, especially in the developing world.

As far as **food shops** were concerned, we were particularly interested in wholefood and health foods, organic fruit and vegetables, cruelty-free meat, free-range eggs and so on. When shops had policies on returnable bottles, low-level packaging, recyclable and recycled paper, we wanted to hear about that too.

For **restaurants, cafés and take-aways,** we list those that provide in their menus a wide and comprehensive choice of wholesome organic food, or provided full vegetarian or vegan menus. Many restaurants, notably Indian and Chinese, do offer some vegetarian choices, but we did not include all these unless they were particularly specialising in such dishes.

We searched for **electrical shops** that sell energy-efficient and low energy domestic appliances (and low energy lightbulbs) and for **chemists** and other shops that offer a wide range of cosmetics and toiletries that are not tested on animals and cause low environmental damage in their manufacture, use and disposal. We were also interested in outlets for unbleached and recycled **paper** and for **household items,** such as cleaning materials and washing powders, that cause low environmental damage.

**Charity shops** serve many environmental purposes as well as providing funds for their organisations. Selling second hand clothes and other items is good 'recycling', while the textiles in those unfit for wear can be used in the making of blankets, quilts, upholstery etc and for paper. Shops such as Oxfam also sell craft goods from the developing world and are careful to avoid exploitation.

In the **wood** section, we used the latest research for the new Good

Wood Guide, published by Friends of the Earth, together with the National Association of Retail Furnishers. Strict criteria are laid down for retailers and manufacturers who have to show that they are actively helping to save rainforests by obtaining timber 'from an ecologically benign source'. Also included in this section are architects, planners and designers who utilise such timber in their work. We also thought that Habitat were worthy of inclusion because of their recent decision no longer to purchase any hardwood furniture and their clearance of all stocks of furniture made from endangered tropical hardwoods. And we commend their work towards the use of recycled materials for all their packing.

The London Cycle Campaign has kindly provided a list of all the **bike shops** in Central London, which we have also broken down area by area.

We have not included addresses of supermarkets and chain stores (with the exception of The Body Shop and Holland and Barrett, see below), because although many of them are now offering a wider range of green products, none do so exclusively. There is no denying that for many of us they are the most convenient way to do the family shopping, but at the same time, in their structure and organisation, supermarkets and other chain stores cannot be regarded as 'green': they transport their supplies in massive lorries that pollute the environment, many use a lot of unnecessary packaging and sell goods and products which are environmentally-unfriendly in their processes of manufacture, in their use, in the difficulties of disposal and in exploitation of labour in the developing world. We have, however, seen big changes in supermarket and store policies, due in no small measure to consumer pressures, and no doubt will see more in the 1990s. But until supermarkets and chains can be seen to be more overwhelming green in their overall practices and policies, they will not merit individual inclusion in this guide.

It is important also to note that while growing numbers of products in the supermarkets are labelled as 'environmentally-friendly', these claims are usually made by the advertising agencies and marketing men of the producers and retailers and often do not stand up to objective scrutiny. There is a pressing need for an official, objective labelling system for such products so that we can make a much more informed choice while wheeling our trolleys past their shelves.

Nonetheless, we should give credit where it is due, and we do applaud the recent progress that has been made. We have, therefore, enquired about the practices and policies of the major chains and we outline their responses below. We asked the supermarkets about their company policies on wholefoods and organic foods and how widely available and expensive such produce was in their stores; about labelling, additives and preservatives; about policies on selling foods from countries like South Africa; whether they would sell irradiated food; about their general policies on environmental issues and on recycling.

We asked the chemists' chains about animal testing and products that threatened endangered species and damaged the environment (particularly detergents and household cleaning products) and about packaging and recycling.

The electrical shops were asked about energy-saving and energy-efficient appliances; about fridges and freezers and CFCs; and about packaging and recycling.

Clearly, in this fast-changing area, there will be new developments during the year and we will update these entries for the next guide.

# SUPERMARKETS AND FOOD

## Asda

Organically-grown fruit and vegetables (defined as 'grown in soil which has had no artificial chemical fertilisers and pesticides added for at least two years and not subsequently treated with chemicals') are available in some 54 stores. Organic bread and wine is sold in all stores, organic cheese in some. Only a small, but growing, percentage of food sales are organic. Additives and preservatives are not used in own-label products 'unless it is absolutely necessary'. Asda has no immediate plans to sell irradiated food. The company does not ban produce or goods from any country, leaving choice to the customer. Aerosols are CFC-free, as are meat and poultry trays; own-brand batteries are mercury-free; nappies are non-chlorine bleached; household cleaners etc., are biodegradable (a phosphate-free product is being introduced); toilet tissues, kitchen rolls etc., are made from recycled paper. A recycled stationery range is being introduced. A wide range of recycling facilities is available at Asda stores, with bottle banks (73 stores), paper banks, can banks and plastic bottle banks all expanding.

## Co-op

Local Co-ops are supplied by the Co-operative Wholesale Society (CWS), which has its own-label brands. As well as purely local co-ops there is also Co-operative Retail Services Ltd., with a national chain of food stores, and its own retailing policies. CWS has introduced a limited range of organic products (as defined by the Soil Association), available at superstores and large supermarkets. Organic food accounts for about two per cent of fresh food sales. It is more expensive. Other food products have 'Consumer Care' labels with information on nutrition, additives etc. Additives in own-label products have been reduced or eliminated. All the evidence for and against irradiation 'is being carefully weighed'. CWS is taking further steps to eliminate all trade with South Africa, while CRS has banned all South African products. Their policy on animal testing is only to use, wherever possible, ingredients and formulation that have not been animal tested in the last five years. Own-brand aerosols are CFC-free, CFC packaging was been withdrawn and less damaging coolants are used in freezer and chiller units. Own-label detergents are biodegradable; phosphate-free detergents are being introduced; non-chlorine bleached nappies and sanitary products, non-PCDB toilet blocks and recycled paper toilet tissues are all available.Recycling symbols are used on products, including the identification of plastics. Easier-to-recycle PET is used instead of PVC in plastic squash bottles. Recycled material is used for egg, washing powder and other cartons. All Co-op vehicles will run lead-free.The Co-op has also appointed David Bellamy Associates to advise on environmental issues. As Britain's biggest farmer, it has launched an organic farming experiment at its Stoughton Lodge Farm.

## Iceland

Iceland Frozen Foods, which now incorporates the Bejam Group, does not sell fresh fruit and vegetables, but has a range of frozen fish and vegetables that do not contain additives and preservatives. All own-label products are labelled for additives as needed. Some additives have been removed. Suppliers have been asked to guarantee no/low pesticide levels and are regularly monitored. Irradiated foods will 'probably' be sold, 'when this method is proven and acceptable'. Regular checks on company refrigeration equipment are carried out to prevent leaks of CFCs. CFC refrigerants are recycled. Iceland is a large supplier of domestic fridges and freezers and offers to remove old models free of charge on sale of new ones, and removes CFCs for recycling. The majority of new fridges and freezers have reduced CFC insulation. Iceland does not buy from South Africa as a matter of principle. Recycled cardboard is being tested for food packaging. Empty cases at stores are recycled. Recycling of plastic carrier bags is encouraged by a large message on the bags. The company car fleet runs lead-free, and the company will pay for conversion of all employees' cars.

## Londis

Londis acts as a wholesaler and neither owns or manages stores nor manufactures products itself. It does, however, recommend guidelines on what its stores sell and makes suggestions to manufacturers, particularly in the specifications for its own-brand goods, where it is 'making a concerted effort to ensure our own-label range is manufactured in an environmentally-friendly manner'. New nappies and sanitary towels are non-chlorine bleached. No own-label products come from South Africa.

## Marks and Spencer

Marks and Spencer sell a range of organic produce, which they define as 'products grown on farms using organic principles and employing traditional methods of farming and crops rotation. No artificial fertilisers or chemical sprays are used.' Such produce has been available at 10 stores in the south-east and will be in 50 stores nationally in early 1990. The percentage of sales of organic produce is 'confidential'. It is more expensive. Nutritional labelling has been introduced and the use of additives reviewed and changes made. Foods are monitored for pesticide and other residues. Marks and Spencer will not sell irradiated food. Its policy is to buy British wherever possible, but clearly foods are bought on a worldwide basis. There are no bans on food from any country: 'We do not believe that we should impose any specific view on our customers; we believe that they should be free to choose as they wish.' Packaging is considered essential to protect quality, safety and hygiene, but constantly reassessed: all is now CFC-free and 95 per cent of eggs are sold in pulp boxes; trials of recycled board for some recipe dishes are underway. Cosmetic, toiletry and homecare products are not tested on animals. All M & S aerosols are CFC-free; toilet paper and kitchen roll is made with up to 30 per cent recycled paper; nappies contain 'environmentally-friendly' pulp. Washing powders contain 30 per cent less phosphates; phosphate-free products are being investigated. Detergents used are biodegradable. Some furniture sold uses tropical hardwoods, usually as veneers. No new ranges contain rainforest timber. A limited range of energy-efficient electrical appliances is available.

## Safeway

Safeway sells organically-grown produce (as defined by the Soil Association) in all its stores and it accounts for about two per cent of all produce sales. It is generally more expensive. Nutritional labelling is being added to all the company's products. Since 1985 Safeway has been removing 'all unnecessary ingredients and alleged contentious food additives' from its own label products. Irradiated food would only be sold subject to strict conditions. The company does not ban products from any particular country, leaving the decision 'entirely at the discretion of customers.' Alternative choices are available.Many lines are now sold in recycled packaging, and this is increasing. Cardboard boxes are recycled and new re-usable plastics trays have replaced cardboard in much of the fresh produce delivery system. Recycled plastic packaging has been tried, but with limited success. The car fleet policy is to run on lead-free petrol. Bottle banks have been set up at many stores.

## Sainsbury's

Sainsbury's offers a good range of organic produce, as defined by the Soil Association. Nutritional labelling has been introduced. Other fruit and vegetables are monitored for pesticide levels. The company policy is to introduce increasing numbers of 'environmentally-friendly' products: 'The company has reacted to increased concern on environmental matters.' All CFCs have been removed from own-label products and no CFC proprietary brands are sold. All cold stores and distribution depots now use refrigerants less damaging to the ozone layer and this use is being extended to all new stores and refurbishments. Phosphate-free detergents, non-chlorine bleached nappies and mercury-free batteries, PDCB-free toilet blocks, recycled stationery, toilet tissues and kitchen towels are all available. Meat packaging trays have been switched to those not using CFCs in their production. In general packaging, the company looks for recyclable products. It is investigating photodegradable and biodegradable plastic carrier bags, but will probably go for recyclable bags. Sainsbury's has introduced award-winning energy-efficiency schemes at many of its stores: the new ones use 60 per cent of those built ten years ago. There are bottle banks at some 100 stores, plus a few can banks and paper banks. Cardboard cartons are recycled where possible and polythene is now being collected at many stores, for re-processing. The company car fleet runs lead-free. Sainsbury's won the Grocer Green Award in 1989, as the retailer 'with the greatest commitment to the environment.'

## Tesco

Tesco sells organic produce (as defined by the Soil Association) in 58 of its stores nationwide and it now accounts for about one per cent of produce sales from all their retail outlets. Prices of such foods are generally more expensive. The company has also tried to remove additives from as many of their own brand products as possible. Nutritional labelling has been introduced. Tesco will not sell irradiated food. All Tesco aerosols are CFC-free, as are meat and produce packaging trays. Recycled paper, non-chlorine bleached and phosphate-free products are available. No South African foods are sold except for produce 'where no alternative source is available'. Tesco has also been active in promoting recycling, with more than 100 bottle banks at stores as well as Save-a-Can collection points. The company is also setting up a nationwide chain of aluminium can recycling pick-up points.

## Waitrose

A range of organic fruit and vegetables, as defined by the Federation of Organic Agricultural Movements, is available in all 85 stores. They are more expensive. Additives in other foods have been removed or replaced and suppliers are encouraged to minimise pesticide use. Waitrose has no plans to sell irradiated food. Most plastic bottles and some plastic trays are made with PET plastic, which is easier to recycle. Recycled paper is used in most paper products, except where packaging is in direct contact with food. Most branches reclaim cardboard for recycling.

## Other supermarkets and food stores

**7-Eleven** told us they were 'convenience stores, not supermarkets, and are therefore limited to space. They were unable to answer our specific questions, but said: 'Our current buying policy is to support environmentally-friendly products where at all commercially viable and when they fit within our ranging policies.'
**Budgens, Cullens, Europa, Lowcost and Shepherd Foods** were unable or unwilling to answer our questions.

# COSMETICS, TOILETRIES, CLEANING MATERIALS, MOTHER AND BABY PRODUCTS

## Boots (including Underwoods)

Boots own-brand toiletries and cosmetics have not been tested on animals for many years. The company was one of the first to announce the withdrawal of CFCs from its aerosols and all but one or two are now CFC-free. Boots is attempting to move away from chlorine bleaching in a wide range of its products and hard detergents have not been used in its own brands since the late 1960s. A range of recycled paper products was introduced last year and there are plans to extend it. Recycled paper and envelopes are used.

## Mothercare

From the middle of 1989 all Mothercare disposable nappies and maternity pads have been produced using an oxygen bleaching process and from September of that year, all mattresses were filled with CFC-free foam. The Natural Products toiletries range has opticite labels. Trials began late in 1989 on carrier bags using 25 per cent recycled material and photo-degradable counter bags were being introduced in all stores. Computer paper and mail-order warehouse cardboard packaging is recycled. Company cars run lead-free where possible and an energy conservation scheme has been introduced in all stores. Recycled paper is used internally and computer paper, printing waste paper and card are recycled.

## Superdrug

Superdrug began in 1988 to alter the formulations on all its aerosol products and was no longer purchasing CFC aerosols after September 1989. Stores offer a range of recycled paper products, from toilet rolls to writing paper. Cardboard delivery boxes are recycled and the recycling of polythene packaging is being investigated. The company is investigating the possibility of biodegradable bin-liners. Superdrug sells non-chlorine bleached nappies, cadmium- and mercury-free batteries, phosphate-free cleaning materials and PDCB-free toilet blocks. Company cars are unleaded where possible.

# ELECTRICAL STORES

## Comet

Comet is now actively promoting specific energy-saving products, notably washing machines and dryers. It will highlight energy-efficient models. As far as recycling is concerned, the company says: 'As Comet is not a manufacturer, we are not involved in these aspects'. It does sell fridges and freezers with reduced CFCs in the insulation.

## Dixons (including Currys)

Dixons say that they try to persuade their suppliers to produce energy-saving and energy-efficient products. On energy labelling they 'accept the manufacturers lead on this practice'. They feel, too, that they have little real control over packaging and 'can only encourage our suppliers to change where possible'. They have actively promoted the production of refrigerators with reduced CFCs and these now make up the majority of the products they stock.

## London Electricity

London Electricity does not display energy-efficiency labels as a matter of course, although it says: 'wherever practical, we highlight energy-efficiency and energy-saving.' By and large it relies on manufacturers' literature and leaflets and it sees other features, such as colour, having more influence on customer choice. New washing machines using less water have been introduced. As a retailer and user of electrical goods, London Electricity sees itself as dependent on manufacturers for environmental improvements, but is having 'discussions' with suppliers. It now tries to sell refrigeration systems with less CFCs in their insulation and is buying an extraction plant to remove CFCs from trade-in fridges and freezers, to sell back to the makers. Most of its waste paper is recycled and it has begun to convert more than 2,000 vehicles in its fleet to lead-free petrol.

# THE GREEN PIONEERS

## The Body Shop

The Body Shop has long had impeccable environmental credentials and since its inception in 1976 has operated on a non-exploitative basis, **not** selling or using products which: consume a disproportionate amount of energy in manufacture or use; cause unnecessary waste; use materials from threatened species or environments; involve cruelty to animals or adversely affect other countries, particularly in the Third World. It sells more than 300 products conforming to these criteria. All are biodegradable and none are tested on animals, but on human volunteers, where necessary. Packaging is minimal and most products are refillable at shops. Plastics are used, but efforts are being made to re-use them. By 1991 a bottle-blowing plant should have been established to re-use glass from bottles returned by customers. The Body Shop recycles as much as it possibly can, notably paper and card and some plastic containers. Shops have links with local groups and schools for further recycling schemes. A recycling 'port' for newspapers and aluminium is being set up at the warehouse. Only recycled paper is used throughout the organisation. No tropical hardwoods are sold and no CFC foams for insulation purposes. Energy-efficient lighting is used. Recycled paper is now being used for carrier bags and there is one small bag in biodestructible plastic. Body Shop also encourages its employees to campaign for environmental improvements and keeps it customers informed about the causes it actively supports, among them Save the Whale (with Greenpeace), Helping the Earth Fight Back (with Friends of the Earth), countryside affairs, the ozone layer and CFCs, and tropical rainforests. It also fights for the survival of tribal cultures and believes in 'Trade not Aid', the policy of producing sustainable growth in the developing world.

Because of this impressive list of policies and the quality of its products, the addresses of all Body Shops in the London area are listed in this guide.

## Holland and Barrett

Holland and Barrett's policy is to stock vegetarian foods, free from animal derivatives and not containing any artificial additives. They were the first to go into the market with organic vegetables three or so years ago, but felt that the price premium was too great and discontinued. The situation is under review. Some 20 other organic products (as defined by the Soil Association) are stocked. 40 per cent of their sales are wholefood. Most wholefood and organic products are available at all 200 stores. The company is 'apolitical as far as green issues are concerned', but by its practices has been involved in the green debate for more than 70 years. It does not, however, stock any South African or Chilean products, 'something that our customers would expect of us'. It will not stock irradiated foods in the foreseeable future, although their sale will be reviewed. Packaging is kept to a minimum and the company tries to ensure that materials are recyclable . Toiletries bottles are easily recyclable and carrier bags are either in recyclable paper or biodegradable plastic. All company cars run on unleaded fuel and all office stationery is recycled.

Because of their policies and practices, all Holland and Barrett stores in the Greater London area are listed in this guide.

# WEST END AND CITY
*Incorporating Postal Districts EC1–EC4, WC1, WC2, W1*

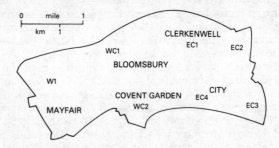

## *FOOD SHOPS AND EVERYDAY PRODUCTS including: cleaning items, cosmetics, recycled paper and energy-efficient electrical goods*

**Alara Wholefoods** 58 Marchmont Street WC1 (071) 837 1172
**Barbican Natural Health Ltd** 122 Whitecross Street EC1 (071) 628 6139
**Body Shop** The Mall, Liverpool Street Station, Broadgate EC2 (071) 638 2304
**Body Shop** 22/23 Cheapside EC2 (071) 248 3410
**Body Shop** Unit 18 Covent Garden Market WC2 (071) 836 3543
**Body Shop** 32/34 Great Marlborough Street W1 (071) 437 5137
**Body Shop** Unit G3, The London Pavilions, No.1 Piccadilly W1 (071) 494 0485
**Body Shop** 18/26 Long Acre WC2 (071) 836 4901
**Body Shop** 66 Oxford Street W1 (071) 631 0027
**Body Shop** 268 Oxford Street W1 (071) 629 9365
**City Papers** 7 Curtain Road, London (071) 377 5112
  Recycled stationery suppliers
**Clear Spring Natural Grocer** 196 Old Street EC1 (071) 250 1708
  Wide selection from Soil Association sources. Good selection of organic items
**Cranks Health Foods** 8 Adelaide Street WC2 (071) 836 0660
**Cranks Health Foods** 31 The Circle, Broadgate EC2 (071) 256 5044
  Due to open in early 1990. Take-away/shop
**Cranks Health Foods** 13 Leadenhall Market EC3 (071) 626 0853
  Due to open in early 1990. Take-away/shop
**Cranks Health Foods** 11 The Market, Covent Garden WC2 (071) 379 6508
**Cranks Health Foods** 8 Marshall Street W1 (071) 437 2915
**Cranks Health Foods** 9 Tottenham Street W1 (071) 631 3912
**Farm Shop** No.1 Neal's Yard, Covent Garden WC2 (071) 836 1066
**Golden Orient Ltd** 17 Earlham Street WC2 (071) 836 5545
**Health Food Centre** 11 Warren Street W1 (071) 387 9289
  Organic vegetables, free-range eggs, plant and natural cosmetics. There is also a hot food take-away
**Holland & Barrett** 78 Baker Street W1 (071) 935 3544
**Holland & Barrett** 36 Brunswick Shopping Centre WC1 (071) 278 4640

**Holland & Barrett** 19 Goodge Street W1 (071) 580 2886
**Holland & Barrett** c/o Selfridges, Oxford Street W1 (071) 629 1234
**Holland & Barrett** Unit C/12 West One Shopping Centre, Oxford Street W1
   (071) 493 7988
**Leon Miller & Co** 9 Tower Place, London EC3 (071) 626 0261
   Sells 'real' meat, free of artificial additives and hormones. Free-range eggs
**Neal's Yard Wholefood Warehouse** 21/23 Shorts Gardens WC2 (071) 836 5151
   Wholefood warehouse stocks organic fruit and veg. and cheeses
**Rye Wholefoods** 35a Myddleton Street EC1 (071) 278 5878
**Solomon's Mine** 37 Tottenham Street W1 (071) 636 1458
**Thames and Ganges Trading Co** 36 Eastcastle Street W1 (071) 631 4106
**Wholefood** 24 Paddington Street W1 (071) 935 3924
   Sells greengrocery, dairy produce and wholefoods
**Wholefood Butchers** 31 Paddington Street W1 (071) 486 1390
   Sells 'real' meat, free of artificial additives and hormones. Free-range eggs

## *EATING OUT - Restaurants, cafés, take-aways*

**Alistair Little** 49 Frith Street W1 (071) 734 5183  Has good vegetarian starters
   which can double up for main courses
**Ajimura** 51/53 Shelton Street WC2 (071) 240 0178
   Informal, busy Japanese restaurant close to theatres and cinemas. Selection
   of vegetarian dishes. Vegans can be catered for
**Al Sultan** 52 Hertford Street SW1 (071) 408 1155
   Menu has long lists of meatless Lebanese meze food
**Bahn Thai** 2a Frith Street W1 (071) 437 8504
   Authentic Thai cuisine served in the oriental manner and cooked to order to
   ensure freshness of flavour. Vegetarians and vegans catered for
**Bunjies** 27 Litchfield Street WC2 (071) 240 1796
**Burts** 42 Dean Street W1 (071) 439 0972
   Lots of vegetarian dishes
**Café Pelican** 45 St. Martins Lane WC2 (071) 379 0309
   Upmarket brasserie, with an imaginative daily vegetarian set-meal
**Christies** 122 Wardour Street W1
**Compton Green** 14 Old Compton Street W1 (071) 434 3544
   International menu with many vegan dishes
**Country Life Vegetarian Buffet & Natural Food Shop** 123 Regent Street W1
**Country Life** 1 Heddon Street W1 (071) 434 2922
   A virtually vegan restaurant run by Seventh-Day Adventists
**Cranks** 10 Adelaide Street WC2 (071) 379 5919
   Restaurant serving wholefood meals
**Cranks** 23 Barrett Street W1 (071) 495 1340
**Cranks** 31 The Circle, Broadgate EC2 (071) 256 5044
   Due to open early 1990. Take-away/shop
**Cranks** 17/18 Great Newport Street WC2 (071) 836 5226
**Cranks** 13 Leadenhall Market EC3 (071) 626 0853
   Due to open early 1990. Take-away/shop
**Cranks** 11 The Market, Covent Garden WC2 (071) 379 6508
**Cranks** 8 Marshall Street W1 (071) 437 9431
**Cranks** 9-11 Tottenham Street W1 (071) 631 3912
**East West Restaurant** 188 Old Street EC1 (071) 608 0300
   This restaurant is owned by the Community Health Foundation and the staff

are experts on macrobiotics. The food exceeds the requirements of
vegetarians and vegans. Take-away service available

**Food for Health** 15/17 Black Friars Lane EC4

**Food for Thought** 31 Neal Street, Covent Garden WC2 (071) 836 0239
This restaurant provides reasonably priced vegetarian fare to shoppers and
theatre-goers.

**Fourteen Carrots** 14 Old Compton Street W1

**Friths Restaurant** 14 Frith Street W1 (071) 439 3370

**Futures** 8 Botolph Alley EC3 (071) 623 4529
Lunchtime café serving healthy alternatives to fast food and sandwiches.
Vegan options on the daily changing menu. Open 11.30am – 3pm

**Gaylord Restaurant** 79/81 Mortimer Street W1 (071) 580 3615
A licensed Indian restaurant with a good selection of vegetarian dishes.
Vegans and special diets can be catered for

**Govindas Vegetarian Restaurant** 9 Soho Street W1 (071) 437 3663
Established by the International Society for Krishna Consciousness with the
specific aim of supplying tasty and nutritious vegetarian food

**Greenhouse Vegetarian Restaurant** 16 Chenies Street WC1 (071) 637 8038
A counter-service restaurant offering wide range of interesting vegetarian
dishes

**Hare Krishna Curry House** 1 Hanway Street W1 (071) 636 5262
Run by a Hindu family specialising in gujarati style dishes.
Vegans catered for

**Inigo Jones** 14 Garrick Street WC2 (071) 836 6456
Old stained glass factory becomes formal elegant restaurant in August 1990.
Vegetarian menu

**Jamdani** 34 Charlotte Street W1 (071) 636 1178
Indian restaurant with extensive separate vegetarian menu

**Kettner's Restaurant** 29 Romilly Street W1 (071) 734 6112
Licensed restaurant with live music nightly. Vegetarian meals clearly
marked on the menu

**London School of Economics** Students' Union Café, East Building, Houghton
Street WC2 (071) 405 7686 Ext.2880
Very cheap vegetarian and vegan dishes. Caters mainly to students but is
open to public

**Mandeer** 21 Hanway Place W1 (071) 323 0660
An exclusive and romantic Indian vegetarian restaurant. Vegan dishes are
included in the menu

**Melange** 59 Endell Street W2 (071) 240 8077
Vegetarian specials and starters

**Neal's Yard Bakery Co-op** 6 Neal's Yard WC2 (071) 836 5199
A vegetarian wholefood co-op providing a sit-down and take-away service

**New World** 1 Gerrard Place W1 (071) 434 2508
Chinese restaurant with a long-established vegetarian menu.
Vegans catered for

**Nuthouse** 26 Kingly Street W1 (071) 437 9471
Shop and sit-down restaurant offering wide range of salads, soups, hot
dishes. Vegans catered for

**Ragam South Indian Restaurant** 57 Cleveland Street W1 (071) 636 9098
Authentic Indian restaurant near the Post Office Tower specialising in
dishes from the South. Vegans catered for

**Raw Deal** 65 York Street W1 (071) 262 4841

**Sawasdee Thai Restaurant** 26/28 Whitfield Street W1 (071) 631 0289
**Sharuna** 107 Great Russell Street WC1 (071) 636 5922
   Indian vegetarian restaurant
**Smollensky's Balloon Bar & Restaurant** 1 Dover Street W1 (071) 491 1199
   Large restaurant featuring music of the 30s and 40s serving many vegetarian
   dishes
**Shan Vegetarian Restaurant** 200 Shaftesbury Avenue WC2 (071) 240 3348
   Good, inexpensive Indian vegetarian food. Café-style decor
**Slenders** 41 Cathedral Place EC4 (071) 236 5974
**Sutherland's** 45 Lexington Street W1 (071) 434 3401
   Restaurant with good vegetarian choice on menu
**Unicorn Café/Bar** Arts Theatre Basement
   Great Newport Street WC2 (071) 836 3334
**The Veeraswanny** 99/101 Regent Street W1 (071) 734 1401
   Smart comfortable restaurant with a good choice of vegetarian thalis
**Woodlands** 77 Marylebone Lane W1 (071) 486 3862
   First-class Indian vegetarian food, with some unusual choices
**Yours Naturally** London Ecology Centre, 45 Shelton Street
   Covent Garden WC2 (071) 497 2723
   Family-welcoming, live music at weekends. Very vegan
**ZZZ's Café** 238 Grays Inn Road WC1 (071) 833 4466
   Pretty, intimate café serving vegan and vegetarian dishes. Wholefood/
   organic ingredients are used and meals are inexpensive

## CHARITY SHOPS

**British Red Cross Society** 106 Crawford Street W1 (071) 935 3416
**Imperial Cancer Research** 98 Marylebone High Street W1 (071) 486 0018
**Oxfam** 26 Ganton Street W1 (071) 437 7338
**Oxfam** 13/13a Marylebone High Street W1 (071) 487 3852
**Oxfam** 23 Drury Lane, Covent Garden WC2 (071) 240 3769
**Royal National Institute for the Blind** 224 Great Portland Street W1
   (071) 388 1266 Ext.2339
**Sue Ryder** 2 Crawford Street W1
**Sue Ryder** 22 New Cavendish Street W1 (071) 935 6547
**YMCA** 22 Goodge Street W1 (071) 323 5073

## WOOD

**Asif Malik** 5 Dryden Street WC2 (071) 240 2430
   Architect
**BDP Landscape** P.O. Box 4WD, 16 Gresse Street W1
   Landscape architects
**Carrick Howell & Lawrence** 16 Little Portland Street W1 (071) 631 1732
   Architects
**Child Wilson Associates Ltd** 33 Fitzroy Street W1 (071) 636 2822
   Architects
**Chris Wilkinson Architects** 1 Horseshoe Yard, Brook Street W1 (071) 409 2887
   Architect
**Dunthorne Parker** 8 Seymour Place W1 (071) 402 2053
   Architects and designers
**Habitat** 196 Tottenham Court Road W1 (071) 631 3880

**Hood Story Partnership** 71 Golden House, 29 Great Pulteney Street W1
   (071) 437 4581
   Architects
**Julian Bicknell** Monro House, 40/42 King Street WC2
   Architects
**Le-Plan Limited** 38 Park Street W1 (071) 491 8029
   Design consultants and architects
**MacFarlane Lack Lawson** 55 Welbeck Street W1
   Architect
**Naturally British** 13 New Row, Covent Garden WC2 (071) 240 0551
   Craft Shop
**SCP Ltd** 135/139 Curtain Road EC2
   Modern furniture manufacturers (071) 739 1869
**Timothy Associates** 20/22 Maddox Street W1 (071) 409 3379
   Architects

## BIKE SHOPS

**Angel Cycles** 397 St. John Street, Islington EC1 (071) 278 7793
**Avis Cycling & Leisure** 21 Clerkenwell Road EC1 (071) 250 1534
**Bike Peddlars** 50 Calthorpe Street WC1 (071) 278 0551
**Bike UK** Youth Hostel Association Shop, 14 Southampton Street, Covent
   Garden WC2 (071) 497 2299
**Bike UK** Lower Robert Street, Off York Buildings, Strand WC2 (071) 839 2111
**Condor Cycles** 144 Grays Inn Road WC1 (071) 837 7641
**Covent Garden Cycles** 2 Nottingham Court, Off Shorts Gardens, Covent
   Garden WC2 (071) 836 1752
**Cycle Logical** 136 New Cavendish Street W1 (071) 631 5060
**On Your Bike** 5th Floor, Lillywhites, 34/36 Regent Street W1 (071) 930 3181
**Paolo Garbini** 36 Great Pulteney Street W1 (071) 734 9912
**Pindisports** 14/18 Holborn EC1 (071) 242 3278
**Porchester** 8 Porchester Place, Marylebone W2 (071) 723 9236
**Selfridges** 400 Oxford Street W1 (071) 629 1234

# CENTRAL WEST

*Incorporating Postal Districts SW1, SW3, SW5–SW7, SW10 W2,
W8, W9–W11, W14*

## FOOD SHOPS AND EVERYDAY PRODUCTS *including:
cleaning items, cosmetics, recycled paper and energy-efficient
electrical goods*

**Angie** The Wren, 35 Jermyn Street SW1
**Body Shop** 15 Brompton Road SW3 (071) 589 0170
**Body Shop** 203 Kensington High Street W8 (071) 937 1890
**Body Shop** 54 King's Road SW3 (071) 584 0163
**Body Shop** 194 Portobello Road W11 (071) 229 3928
**Body Shop** Unit 9, Victoria Place SW1 (071) 828 2778

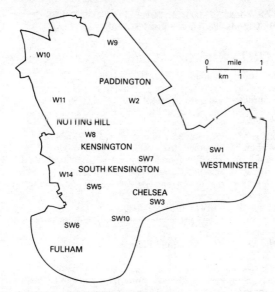

**Body Shop** 113 Victoria Street SW1 (071) 630 5588
**Body Shop** Unit 10, Whiteleys Shopping Centre, Queensway W2 (071) 792 0029
**Brixton Wholefoods** 27 Arcade, Brixton SW6
**Ceres Grain Shop** 269a Portobello Road W11 (071) 229 5571
**Cornucopia** 51 Chelsea Manor Street SW3 (071) 352 7403
**Friends Foods** 113 Notting Hill Gate W11 (071) 221 4700
**Harrods Ltd** (Health Food Dept), Lower Ground Floor, Knightsbridge SW1
    (071) 730 1234
**Health Craze** 24 Old Brompton Road SW7 (071) 589 5870
**Health Foods** 767 Fulham Road SW6 (071) 736 8848
**Health & Diet Centre** 5 Jerdan Place SW6 (071) 385 0015
**Health Place at Victoria** 11/13 Strutton Ground SW1 (071) 222 4588
**Holland & Barrett** 220 Fulham Road SW10 (071) 352 9939
**Holland & Barrett** 139 Kensington Church Street W8 (071) 727 9011
**Holland & Barrett** 260 Kensington High Street W8 (071) 603 2751
**Holland & Barrett** 10 Warwick Way SW1 (071) 834 2711
**Holland & Barrett** 139 Kensington Church Street W8 (071) 727 9011
**Nick's Yard** 93 Wandsworth Bridge Road SW6
**Olivers Wholefood Store** 243 Munster Road SW6 (071) 381 5477
**Portobello Wholefoods Ltd** Unit 1, 266 Portobello Road W10 (071) 960 1840
**Rockspring Ltd** 1st Floor, 27/29 Westbourne Grove W2 (071) 727 1844
**Sloane Health Shop** 64 Gloucester Road SW7 (071) 584 4815
**Sloane Health Shop** 32 Sloane Square SW1 (071) 730 7046
**Victoria Health Food and Grocers** 17 Elizabeth Street SW1 (071) 730 7556
**The Well** 2 Eccleston Place SW1 (071) 730 7303
    Also good-value self-service restaurant
**Western Wholefoods** 6 Charleville Road W14
**'Wild Oats'Whole Foods** 210 Westbourne Grove W11 (071) 229 1063

**Wilkins Natural Foods** 53 Marsham Street SW1 (071) 222 4038
**Windmill Wholefoods** 486 Fulham Road SW6 (071) 385 1570

## *EATING OUT* - *Restaurants, cafés, take-aways*

**Asia Grill**  26 Pembridge Road W11 (071) 727 5868
    An Indian restaurant offering some vegetarian dishes
**Baalbek Restaurant** 18 Hogarth Place SW5 (071) 373 7199
    Fully licensed Lebanese restaurant serving a wide range of vegetarian
    dishes. Take-away service
**Byblos Restaurant** 262 Kensington High Street W8 (071) 603 4422
**Ceres Coffee Shop** 74 Tavistock Road W11 (071) 229 5571
    Brand new addition to wholefood shop of same name in Portobello Road
**Down Mexico Way** 10 Smedley Place SW1 (071) 824 8224
    Mexican restaurant that caters for vegetarians with some vegan options.
    Licensed. Take-away service
**Dynasty II** 15 Lots Road SW10 (071) 351 1020
    Luxurious Chinese restaurant in converted grain mill on Thames at Chelsea.
    Good vegetarian selection
**Ethiopia in the Year 2002** 1 Woodfield Place, off Harrow Road W9
    (071) 286 5129
    Ethiopian restaurant offering interesting vegetarian menu. Dishes are
    cooked daily using fresh wholefood ingredients and can cater for vegans
**The Inn of Happiness** St. James Court Hotel, Buckingham Gate SW1
    Szechuan, Peking, Cantonese cuisine with vegetarian menu
**Kwality Tandoori Restaurant** 38 Thurloe Place SW7 (071) 589 3663
    Restaurant with a meat and chicken-based North Indian cuisine, but
    vegetarians are well catered for
**L'Auberge de Provence** 41 Buckingham Gate SW1 (071) 821 1899
    French restaurant with several vegetarian dishes on the menu
**Launceston Place** 1a Launceston Place W8 (071) 937 6912
    Vegetarian dishes on the menu
**Leith's** 92 Kensington Park Road W11 (071) 229 4481
    Owned by writer-broadcaster Prue Leith. Vegetarian menu available
**Maxie's Wine Bar and Restaurant** 143 Knightsbridge SW1 (071) 225 2553
**Ménage à Trois**  15 Beauchamp Place, Knightsbridge SW3 (071) 589 4252
    Some vegetarian dishes on the menu
**Mijanou** 143 Ebury Street SW1 (071) 730 4099
    Vegetarian dishes on the menu
**Pembridge Hotel** 64 Pembridge Gardens W2 (071) 229 9977
**Phoenicia Restaurant** 11/13 Abingdon Road W8 (071) 937 0120
    Lebanese restaurant serving interesting vegetarian dishes.
    Vegans catered for
**Pizza Place** 5 Lanark Place, Little Venice W9 (071) 289 4353
    Italian-American style pizza house, strong on take-aways and home delivery
**Pigeon Restaurant** 606 Fulham Road SW6 (071) 736 4618
    A bistro offering some vegetarian options on an essentially French menu
**Wilkins Natural Food**  61 Marsham Street SW1 (071) 222 4038
    International-style cooking at this vegetarian café. Dishes are changed daily
    and prepared from wholefood ingredients. Take-away service. Vegans and
    special diets catered for
**Windmill Vegetarian Restaurant** 486 Fulham Road SW6 (071) 385 1570

Vegetarian licensed restaurant with a wide range of dishes. Vegans catered for. Large selection of organic wines, ciders and beers. Special diets can be catered for. Take-away service

**Woodlands** 37 Panton Street, Leicester Square SW1 (071) 839 7258
Excellent South Indian vegetarian dishes, with filled pancakes a speciality

## CHARITY SHOPS

**British Red Cross Society** 71 Old Church Street SW3
**Cancer Research Campaign** 350 North End Road, Fulham SW6
Opening Spring 1990
**HAPA (Playgrounds for the handicapped)** 57a Fulham High Street W6
**Imperial Cancer Research** 387 North End Road, Fulham SW6
(071) 381 0497
**Oxfam** 432 King's Road, Chelsea SW10 (071) 351 6863
**Oxfam** 202b Kensington High Street W8 (071) 937 6683
**Oxfam** 15 Warwick Way, Pimlico SW1 (071) 821 1952
**Oxfam** 245 Westbourne Grove W11 (071) 229 5000
**Oxfam** 240 Edgware Road W2 (071) 724 0332
**The Spastics' Society** 346 North End Road, Fulham SW6 (071) 385 3853
**Sue Ryder** 49 Parliament Street SW1

## WOOD

**Austin Vernon Associates** 17 Denbigh Street, Pimlico SW1
Architects and planners
**CLS** 9 Thorpe Close, Portobello Green W10
Architects and planners (081) 968 3795
**Fulham Kitchen Centre** 19 Carnwath Road SW6
English and continental design kitchens (071) 736 9935
**Futon Company** 138 Notting Hill Gate W11
Manufacturer, retailer, exporter of futons and furniture (071) 727 9252
**The First Floor Company** Unit 1, Imperial Studios, Imperial Road SW6
Reclaimed hardwood flooring
**Habitat** 110/111 Kensington High Street (in BHS) W8 (071) 376 1221
**Habitat** 208 King's Road SW3 (071) 351 1211
**Lloyd Christie** 22 Doria Road, Parsons Green SW6
Garden architecture and trelliswork
**Robin Thomson Furniture** Floor 3, Block 6/8, Avon Trading Estate, Avonmore Road, Earls Court W14
Furniture design and manufacture
**The House of Shutters** 296 Wandsworth Bridge Road SW6
Manufacturer of window shutters
**Geoffrey Sarson Architects,** The Coach House, 14a St Lukes Road W11
Architects
**Somerville of Drum** 23 Eustace Road, Fulham SW6
Timber merchants, designer and cabinet maker
**Susan Walker Architects** 15 Cromwell Road SW7 (071) 584 9020
Architects

## BIKE SHOPS

**Barnes** 285 Westbourne Grove W11 (071) 727 5147
**Belgravia Cycles** 18 Gillingham Street, Victoria SW1 (071) 828 4040
**Bicycle Workshop** 27 All Saints Road W11 (071) 229 4850
**Bike** 53 Pimlico Road SW1 (071) 730 6668
**Chelsea Cycles** 15 Park Walk SW1
**Cyclecare** 20 Blythe Road W14 (071) 602 9757
**Days** 213 Dawes Road SW6 (071) 385 3870
**Dial a Bike** 18 Gillingham Street SW1 (071) 828 2626
**Fudge** 564 Harrow Road W9 (081) 969 5991
**Muse Bicycles** 14 The Arches, Munster Road SW6 (071) 731 7012
**Porchester Cycles** 8 Porchester Place W2 (071) 723 9236
**Portobello Cycles** 69 Goldbourne Road W10 (081) 960 0444
**Wheelpower Bike Centre** 849 Fulham Road SW6 (071) 736 7965
**Wiltons** 28 Upper Tachbrook Street, Victoria SW1 (071) 834 1367

# INNER WEST

*Incorporating Postal Districts W3–W7, W12, W13*

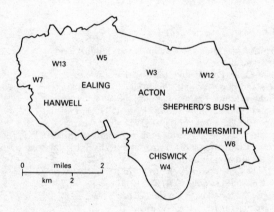

# FOOD SHOPS AND EVERYDAY PRODUCTS *including:*
*cleaning items, cosmetics, recycled paper and energy-efficient electrical goods*

**Anjella Health & Beauty** 3 Leeland Road W13 (081) 567 4638
   Sells a limited range of wholefoods
**Body Shop** Kings Mall, King Street, Hammersmith W6 (081) 748 7651
**Bushwacker** 59 Goldhawk Road W12 (081) 743 2359
   Good range of wholefoods and health foods. Organic food, fruit and
   vegetables. Vegetarian and vegan. Free-range eggs
**Cornucopia Cheese & Coffee** 70 Pitshanger Lane W5 (081) 997 3382
**Cornucopia Wholefoods** 64 St Mary's Road W5 (081) 579 9431

**Earthworks** 1 Devonshire Road W4 (081) 995 0588
    Organic food
**Earthworks** 132 King Street W6 (081) 846 9357
**Hartmoor Herbs Ltd** 66 Margravine Gardens W6 (081) 748 2491
**Holland & Barrett** 416 Chiswick High Road W4 (081) 994 1683
**Holland & Barrett** 3 Kings Mall, Hammersmith W6 (081) 748 1612
**Holland & Barrett** 112 Shepherd's Bush Centre W12 (081) 743 1045
**Holland & Barrett** 6 Ealing Broadway W5 (081) 840 1070
**Holland & Barrett** 61 The Broadway W13 (081) 840 7558
**Market Place Health Foods** 8 Market Place W3 (081) 993 3848
**Natural Food Products Ltd** 10 Barley Mow Passage W4 (081) 994 7185
    Sells a range of packaged wholefood
**Nutriwise** 68 Pitshanger Lane W5 (081) 997 7785
**Old Oak Healthfood Shop** 195 Old Oak Road W3 (081) 743 2348
**The Terrace Health Store** 33 Turnham Green Terrace W4 (081) 994 4997
    Wholefoods, health foods and free-range eggs
**Thorogood** 113 Northfield Avenue, Ealing W13 (081) 567 0339
    Sells a wide range of 'real meat' which can be delivered to the Hillingdon
    area
**Victoria Health Foods** Unit 12b, Ealing Broadway Centre, The Broadway W5
    (081) 840 6949

## EATING OUT - Restaurants, cafés and take-aways

**Angel Gate Vegetarian Restaurant** Temple Lodge, 51 Queen Caroline Street
    W6 (081) 748 8388
**Blah Blah Blah** 78 Goldhawk Road W12 (081) 746 1337
    Vegetarian restaurant
**Breadwinners** Unit A, 18 Greyhound Road W6 (071) 386 8919
    A vegetarian sandwich and snack delivery service
**Earthworks** 132 King Street W6 (081) 846 9357
    Only open in shop hours. Gourmet food at café prices

## CHARITY SHOPS

**Age Concern** Hammersmith Grove W6
**Barnardo's** 70/72 Turnham Green Terrace W4 (081) 994 9931
**Barnardo's** 26a The Broadway, West Ealing W5 (081) 840 0740
**British Epilepsy Association** 151 Princes Gardens W3 (081) 992 4743
**British Red Cross Society** 100 Brook Green, Hammersmith W6
**Cancer Research Campaign** 392 High Road, Chiswick W4
    Opening Spring 1990
**Cancer Research Campaign** 108 King Street, Hammersmith W6
    Opening Spring 1990
**Ealing Day Centre for the Elderly** Ealing Civic Centre, 14/16 Uxbridge Road
    W5 (081) 579 2424 (Ext.53782)
    Takes wool and knitting needles, fabric remnants and games
**Hanwell Salvation Army Centre** Army Hall, Lower Boston Road W7
    (081) 567 6579 (ring beforehand - no fixed hours)
    Takes jumble for jumble sales or for recycling, household fabrics, blankets
    and bric-à-brac
**Imperial Cancer Research** 48 The Broadway, West Ealing W13   (081) 579 0549

**Imperial Cancer Research** 278 Chiswick High Road, Chiswick W4
(081) 742 2501
**Imperial Cancer Research**, 123a King Street, Hammersmith W6
(081) 563 0440
**Kids at Risk** 14 Bond Street W5
New charity shop run by YMCA
**Notting Hill Housing Trust** 76 Askew Road W12 (081) 740 4878
**Notting Hill Housing Trust** 46 Turnham Green Terrace W4 (081) 995 8864
**Notting Hill Housing Trust** 21 High Street W5 (081) 579 5128
**Oxfam** 190 Chiswick High Road W4 (081) 994 4888
**Oxfam** 34 New Broadway, Ealing W5 (081) 579 6532
**Oxfam** 1 The Green, Ealing W5 (081) 567 2152
(This shop specializes in records only)
**Oxfam** 87 King Street, Hammersmith W6 (081) 846 9276
**Oxfam** 99 The Broadway, West Ealing W13 (081) 579 2896
**RSPCA** 48 Uxbridge Road W7 (081) 567 1839
Open Monday–Friday for collection of jumble for jumble sales
**Salvation Army Shop** 40 South Ealing Road W5 (081) 840 6269
Take clothes in nearly new condition only and bric-à-brac. Sell their own
selection of new gift ideas
**The Spastics' Society** 88/88a High Street, Acton W3 (081) 992 9364
**Sue Ryder** 231 Chiswick High Road W4
**Trinity Hospice** 408 Chiswick High Road W4
**YMCA** 14 Bond Street, Ealing W5 (081) 567 3180

## WOOD

**Cubestore Limited** 58 Pembroke Road W8 (071) 602 2001
Storage systems and shelving
**Habitat** West Five Centre, Alliance Road, Western Avenue W3 (081) 993 8261
**Habitat** Kings Mall, Hammersmith W6 (081) 741 7111

## BIKE SHOPS

**Bike UK** 273 High Street, Acton W3 (081) 992 2877
**B & L Accessories** 73 St. Mary's Road W5 (081) 567 4359
**Bob's Bicycles** 327 Greenford Avenue W7 (081) 578 5694
**Ealing Cycles** 16 Bond Street W5 (081) 567 3557
**Fudge** 101 Uxbridge Road W12 (081) 743 5265
**Fudge** 176 Chiswick High Road W4 (081) 994 1485
**Halfords** 49 New Broadway, Ealing W5 (081) 567 3211
**Mo's Enterprise** 84 South Ealing Road W5 (081) 567 3659
**The Mountain Bike Centre** 81 New Broadway, Ealing W5 (081) 579 2382
**Newton** 65 Askew Road W12 (081) 743 4422
**Stuart Bikes** 309 Horn Lane W3 (081) 993 3484
**Woolsey of Acton** 281 Acton Lane, Acton Green W4 (081) 994 6893

# OUTER WEST

*Incorporating Postal Districts UB1–UB10, HA4, HA6, TW3–TW8, TW13, TW14*

## *FOOD SHOPS AND EVERYDAY PRODUCTS including: cleaning items, cosmetics, recycled paper and energy-efficient electrical goods*

**Body Shop** Terminal 1, Heathrow Airport, Hounslow, Middlesex TW6
(081) 759 0243

**Body Shop** Terminal 2, Heathrow Airport, Hounslow, Middlesex TW6
(081) 897 6059

**Food for Thought** 154 High Street, Hounslow, Middlesex (081) 572 0310
Health foods and vegetarian fast food

**Hayes Health Foods** 814c Uxbridge Road, Hayes, Middlesex UB4 (081) 561 1624
Organic food (including vegetarian), goats milk, free-range eggs and
stoneground wholemeal bread daily

**The Health Basket** 4 Botwell Lane, Hayes, Middlesex UB3  (081) 573 5136
Organic food, honey and wheat. Free-range eggs

**Healthy Bite** 5a Windsor Street, Uxbridge, Middlesex UB8 (0895) 810500
Specialises in vegetarian delicatessen, organically-grown products, natural

foods and home baking. Free-range eggs

**Healthcare** 467 London Road, Isleworth, Middlesex TW7 (081) 560 2947
Health products and takeaway food

**Holland & Barrett** 17/19 Pantile Walk, Uxbridge, Middlesex UB8 (0895) 37841

**Hunza Wholefoods** Syon Park, Isleworth, Middlesex TW7 (081) 847 2140
Wholefood and health items

**Manor Health Foods** 81 Victoria Road, Ruislip Manor, Middlesex HA4
(0895) 672386
Organic foods including flour, cereals and honey. Free-range eggs

**Moorpark Fruiterers** 12 Main Avenue, Moorpark, Northwood, Middlesex
(09274) 21707

**Naturewise** 30 Joel Street, Northwood Hills, Middlesex HA6 (09274) 27541
Organic foods including flour, cereals and honey. Free-range eggs

**Northwood Health Foods** 3 Rowland Place, Green Lane, Northwood, Middlesex
HA6 (09274) 24882
Organic food including cheese, juices, yoghurt, cereals, and honey. Free-range eggs

**Ruislip Village Health Store**, 22 High Street, Ruislip, Middlesex HA4
(0895) 638187
Organic food – local and very fresh. Eggs from organically-fed chickens

**F. E. Smith** 31 Swakeleys Road, Ickenham, Middlesex UB10 (0895) 632111
This butcher sells a range of organic fruit and vegetables all year round.
Free-range eggs

**Weigh and Save** 746 Uxbridge Road, Hayes, Middlesex UB4 (081) 561 1218
A wide range of organic/wholefood items are sold, including cereals, dried
fruit, nuts and pulses

## EATING OUT - Restaurants, cafés and take-aways

**Maranatha Christian Bookshop** 22 Windsor Street, Uxbridge, Middlesex UB8
(0895) 55748
Includes 'Martha's Coffee Shop' which serves hot and cold snacks from
9.30am to 5.00pm

**Healthy Bite** 5a Windsor Street, Uxbridge, Middlesex UB8 (0895) 810500
All food vegetarian and a percentage suitable for vegans

## CHARITY SHOPS

**Barnardo's** 25 Swakeleys Road, Ickenham, Middlesex UB10 (0895) 677338

**British Red Cross Society** 90 South Road, Southall, Middlesex UB1
(081) 574 5238
Open Monday–Friday 10.30-1.00 and 2.00-4.00

**British Red Cross Society** 195 Pinner Road, Northwood HA6
Saturday morning market 9.45–11.45

**British Red Cross Society** Rear of Clinic, Dawlish Drive, Ruislip Manor HA4
Open Friday and Saturday 10.00–11.30

**Cancer Research Campaign** 125 High Street, Hounslow, Middlesex TW3
Opening Spring 1990

**Cancer Research Campaign** 87 High Street, Ruislip, Middlesex HA4

**Imperial Cancer Research** 1 Coldharbour Lane, Hayes, Middlesex UB3
(081) 573 5188

**Imperial Cancer Research** 106 High Street, Ruislip, Middlesex HA4

(0895) 675337
**Imperial Cancer Research** 47 High Street, Hounslow, Middlesex TW3
(081) 570 9813
**Oxfam** 26 High Street, Hounslow TW3 (081) 572 1024
**Oxfam** 1213 Greenford Road, Greenford, Middlesex UB6 (081) 422 0600
**Oxfam** 30 The Broadway, Greenford, Middlesex UB6 (081) 575 9047
**Oxfam** 10 Joel Street, Northwood Hills, Middlesex HA6 (09274) 27981
**Oxfam** 8a Ickenham Road, Ruislip, Middlesex HA4 (08956) 74845
**Oxfam** 19 Victoria Road, Ruislip Manor, Middlesex HA4 (08956) 75776
**Salvation Army Centre** 46 Mansell Road, Greenford, Middlesex UB6
(081) 578 7849 (Ring beforehand)

## WOOD

**ICTC** Fleming Way, Isleworth, Middlesex TW7
Importers/distributors of tableware products to the retail trade
**Park Green & Co** Eskdale Road, Uxbridge, Middlesex UB8 (0895) 53531
Manufacturer of pepper mills

## BIKE SHOPS

**Cycle Centre**, 122 The Broadway, Southall UB1 (081) 574 1782
**Hayes Cycle Centre** 13 Coldharbour Lane, Hayes, Middlesex UB3
(081) 573 2402
**Ken Rogers** 71 Berkeley Avenue, Cranford, Hounslow, Middlesex TW5
(081) 897 9109
**Moore Bros** 3/5 St. John's Road, Isleworth, Middlesex (081) 560 7131
**Richardsons** 7 Rochester Parade, High Street, Feltham, Middlesex
(081) 890 4399
**Richardsons** 128 The Centre, Feltham, Middlesex TW13 (081) 890 4399
**Viscount** 492 Church Road, Northolt UB5 (81) 845 6144

# INNER SOUTH-WEST

*Incorporating Postal Districts SW2, SW4, SW8, SW9,*
*SW11–SW20*

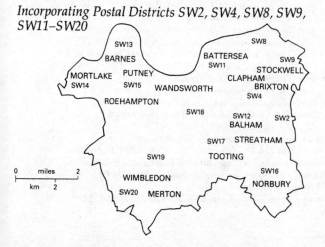

## FOOD SHOPS AND EVERYDAY PRODUCTS *including: cleaning items, cosmetics, recycled paper and energy-efficient electrical goods*

**Abraxas (Streatham Greenpeace)** 7 Shrubbery Road SW16
**Balham Wholefood & Health Store** 8 Bedford Hill SW12 (081) 673 4842
**Barnes Health Foods** 60 Barnes High Street SW13 (081) 876 5476
**Bedford Hill Gallery** 50 Bedford Hill, Balham SW12 (081) 675 5446
**Bella-Donna** 5 Westbury Parade SW12 (081) 673 3121
**Bodycare**, 266 Lavender Hill SW11
**Body Shop** 77 High Street, Putney SW15 (081) 785 4780
**Body Shop** 464/470 Brixton Road SW9 (071) 738 4468
**Body Shop** 1a White Hart Lane, Barnes SW13 (081) 876 1002
**Brixton Healthfoods** 30 Granville Arcade, Coldharbour Lane SW9
**Brixton Wholefoods** 56 Atlantic Road SW9 (071) 737 2210
**Broadway Health Shop** 22 The Broadway SW19 (081) 947 8740
**Cordon Vert** 136 Merton Road, South Wimbledon SW19 (081) 543 9174
**Country Wholefoods** 47 The Broadway SW19
**Dandelion** 254 Battersea Park Road SW11
**Dandelion Natural Foods** 120 Northcote Road, Battersea SW11
**Di's Larder** 62 Lavender Hill SW11
**Fab-Foods** 1 Station Buildings, Wimbledon Chase Station, Kingston Road SW20 (081) 540 5923
    Various wholefoods, herbal medicines and natural dairy products
**Health & Diet Centre** 151 Putney High Street SW15
    (081) 788 0944
    Organic vegetables, herbal teas, free-range and organic eggs, literature
**Health & Diet Centre**, 194 Upper Richmond Road West, East Sheen SW14
    (081) 876 6440
    Organic vegetables, herbal teas, free-range and organic eggs, literature
**Holland & Barrett** 68 The Broadway SW19 (081) 542 7486
**Holland & Barrett** 110 Streatham High Road SW16 (081) 769 1418
**Holland & Barrett** 5 Arndale Walk SW18 (081) 874 3598
**Holland & Barrett** 51 St. John's Road SW11 (071) 228 6071
**Lifecycle Ltd** Unit 29, The Arndale Centre SW18 (081) 871 3706
**Linkers** 90 Clapham High Street SW4 (071) 720 4567
**Nature Freight** 63 Tremadoc Road SW4 (071) 622 1210
**Nature's Way Ltd** 252 Streatham High Road SW16 (081) 769 0065
**Odin** 32 Fruit & Veg. Market, New Covent Garden SW8 (071) 622 3099
    Organic fruit and vegetables – open two days a week to the public
**Oliver Wholefood Store** 256 Battersea Park Road SW11 (071) 223 9211
**The Organic Shop** 120 Ferndale Road SW4 (071) 737 1365
    Large range of food and beverages
**Pamela Price Here is Food Delicatessen** 26 The Pavement SW4 (071) 622 6818
    Wholefood and vegetarian products and free-range eggs
**C.K. Patel** 29 Clapham High Street SW4 (081) 543 3999
    'Plamil' vegan foods and general vegetarian foods
**Premier Fruit and Nut Ltd** 72 Tankerville Road SW16 (081) 679 8226
**Pure Grace Natural Foods Ltd,** 153 Clapham High Street SW4 (071) 622 1304
**Putney Healthfoods** 28 Upper Richmond Road, Putney SW15
**Realfoods** 110 Streatham High Road SW16
**Rupe Food Store** Grand Drive, Raynes Park SW20 (081) 542 3332

**South London Bakers Co-op** 639 Garrett Lane SW18 (081) 947 5264
**Terrapin Station** 76 Effra Road SW19 (081) 543 3999
  'Plamil' vegan foods and general vegetarian foods
**Todays Living** 92 Clapham High Street SW4 (071) 622 1772
**Top Food** Coombe Lane, Raynes Park SW20
  Organic fruit and vegetables
**Trees** 9 Horseford Road SW2
**Treohan's** 56 Abbeville Road SW4 (081) 673 2738
  Stock free-range eggs, various wholefood items
**Vauxhall Housing Co-op** 56 Bonnington Square SW8

## EATING OUT - Restaurants, cafés and take-aways

**Bedford Hill Gallery** 50 Bedford Hill, Balham SW12 (081) 675 5446
  Vegetarian café. Open Monday–Saturday 10-4
**Brixton Wholefoods** 56 Atlantic Road SW9 (071) 737 2210
**Cordon Vert** 136 Merton Road, Wimbledon SW19 (081) 543 9174
  Reasonably priced vegetarian restaurant where you can bring your own
  drink
**Di's Larder** 62 Lavender Hill SW11
**The Gourmet** 2a Kings Road, Wimbledon SW19 (081) 543 6416
  Vegetarian and fish restaurant serving lunch and dinner
**The Green Café** The Broadway, Wimbledon SW19
  Light vegetarian meals and snacks served throughout the day, but not open
  for dinner
**Jacaranda Garden** 11 Brixton Station Road SW9 (071) 274 8383
  Serves mainly snacks
**Klaro** 4 Upper Richmond Road SW15 (081) 874 7251
  Caribbean food with good vegetarian selection
**Kastoori** 188 Upper Tooting Road SW17 (081) 767 7027
  Small menu but excellent choice in this pure vegetarian restaurant
**Myra's Restaurant** 240 Upper Richmond Road, Putney SW15 (081) 788 9450
  Small restaurant with vegetarian dishes
**The Nature Garden** 52 Lavender Hill, Battersea SW11 (071) 223 4618
  Vegetarian restaurant offering home-made soup, pizza, quiche and
  sandwiches during the day. In the evening the only Chinese vegetarian
  restaurant south of the river. Bring your own wine
**No.1 Bedford Hill** 1 Bedford Hill, Balham SW12
  Vegetarian restaurant.
**The Organic Shop** 120 Ferndale Road SW4 (071) 737 1365
  Serves mainly snack meals
**Shahee Bhelpoor** 1547 London Road, Norbury SW16 (081) 679 6275
  Indian Vegetarian restaurant
**Sree Krishna** 194 Tooting High Street SW17 (081) 672 4250
  South Indian restaurant, mainly vegetarian. Superb value
**Twenty Trinity Gardens** 20 Trinity Gardens SW9 (071) 733 8838
  Small friendly restaurant with outside tables. Vegetarians catered for
**Whole Meal Café** 1 Shrubbery Road SW16 (081) 769 2423
  Vegetarian café - no smoking please

## CHARITY SHOPS

**Age Concern** 1/5 Acre Lane SW2 (071) 274 7722
**Age Concern** 202 High Street, Wandsworth SW17 (081) 767 5419
**Age Concern** 112 Mitcham Road, Tooting SW17 (Not on telephone)
**Barnardo's** 3 Parkway House, Sheen Lane SW14 (081) 876 5620
**Barnardo's** 414 Brixton Road, Brixton SW9 (071) 274 4165
**British Red Cross Society** 28 Worple Road, Wimbledon SW19 (081) 946 1970
**British Red Cross Society** 106 Clapham Road, Lambeth SW9
  Open Monday–Friday 10.30–12.30
**British Red Cross Society** 5 Bridge Parade, Streatham SW16
  Open Monday–Saturday 10.30–4.00
**British Red Cross Society** 332 Kingston Road, Merton SW20
**British Red Cross Society** 54 Fairfield Street, Wandsworth SW18
**Cancer Research Campaign** 18 The Broadway, Wimbledon SW19
**The Childrens Society Shop** 3 Victoria Crescent SW19 (081) 946 2808
**Dr. Barnardo's Gift Shop** 414 Brixton Road SW9 (071) 274 4165
**Help 71** 95 Acre Lane SW2 (071) 737 1419
**Imperial Cancer Research Campaign** 65 Streatham High Road SW16
  (081) 677 3442
**Imperial Cancer Research Campaign** 58 The Broadway, Wimbledon SW19
  (081) 543 8137
**Imperial Cancer Research Campaign** 224 Upper Richmond Road West, East
  Sheen SW14 (081) 876 2255
**Imperial Cancer Research Campaign** 1390 London Road, Norbury SW16
  (081) 679 1422
**Imperial Cancer Research Campaign** 83 St. John's Road, Clapham SW11
  (071) 223 5349
**MIND** 106 Merton High Street SW19 (081) 542 8499
**MIND** 463/465 Wandsworth Road SW8 (071) 622 3442
**Notting Hill Housing Trust** The Charity Shop, 19 The Broadway, Wimbledon
  SW19 (081) 946 0406
**Oxfam** 333 Upper Richmond Road West, East Sheen SW14 (081) 876 9735
**Oxfam** 149 Putney High Street, Putney SW15 (081) 789 3235
**Oxfam** 4 Replingham Road, Southfields SW18 (081) 870 2676
**Oxfam** 320 Streatham High Road, Streatham SW16 (081) 769 1291 (This shop
  specialises in electrical goods only)
**Oxfam** 110 The Broadway, Wimbledon SW19 (081) 540 5606
**Oxfam** 7 Astoria Parade, Streatham High Road SW8 (081) 769 0515
**Oxfam Shop** 93 High Street, Wimbledon Village SW19 (081) 946 7344
**Oxfam Shop** 365 Kingston Road, Wimbledon Chase SW20 (081) 540 8456
**Red Cross Shop** 106 Clapham Road SW9 (071) 582 5444
**RNLI,** c/o 72c Leopold Road, Wimbledon SW19 (081) 947 5172
  This is not a shop but a private address where goods suitable for recycling
  can be taken
**Save The Children** 36 Clapham High Street SW4 (071) 978 2542
**Street Level** All Saints Charity Shop, 226 Brixton Hill SW2 (081) 674 6138
**Sue Ryder** 87 Balham High Road, Balham SW12
**Trinity Hospice Charity Shops** 184 Clapham High Street SW4 (071) 622 9481
**Trinity Hospice Charity Shops,** 9 The Old Town, Clapham SW4
**Trinity Hospice Charity Shops** Wilcox Street SW9

# WOOD

**Futon South** 109 Balham High Road SW12 (081) 675 6727
   Retailer of futons
**The Good Wood Shop** 100 Haydons Road SW19
   Furniture retailer
**Nowell & Cole** 44C St. John's Hill Grove SW11
   Architects
**Ovans Pownall Timber Ltd** 8 Fitzgerald Avenue SW14 (081) 876 9948
   Importer of temperate hardwoods
**Scallywag Antique and Country Pine** 187 Clapham Road SW9 (071) 274 0300
   Retailer of antique and country pine
**Smith & Redfern** 25 Badminton Road SW12
   Sign consultancy
**The Treske Shop** 5 Barmouth Road SW18 (071) 874 0050
   English hardwood furniture maker

# BIKE SHOPS

**ACTIV (LONDON ATB Centre)** 553 Battersea Park Road SW11 (071) 223 2590
**Astoria Cycles** 2 Central Hall Building, Durnsford Road SW19 (081) 947 5575
**Algurns** 569 Garrett Lane SW18 (081) 946 7921
**AW Cycles** 23 Abbey Parade, Merton High Street SW19 (081) 542 2534
**Bike UK** 40 Clapham High Street SW4 (071) 622 1334
**Bike UK** 296 Upper Richmond Road SW15
**Brixton Cycle Co-op** 433 Coldharbour Lane SW9 (071) 733 6055
**Cycle City** 57 Approach Road SW20 (081) 542 4076
**DeVer Cycles** 630 Streatham High Road SW16 (081) 679 6197
**Edwardes** 261 Mitcham Lane SW16 (081) 769 6423
**Edward Warner & Son** 24 High Street, Colliers Wood SW19 (081) 540 6125
**Halfords** 307 Lavender Hill SW11 (071) 228 6618
**Halfords** 254 Streatham High Road SW16 (081) 769 7525
**Halfords** 60 High Street SW17 (081) 672 7796
**Halfords** 66 Putney High Street SW15 (081) 789 3561
**Halfords** 9 Wimbledon Hill Road SW19 (081) 946 1775
**Holdsworth** 132 Lower Richmond Road SW15 (081) 788 1060
**Saviles** 99 Battersea Rise SW11 (071) 228 4279
**Smith Bros** 14 Church Road SW19 (081) 946 2270
**South Bank Bicycles** 194 Wandsworth Road SW8 (071) 622 3069
**Strattons** 101 East Hill, Wandsworth SW18 (081) 874 1381
**Stuart's Lightweight Cycles** 1 Ascot Parade, Clapham Park Road SW4  (071)
   622 4818
**Wheel Power Bike Centre** 264 Grand Drive SW20 (081) 543 0321

# OUTER SOUTH-WEST

*Incorporating
Postal Districts
TW1, TW2,
TW9–TW12,
KT1–KT6, KT9*

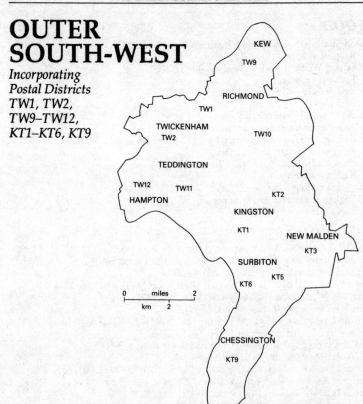

## *FOOD SHOPS AND EVERYDAY PRODUCTS including: cleaning items, cosmetics, recycled paper and energy-efficient electrical goods*

**All Manna** 179 Sheen Road, Richmond, Surrey TW9 (081) 948 3633
  Long-established shop selling a large variety of organic fruit and vegetables, organic dairy produce including sheep's milk. They also stock a range of macrobiotics and Martin Pitt eggs.
**Bay Tree** 190 Stanley Road, Teddington, Middlesex TW11
**Body Shop** 50a George Street, Richmond, Surrey TW9 (081) 940 0310
**Body Shop** 6/8 Thames Street, Kingston-upon-Thames, Surrey KT1
  (081) 541 4372
**Food for Thought** 38 Market Place, Kingston-upon-Thames KT3 (081) 546 7806
  Wholefoods, organic produce and free-range eggs
**Gaia** 123 St Margaret's Road, Twickenham, Middlesex TW1 (081) 892 2262
**Good Nature** 5 Station Approach, Kew TW6
**Health Food Centre** 62 The Broadway, Surbiton, Surrey KT6 (081) 399 3932
**Holland & Barrett** 95 High Street, New Malden KT3 (081) 942 6694

**Holland & Barrett** 12/13 Apple Market, Kingston-upon-Thames KT1
   (081) 541 1378
**Holland & Barrett** 50a George Street, Richmond, Surrey TW9 (081) 940 1007
**Holland & Barrett** 25 Heath Road, Twickenham, Middlesex TW1
**Kingston Wholefood Co-op** 34 Vicarage Road, Kingston-upon-Thames KT1
**Natural Food Butchers Shop** 90 Elm Road, Kingston-upon-Thames KT2
   (081) 546 1556
**Naturally Wholefoods** 70 High Street, Hampton Wick, Middlesex TW12
**Sesame Health Food Store** 10 Seaforth Avenue, New Malden, Surrey KT3
   (081) 949 0327
   Various health foods and products
**Sunshine Health Food Stores** 26 Cheam Common Road, Worcester Park, Surrey
   KT4 (081) 337 3508
**Surbiton Whole Foods** 14 Claremont Road, Surbiton, Surrey KT6 (081) 399 2772
   Freshly baked organic bread
**Teddington Wholefood Co-op** Normansfield Avenue, Teddington, Middlesex
   TW11
   Open Friday and Saturday only
**Tolworth Healthfoods** 62 Broadway, Tolworth, Surrey

## EATING OUT - Restaurants, cafés and take-aways

**Chatteries** Motspur Park, Surrey KT3
**The Pavement** 165 Ewell Road, Surbiton, Surrey KT6 (081) 390 0320
   Totally vegetarian restaurant
**La La Pizza** 138 London Road, Kingston-upon-Thames KT2 (081) 546 4888
   Pizza restaurant/takeaway which serves some vegetarian dishes.
**Yellow Heaven Soup Kitchen** 74 Richmond Road, Kingston-upon-Thames KT2
   (081) 546 6691
   Theme restaurant and bar serving some vegetarian and vegan dishes

## CHARITY SHOPS

**British Red Cross Society** Red Cross Centre, King Charles Crescent, Surbiton
   KT5 (081) 399 1673
   Open Thursdays 10.00–5.00
**British Red Cross Society** 59 King Street Parade, Twickenham TW1
   (081) 892 6345
**Cancer Research Campaign** 1 Hill Street, Richmond, Surrey TW9
   Opening Spring 1990
**Cancer Research Campaign** 48 King Street, Twickenham TW1 (081) 744 1817
**Cancer Research Campaign** 118 Central Road, Worcester Park, Surrey KT4
   (081) 337 2108
**Helping Hand** 1 Lichfield Terrace, Sheen Road, Richmond, Surrey TW9
   (081) 940 1800
**Imperial Cancer Research** 43 Broad Street, Teddington, Middlesex TW11
   (081) 977 0271
**Imperial Cancer Research** 12 Heath Road, Twickenham, Middlesex TW1
   (081) 892 7128
**Imperial Cancer Research** 100 Central Road, Worcester Park KT4
   (081) 337 4851
**Imperial Cancer Research** 21 Victoria Road, Surbiton, Surrey KT6

(081) 390 6650

**Imperial Cancer Research** 36 Eden Street, Kingston-upon-Thames, Surrey KT3
(081) 541 5268

**Imperial Cancer Research** 85 High Street, New Malden, Surrey KT3
(081) 949 5351

**MentalAid** 426 Ewell Road, Tolworth KT6 (081) 399 3136

**MentalAid** 1a St. Andrews Road, Surbiton, Surrey KT6 (081) 390 5597

**MIND** 35 Richmond Road, Kingston, Surrey KT2 (081) 546 9050

**MIND** 33 Heath Road, Twickenham, Middlesex TW1 (081) 892 5414

**Oxfam** 16 Castle Street, Kingston-upon-Thames, Surrey KT1 (081) 546 5939

**Oxfam** 30 London Road, Kingston-upon-Thames, Surrey KT2 (081) 549 3559

**Oxfam** 62 Victoria Road, Surbiton, Surrey KT6 (081) 390 7528

**Oxfam** 104 High Street, New Malden KT3 (081) 942 1581

**Oxfam** 6 The Quadrant, Richmond, Surrey TW9 (081) 948 7381

**Oxfam** 46 King Street, Twickenham, Middlesex TW1 (081) 892 4605

**Oxfam** 88 Central Road, Worcester Park KT9 (081) 330 7527

**Oxfam** 56 Broad Street, Teddington TW11 (081) 943 3196

**Princess Alice Hospice Charity Shop**, London Road, Kingston-upon-Thames,
Surrey KT2

**Princess Alice Hospice Charity Shop**, 4 Claremont Road, Surbiton, Surrey KT6
(081) 390 5380

**YMCA** 3 London Road, Twickenham, Middlesex TW1 (081) 744 2446

## BIKE SHOPS

**Kingston Cycles (F.W. Evans)**, 48 Richmond Road, Kingston KT5 (081) 549 2559

**Richmond Cycles** 425/427 Richmond Road, East Twickenham TW1
(081) 892 4372

**Richmond Cycles** 36 Hill Street, Richmond, Surrey TW9 (081) 940 6961

# OUTER SOUTH

*Incorporating Postal Districts SM1–SM6, CR0, CR2, CR4*

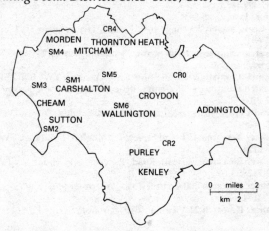

## FOOD SHOPS AND EVERYDAY PRODUCTS *including: cleaning items, cosmetics, recycled paper and energy-efficient goods*

**Aquarius** 51 Lower Addiscombe Road, Croydon, Surrey CR0

**Better Fare** 73 Banstead Road, Carshalton, Surrey

**Body Shop** 1037 The Whitgift Centre, Croydon, Surrey CR0 (081) 688 4751

**Body Shop** 4 Rothschild House, Croydon, Surrey CR0 (081) 680 8318

**Deen City Farm** Batsworth Road, Mitcham, Surrey CR4 (081) 648 1461
  Organically-grown vegetables

**GCB Foods** 3 Eagle Star House, High Street, Sutton SM3

**Health Foods** 60 The Broadway, Cheam, Surrey SM3 (081) 643 5132

**Healthcare** 234 Brigstock Road, Thornton Heath, Surrey CR4

**Healthwise** 5 Woodville Road, Thornton Heath, Surrey CR4 (081) 771 9731

**Healthwise for Health Foods** 2 High Street, Sutton, Surrey SM3 (081) 643 4251

**Hockneys Vegetarian Wholefoods** 98 High Street, Croydon, Surrey CR0
  (081) 688 2899
  Run by the western order of Buddhists to help fund arts programme.
  Provides virtually everything from dry and ready-made foods to snacks.
  Organic free-range eggs

**Holland & Barrett** 100 High Street, Croydon, Surrey CR0 (081) 688 0970

**Holland & Barrett** 1098-99 The Mall, Whitgift Centre, Croydon, Surrey CR0
  (081) 681 5174

**Holland & Barrett** 213 High Street, Sutton, Surrey SM5 (081) 642 5435

**Holland & Barrett** 50 London Road, Morden, Surrey SM4 (081) 685 0375

**Nature's Store** 24 St George's Walk, Croydon, Surrey CR0 (081) 680 1275

**Noah's Health Food Stores** 4 South Parade, Stafford Road, Wallington, Surrey
  SM6 (081) 647 1724
  Wholefood including fresh bread

**Peppers Delicatessen** 94 Stafford Road, Wallington , Surrey SM6 (081) 773 2778
  Wholefood and some organic produce

**Purley Wholefoods** 48 High Street, Purley, Surrey CR2 (081) 668 1293

**Weigh & Save Ltd** 41 The Market, Wrythe Lane, Carshalton, Surrey SM5
  (081) 644 9834
  Specialises in low packaging dried fruits, nuts, cereals etc

## EATING OUT - *Restaurants, cafés and take-aways*

**Hockneys Vegetarian Restaurant** 98 High Street, Croydon CR0 (081) 688 2899
  Lunchtime takeaway counter. Restaurant open in evening serving
  vegetarian food. Booking advisable

**Pizzeria Romana** 54 South End, South Croydon CR0 (081) 688 7124
  Very popular pizzeria offering vegetarian pizzas and lasagne.

**'Roots', The Wholefood Café** Carshalton Park, Carshalton, Surrey SM5
  Based in the park, one can sit at a table outside to eat, or take-away quick
  snack meals.

**The Rose** 305 London Road, West Croydon CR0 (081) 684 1198/1536
  Excellent Indian restaurant catering for both meat-eaters and vegetarians

**Santosh** 830 London Road, Thornton Heath CR4 (081) 683 2447
  Western Indian quality vegetarian cuisine - very popular so worth booking.
  Thalis are a speciality, although kerala (South Indian) and gujerati style is
  also on offer

## CHARITY SHOPS

**British Red Cross Society** 304 High Street, Croydon, Surrey CR0 (081) 681 7934
**British Red Cross Society** Red Cross House, Woodcote Road, Wallington,
Surrey SM6 (081) 647 8265
**Cancer Research Campaign** 20 The Broadway, Cheam, Surrey SM3
(081) 643 7410
**Cancer Research Campaign** 3 Fairgreen Parade, Upper Green West, Mitcham,
Surrey CR4 (081) 648 5863
**Cancer Research Campaign** 919 Brighton Road, Purley, Surrey CR2
(081) 660 0963
**Croydon Guild of Voluntary Organisations** 9 High Street, Purley, Surrey CR2
(081) 668 0246
**Helping Hand** 16/18 Station Road, Croydon, Surrey CR0 (081) 681 1914
**Helping Hand** 542 London Road, North Cheam, Surrey CR0 (081) 641 5477
**Helping Hand** 316 Wrythe Lane, Carshalton, Surrey SM5 (081) 641 6004
**Helping Hand** 329 High Street, Sutton, Surrey SM1 (081) 643 3431
**Imperial Cancer Research** 34/36 Church Street, Croydon, Surrey CR0
(081) 688 4102
**Imperial Cancer Research** 12 Fair Green Parade, Mitcham, Surrey CR4
(081) 640 5484
**Imperial Cancer Research** 954 Brighton Road, Purley, Surrey CR2
(081) 660 6469
**Imperial Cancer Research** 91 High Street, Sutton, Surrey SM1
(081) 643 2844
**Imperial Cancer Research** 19 Woodcote Road, Wallington, Surrey
(081) 647 1063
**MIND** 26 Pampisford Road, Purley, Surrey CR2 (081) 668 2982
**MIND** 135 Addington Road, Selsdon, Surrey CR2 (081) 651 4114
**MIND** 135 Addington Road, Selsdon, Surrey CR2 (081) 651 4114
**MM Missionary Mart** 105 Stafford Road, Wallington, Surrey SM6
(081) 669 3495
**Oxfam Shop** 8 Whitgift Street, Croydon, Surrey CR0 (081) 669 8453
**Oxfam Shop** 172 North End , Croydon, Surrey CR0 (081) 686 2253
**Oxfam Shop** 108a High Street, Croydon, Surrey CR0 (081) 686 0716
**Oxfam Shop** 928 Brighton Road, Purley CR2 (081) 668 8287
**Oxfam Shop** 33 High Street, Carshalton, Surrey SM5 (081) 669 8453
**Oxfam Gift Shop** 10 The Arcade, Sutton, Surrey SM1 (081) 642 6349
**Oxfam** 26 High Street, Cheam, Surrey SM3 (081) 643 1474
**Oxfam** 31 London Road, Morden, Surrey SM4 (081) 640 2754
**PDSA** 5/7 Hurst Road, Croydon, Surrey CR2 (081) 680 4741
This is a collection point for all bric-à-brac, clothes, books, jewellery etc. but
please, no electrical goods
**Salvation Army** Croydon Citadel, Booth Road, Lower Church Street, Croydon,
Surrey CR0 (081) 688 2038
**Save the Children** 25 High Street, Cheam, Surrey SM3 (081) 643 6456
**Save the Children** 131b Cherry Orchard Road, Croydon, Surrey CR0
(081) 688 7250
**The Spastics' Society** 307 Lower Addiscombe Road, Croydon, Surrey CR0
(081) 654 6838
**The Spastics' Society** 39 London Road, Morden, Surrey SM4
(081) 646 5646

## WOOD

**Habitat** 1 Drury Crescent, Purley Way, Croydon CR0 (081) 681 3818

## BIKE SHOPS

**Allins** 57 Whitehorse Road , Croydon, Surrey CR0 (081) 684 1620
**Ayton Cycles** 92 Beulah Road, Thornton Heath CR4 (081) 653 3896
**Broadway Cycles** 65 The Broadway, Stoneleigh, Surrey (081) 393 3256
**Geoffrey Butler** 15 South End, Croydon CR0 (081) 688 5094
**Pearsons** 126 High Street, Sutton, Surrey SM6 (081) 642 2095
**Roberts Cycles** 89 Gloucester Road, Croydon CR0 (081) 684 3370
**Saviles** 243 London Road, Mitcham, Surrey (081) 685 9231
**Townsend Cycle** 57 Stafford Road, Wallington, Surrey SM6 (081) 669 5199

# INNER SOUTH-EAST

*Incorporating Postal Districts SE1–SE28*

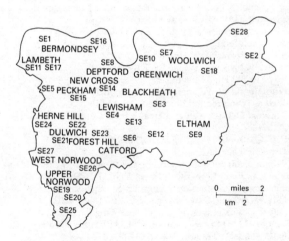

## FOOD SHOPS AND EVERYDAY PRODUCTS *including: cleaning items, cosmetics, recycled paper and energy-efficient electrical goods*

**Abbeywood Wholefoods** 11 Wilton Road SE2 (081) 311 4811
**Baldwins Health Food Centre** 171 Walworth Road SE17 (071) 701 4892
**Beanbags** 152 Maple Road SE20 (081) 659 1242

**Bean Thinking** Greenwich High Road SE10 (081) 692 3083
**Better Health Food Store** 7 Pound Place SE9 (081) 859 3807
**Bodycare Health Centre** 5 Lewis Grove SE13 (081) 852 1970
**Body Shop** Unit 3, Surrey Quay Shopping Centre SE16 (071) 252 3435
**The Brockley Bean** 2 Coulgate Street, Brockley SE4
**Coopers** 17 Lower Marsh SE1 (071) 261 9314
**Court Farm Granaries** 89 Mottingham Road SE9 (081) 857 0857
**Cross Currants** 304 New Cross Road SE14 (081) 692 1290
**Crystal Palace Wholefoods** 74 Church Road SE19 (081) 771 4605
**Fareshares Food Co-op** 56 Crampton Street SE17
**Four County Foods Ltd** 64 Union Street SE1 (071) 403 6626
**Full of Beans** 127 Rushey Green SE6 (081) 698 3283
**The Granary** 11a Delacourt Road SE3 (081) 853 5300
**Greenwich Wholefoods** 19 Greenwich South Street SE10 (081) 305 0203
**Health Farm Shop** 6 Camberwell Church Street SE5 (071) 703 7130
**Health Garden** 35 North Cross Road SE22 (081) 299 3780
**Health Stores & Greengrocery** 25 Half Moon Lane SE24 (071) 274 5759
**Health Trail** Peckham High Street SE15
**Health-wise** 86 Royal Hill SE10 (081) 692 0305
**Jolly Stores** 159 Hamilton Road SE27
**Health & Diet Centre** 24 Transquil Vale, Blackheath SE3 (081) 318 0428
    Organic vegetables, herbal teas, free-range and organic eggs and literature
**Holland & Barrett** 33 Winslade Way SE6 (081) 690 3903
**Holland & Barrett** 198 Eltham High Street SE9 (081) 859 7075
**Living Foods Wholefood Store** 304 New Cross Road SE14
**The Larder** (Julie Waghorn), 55 Upland Road SE22
**Nature's Larder** 340 Norwood Road SE27 (081) 670 0288
**Nature's Way Ltd** 140 High Street SE20
**Nosebag Wholefoods** 19 Wellington Street, Woolwich SE18
**Nunhead Dell & Wholefoods** 120 Evelina Road SE15
**Polka Continental Delicatessen and Health Food Centre** 3 Station Way SE15
    (071) 639 5910
**Provender** 103 Dartmouth Road SE23 (081) 699 4046
**SMBS** 75 Lordship Lane SE22
**Squirrels** 213 Elephant & Castle Shopping Centre SE1 (071) 708 3748
**Surrey Docks City Farm** Rotherhithe Street SE16 (071) 231 1010
    Free-range eggs, sometimes duck eggs. Free-range meat
**Vauxhall City Farm** 24 St. Oswalds Place SE11 (071) 582 4202
    Free-range eggs, sometimes duck eggs. Free-range meat
**Veganomics Ltd** 312/314 Lewisham Road SE13 (081) 852 7978
**Village Health Foods** 31 Tranquil Vale SE3 (081) 318 0448
**Well Bean** 10 Old Dover Road SE3 (081) 858 1319
**Wellbeing** 19 Sydenham Road SE26 (081) 659 2003

## EATING OUT - Restaurants, cafés and take-aways

**The Bombay Mix** 7/9 Woolwich New Road, Woolwich SE18 (081) 854 0035
**Bon Ton Roulet** 127 Dulwich Road, Herne Hill SE24 (071) 733 8701
    Open evenings, bring your own wine
**Café Pelican du Sud** Hays Galleria, Tooley Street SE1 (071) 378 0097
    English owned but very French. Vegans catered for on request
**Dining Room** 1 Winchester Walk SE1 (071) 407 0337

International cuisine. An imaginative menu including organic wine.
Vegans catered for

**Review** Royal Festival Hall, South Bank SE1 (071) 921 0800
With views across the Thames, this Terence Conran designed restaurant
offers vegetarian and vegan dishes

**Veganomics Vegan Restaurant** 314 Lewisham Road SE13 (081) 852 7978
Run by an all-vegan team producing many goodies

**The Veggy Table** 312/314 Lewisham Road SE13

**Well Bean** 10 Old Dover Road, Blackheath SE3  (081) 858 1319
Homemade food served in small vegetarian restaurant

## CHARITY SHOPS

**Barnardo's** 67 High Street, Eltham SE9 (081) 850 8241
**British Red Cross Society** 46 Vanbrugh Park, Greenwich SE3
**British Red Cross Society** 213 Stanstead Road, Lewisham SE23
**British Red Cross Society** 160 Peckham Rye SE22
Open Thursdays 2.00–4.00
**Imperial Cancer Research** 6 Montpelier Vale, Blackheath SE3 (081) 852 0686
**MIND** 265 South Norwood Hill SE25 (081) 653 3547
Nearly new shop open Mon,Tues,Thur, Fri 10.00-3.30,
Wed. 10.00–2.00 and Saturday 10.00–1.00
**MIND** 55 Baring Road SE12 (081) 857 7731
Open Mon-Sat 10.00-4.00
**MIND** 96 Grove Vale, Southwark SE22 (081) 299 4101
**NSPCC** Review Shop, 191 High Street SE20 (081) 659 4314
**Oxfam** 68 Tranquil Vale, Blackheath SE3 (081) 852 6884
**Oxfam** 85 High Street, Eltham SE9 (081) 859 7210
**Oxfam** 97 Sydenham Road, Sydenham SE26 (081) 778 5689
**Save the Children** Unit 3, 8/10 Passey Place, Eltham SE9
**Save the Children** 224 Trafalgar Road, Greenwich SE10 (081) 858 6739
**The Spastics' Society** 42 Denmark Hill, Camberwell SE5 (071) 274 2392
**The Spastics' Society** 50 High Street, Eltham SE9 (081) 850 2071
**The Spastics' Society** 2/4 Eltham Courtyard SE9 (081) 859 2378
**The Spastics' Society** 7 Lewis Grove, Lewisham SE13 (081) 852 5334
**The Spastics' Society** 93 High Street, Peckham SE15 (071) 639 5646
**The Spastics' Society** 131 Sydenham Road SE26 (081) 778 1442
**The Spastics' Society** 30 Hare Street, Woolwich SE18 (081) 317 7850

## WOOD

**M. Burns** Unit 1144, 41 Norwood Road SE24 (081) 671 7551
Carpentry and joinery
**Fireweed Furniture** c/o 137 Auckland Hill SE27
Furniture designer and maker
**Robin Thomson** Unit 5, Pottery Lane, Warham Street, Kennington SE5
Furniture design and manufacture

## BIKE SHOPS

**Ken Bird Cycles** 37 Anerley Road SE19 (081) 854 2383
**Central Cycle Stores** 7 Central Hill E19 (081) 670 1780

**Chris Compton Cycles** 23 Catford Hill SE6 (081) 690 0141
**Cycle World** 46 Rushey Green, Catford SE6 (081) 690 4756
**Donington Cycles** 55 High Street SE20 (081) 778 7714
**Edwardes** 223 Camberwell Road SE5 (071) 703 3676
**F.W. Evans** 77 The Cut SE1 (071) 928 4785
**Halfords** 70 Rye Lane SE15 (071) 639 2782
**Halfords** 139 Lewisham High Street SE13 (081) 852 8413
**Halfords** 82 Eltham High Street SE9 (081) 850 5176
**Halfords** 81 Powis Street SE18 (081) 854 0650
**Hill** 57 Well Hall Road SE9 (081) 850 2446
**London Bridge Cycles** 41 Railway Approach SE1 (071) 403 1690
**On Your Bike** 52 Tooley Street SE1 (071) 407 1309
**On Your Bike** 22 Duke Street Hill, London Bridge SE1 (071) 378 6669
**Harry Perry Cycles** 8 Wellington Street SE18 (081) 854 2383
**Geoff Roberts Cycles** 49 Honor Oak Park SE23 (081) 699 8711
**Swift Cycles** 15 Dartmouth Road, Forest Hill SE23 (081) 699 2961
**Wilson** 32 Peckham High Street SE15 (071) 639 1338
**Witcomb** 25 Tanners Hill SE8 (081) 692 1734
**Young's** 290 Lee High Road SE13 (081) 852 1848

# OUTER SOUTH-EAST

*Incorporating Postal Districts BR1–BR7, TN16, DA5–DA8, DA14 - DA18*

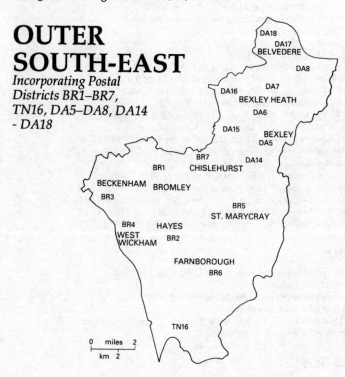

# FOOD SHOPS AND EVERYDAY PRODUCTS *including: cleaning items, cosmetics, recycled paper and energy-efficient electrical goods*

**Better Health Food Store** 208a Broadway, Bexleyheath, Kent DA6
(081) 303 6792

**Better Health Food Store** 1 St. John's Parade, Sidcup, Kent DA14
(081) 300 1593

**Body Shop** 39 Broadway Shopping Centre, Bexleyheath, Kent DA7
(081) 303 1535

**Farrington's Health Foods** 9 Beckingham Road, West Wickham, Kent BR4
(081) 777 8721

**Food for Living** 8 Wellington Parade, Blackfen Road, Sidcup, Kent DA15
(081) 304 3874

**Health Centre** 54 Widmore Street, Bromley, Kent (081) 460 3894
Long established independent health/wholefood shop selling loose from the sack

**Health & Diet** The Walnuts, Orpington, Kent BR5

**Holland & Barrett** 56 High Street, Bromley, Kent BR1 (081) 460 3883

**The Honey Tree** 34 Chatsworth Parade, Petts Wood, Kent (0689) 24953

**Life Cycle** 219 High Street, Orpington, Kent (0689) 74773

**Nature Quest** 82 High Street, Beckenham BR3 (081) 650 3813

**Queensway Fruiterers** 125 Queensway, Petts Wood, Kent (0689) 36675

**The Wholefood Emporium** The Old Coach House, Coach House Mews,
r/o 39/41 High Street, Bromley, Kent BR1

**William Swift** 127 Queensway, Petts Wood, Kent (0689) 22242
Range of organically produced meat

## EATING OUT - *Restaurants, cafés and take-aways*

**Pure & Healthy** Westmoreland Place, Bromley (081) 464 2913
Previously totally vegetarian, this café now has half its menu for vegetarian dishes

# CHARITY SHOPS

**British Red Cross Society** 4 Alma Road, Sidcup, Kent DA14 (081) 302 6209

**British Red Cross Society** 111 Masons Hill, Bromley, Kent BR2

**British Red Cross Society** Hornbrook House, High Street, Chislehurst BR7

**British Heart Foundation** 244a Broadway, Bexleyheath, Kent DA6
(081) 303 0804

**Cancer Research Campaign** 316 High Street, Orpington, Kent BR6
(0689) 890119

**Imperial Cancer Research** 227 High Street, Orpington, Kent BR6 (0689) 22815

**Imperial Cancer Research** 100 High Street, Sidcup, Kent DA14 (081) 302 2618

**Imperial Cancer Research** 50 Bellegrove Road, Welling, Kent DA16
(081) 301 2097

**Oxfam** 148 High Street, Beckenham, Kent BR5 (081) 658 9680

**Oxfam** 91 Burnt Ash Lane, Bromley, Kent BR1 (081) 464 2534

**Oxfam** 12/14 High Street, Bromley, Kent BR1 (081) 290 6711

**Oxfam** 340 High Street, Orpington, Kent BR6 (0689) 31929

**Oxfam** 19 High Street, Sidcup, Kent DA14 (081) 302 2623
**Oxfam** 53 High Street, West Wickham BR4 (081) 777 6045
**Save the Children** 431 Croydon Road, Beckenham, Kent BR3 (081) 650 1041
**Save the Children** 104 High Street, Orpington, Kent BR6 (0689) 890435
**The Spastics' Society** 222 High Street, Beckenham, Kent BR3 (081) 650 0514
**The Spastics' Society** 1 Station Square, Petts Wood, Kent BR5 (0689) 21167
**The Spastics' Society** 103 High Street, West Wickham, Kent BR4 (081) 777 0223

## BIKE SHOPS

**Cycleland** 27 Widmore Road, Bromley BR1
   (081) 460 4852
**Welling Cycles** 69 Bellegrove Road, Welling
   (081) 304 2832

# INNER EAST

*Incorporating Postal
Districts E1–E18*

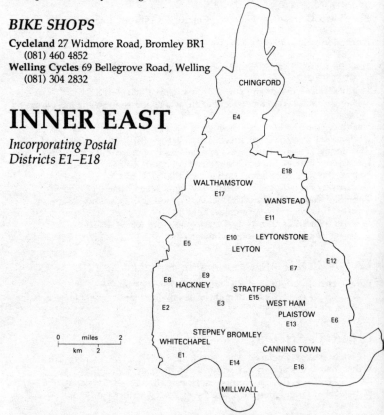

# FOOD SHOPS AND EVERYDAY PRODUCTS *including:*
*cleaning items, cosmetics, recycled paper and energy-efficient electrical goods*

**Apples 'n Pears** Ronan Road E2
   Stocks organic fruit and vegetables
**Apples & Spice** 119 Plaistow Road E15 (081) 536 1711
**Body Shop** 5 Balkan Walk, The Highway, Tobacco Dock E1 (071) 481 2289
**Coopers Health Food Stores** 25 Aldgate Bars, 1 Whitechapel High Street E1
   (071) 481 3791

**Docklands Wholefoods** Poplar High Street E14
   Wholefood retailer
**Easy Weigh** Stratford Shopping Centre E15
   Sells self-weigh wholefoods
**Friends Foods** 51 Roman Road E2 (081) 980 1843
   Small, pleasant wholefood shop run by the attached Buddhist centre
**Ghir Health Foods** 426 Barking Road, East Ham E6 (081) 471 7576
**Granary Health Foods** 165 High Street North E6 (081) 552 5988
**Health Food Centre** 114a Lower Clapton Road E5 (081) 985 2611
**Health Mine** 148 Earlham Grove E7
**Health Nuts** Water Lane, Stratford E15
**Natural Foods** Unit 14, Hainault Road Industrial Estate, Hainault E11
   (081) 539 0134
   Delivers across Greater London, organic meat, fruit and vegetables, dairy
   produce and wholefoods
**Only Natural** 108 Palmerston Road, Walthamstow E17 (081) 520 5898
   Good selection of wholefoods, vegetarian and vegan foods. Select your own
   fresh fruit and vegetables. Friendly atmosphere and orders can be taken for
   delivery
**Paperback Ltd** Business Centre, Bow Triangle, Unit 2, Elenor Street, London
   Recycled stationery suppliers
**Peaches** 143 High Street, Wanstead E11 (081) 530 3617
   Wholefoods, organic produce, free-range eggs, wholemeal breads and cakes
   and organic wines
**The Scotch Beef Centre** 52 Old Church Road E4 (081) 529 2200
   Supplied by Dorset Farms Ltd, this butcher gives non-vegetarians the chance
   to eat meat and meat products raised in conditions as natural as possible. On
   request, sausages, burgers etc. made to your own recipe
**Toast Health Food** 565 Lea Bridge Road E10 (081) 539 3245
   Vegetarian wholefoods, organically-grown products and free-range eggs
**Towards Jupiter** 191 Mare Street E8 (081) 985 5394
**Vanns Health Store** 28 Kirkdale Road, Leytonstone E11 (081) 539 4196
   This shop stocks organically-grown wholefoods along with other vegetarian
   and health foods
**Village Health Foods** 59 Station Road E4 (081) 529 1044
   This shop provides some organically-grown cereals and pulses amongst its
   wide range of vegetarian and wholefood supplies
**The Wholemeal Shop** 190 Well Street E9


# EATING OUT – Restaurants, cafés and take-aways

**The Blue Gardenia** 136 Barking Road E6 (081) 471 6685
   This is a West Indian restaurant, very friendly, with a separate vegetarian
   menu
**Chats Palace** 42 Brooksby Walk E9
**The Cherry Orchard Restaurant** 241/245 Globe Road, Bethnal Green E2
   (081) 980 6678
   Exclusively vegetarian restaurant run by attached Buddhist centre.
   Wholefood ingredients used to prepare the dishes on a daily-changing
   menu. There is always at least one vegan dish
**Health Nuts** 39 Water Lane, Stratford E15 (081) 519 3228
   Wholefood sandwich bar

**Le Soleil** 110/112 Palmerston Road, Walthamstow E17 (081) 520 5898
  Le Soleil is Walthamstow's first wholefood, almost vegetarian restaurant.
  Most dishes are vegan. Bring your own wine
**Oasis** 113 Lower Clapton Road E5 (081) 985 2675
  Wine bar with vegetarian menu
**Poppy Seeds Café** 74 St. Mary Road, Walthamstow E17 (081) 520 1257
  A wholefood and vegetarian café providing a varied menu. Monday to
  Saturday there is a lunchtime menu plus take-away and on Fridays only it
  opens from 7pm to 11pm for a 'gourmet' evening
**Poppy Seeds Catering** 74 St. Mary Road, Walthamstow E17 (081) 520 1257
  Adjoining café above. This is a popular and expanding business providing a
  mixture of traditional and vegetarian dishes for weddings, conferences etc
**Ronak** 317 Romford Road E7 (081) 519 2110
  Vegetarian restaurant
**Rowley's Café** 59 Orford Road, Walthamstow E17
**Whitechapel Café** 80 Whitechapel High Street E1 (071) 377 6182
  This café provides snacks and lunches varying daily. Caters for vegans and
  provides at least two hot main course choices to vegetarians

## CHARITY SHOPS

**Abbeyfield Trust** 141 Wanstead High Street E11 (081) 989 9585
**Age Concern** 644 Leytonstone High Road E11 (No telephone)
**Age Concern** 22 Dalston Lane E8 (071) 254 6195
**Age Concern** 140 Barking Road, Newham E16 (071) 473 2678
**Barnardo's** 3/5 Barking Road E6 (081) 472 5342
**Barnardo's** 70 Old Church Road, Chingford E4 (081) 529 7232
**Barnardo's** 70 High Street, Wanstead E11 (081) 989 3641
**Barnardo's** 101 George Lane, South Woodford E18 (081) 989 9125
**Barnardo's** 50 Station Road, Chingford E4 (081) 524 8961
**British Red Cross Society** 49 Station Road, Chingford E4 (081) 524 8318
**British Red Cross Society** 44a Dalston Lane, Hackney E8
**The Children's Society** South Woodford, George Lane E18
**Imperial Cancer Research** 96 High Street, Walthamstow E17 (081) 509 3704
**MIND** Woodgrange Road E7
**Oxfam** 151 High Street, South Woodford E18 (081) 505 7771
**Oxfam** 570/572 Kingsland Road, Dalston E8 (071) 923 1532
**Oxfam** 21 Old Church Road, Chingford E4 (081) 524 1229
**RSPCA** Barking Road E6 (next door to Bingo Hall)
**The Spastics' Society** 4 Morning Lane, Hackney E9 (081) 985 5825
**The Spastics' Society** 210 High Street E17 (081) 520 5273
**Sportsman's Fund for Injured & Handicapped Children** (opposite West Ham
  Football Club) Green Street E13
**Sue Ryder** 163 Barking Road, Canning Town E16
**Sue Ryder** 198 Kenton Road, Kenton E9

## WOOD

**Home Grown Hardwoods** 1/5 Chance Street E1
  Timber merchants

## *BIKE SHOPS*

**Ash** 99 Station Road, North Chingford E4 (081) 524 0063
**Bates** 589 Barking Road E13 (081) 472 3483
**Bellchamber** 80 Palmerston Road E17 (081) 520 6051
**Cycle Plus** 181 Lower Clapton Road E5 (081) 986 2065
**Cycle Sales** 92 Old Church Road, Chingford E4 (081) 529 0650
**Daycock Cycles** 201 Roman Road, Bethnal Green E2 (081) 980 4966
**Daycock Cycles** 1 Chatsworth Road, Hackney E5 (081) 985 0042
**Daycock Cycles** 427 Barking Road E6 (081) 472 0918
**Daycocks - A.A. Cycles** 717 High Road, Leytonstone E11 (081) 558 3860
**Discount Cycles** 65 Station Road, North Chingford E4 (081) 529 1515
**Ditchfields** 790 Leyton High Road E10 (081) 539 2821
**Etty & Tyler** 83 Upton Lane E7 (081) 472 5797
**Halfords** 403 Barking Road E6 (081) 472 3273
**Halfords** 53 The Mall E15 (081) 519 0808
**Halfords** 147 Hoe Street E17 (081) 520 3304
**Heales** 477 Hale End Road, Highams Park E4 (081) 527 1592
**J. A. Cycles** 110 Markhouse Road E17 (081) 509 0131
**Martins Mart** 159 Leytonstone Road E15 (081) 534 1166
**McCalls** 185 Mare Street Hackney E8 (081) 985 2653
**W. Norris** 252 Barking Road E6 (081) 472 1543
**Riley & Son** 246 Higham Hill Road E17 (081) 527 2045
**Roberts** 241 East India Dock Road E14 (071) 987 2922
**Robins Bikes** 520 Forest Road E17 (081) 521 5812
**J.A. Rose** 149 Bethnal Green Road E2 (071) 739 6724

# OUTER EAST

*Incorporating Postal Districts RM1–RM3, RM5–RM14, IG1–IG6, IG8, IG11*

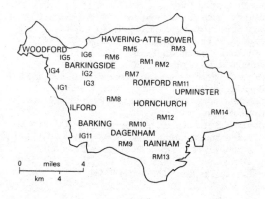

## FOOD SHOPS AND EVERYDAY PRODUCTS *including: cleaning items, cosmetics, recycled paper and energy-efficient electrical goods*

**Body Shop** 14 South Street, Romford, Essex RM1 (0708) 24032
**Conkers Ltd** 18 Greenstead Avenue, Woodford Green, Essex IG8 (081) 505 0114
   Recycled stationery suppliers
**Country Store** 90 Snakes Lane East, Woodford Green, Essex IG5 (081) 505 6793
   Organic and wholefood products. Free-range eggs
**Food for Thought** 4 Cameron Road, Seven Kings, Ilford, Essex IG3
   (081) 597 4388
**Holland & Barrett** 21 Laurie Walk, Romford, Essex RM1 (0708) 21176
**Holland & Barrett** 52 Cranbrook Road, Ilford, Essex IG1 (081) 553 2808
**Whole and Natural Foods** 116 High Street, Barkingside, Essex

## EATING OUT *– Restaurants, cafés and take-aways*

**Sabra** 3 State Parade, High Street, Barkingside, Ilford, Essex (081) 551 5550

## CHARITY SHOPS

**Barnardo's** 39 The Broadway, Elm Park, Hornchurch, Essex (04024) 76440
**Barnardo's** 43/45 Ripple Road, Barking, Essex (081) 594 2986
**Barnardo's** 246/248 Heathway, Dagenham, Essex (081) 593 7830
**Helping Hand** 204 High Street, Hornchurch, Essex RM12 (04024) 40421
**Helping Hand** 33 High Street, Romford, Essex RM1 (0708) 44117
**Helping Hand** 181 St. Mary's Lane, Upminster, Essex RM14 (04022) 23162
**Imperial Cancer Research** 15 East Street, Barking, Essex IG11 (081) 594 6676
**Imperial Cancer Research** Unit 5, 3/19 High Street, Barkingside, Essex IG6
   (081) 551 8124
**Imperial Cancer Research** 8 Station Road, Hornchurch, Essex RM12
   (04024) 49998
**Imperial Cancer Research** 102 South Street, Romford, Essex RM1
   Shop acquired, opening 1990
**Imperial Cancer Research** 36 Cranbrook Road, Ilford, Essex IG1 (081) 553 0903
**Oxfam** 118 High Street, Barkingside, Essex IG6 (081) 551 6327
**Oxfam** 24 Station Lane, Hornchurch, Essex RM12 (04024) 77434
**Oxfam** 451 Cranbrook Road, Ilford, Essex IG2 (081) 554 5292
**Oxfam** 82 South Street, Romford, Essex RM1 (0708) 751346
**Oxfam** 3 Corbetts Tay Road, Upminster, Essex RM14 (04022) 23102
**PDSA** Woodford Bridge Road, Redbridge, Ilford, Essex (081) 551 4714
   This is a collection point for all bric-à-brac, clothes, books, jewellery etc. –
   but not electrical goods
**Save the Children** 46 Station Lane, Hornchurch, Essex RM12 (04024) 44881
**The Spastics' Society** 56 Longbridge Road, Barking, Essex IG11 (081) 594 2379
**The Spastics' Society** 151 High Street, Barkingside, Essex IG6
**Sue Ryder** 289 Heathway, Dagenham RM10
**Sue Ryder** 85 Corbetts Tay Road, Upminster RM14

## BIKE SHOPS

**Crown Cycles** 183 London Road, Romford, Essex RM1
**Discount Cycles** 1088/1090 High Road, Chadwell Heath, Romford, Essex
  (081) 597 6834
**Johns of Romford** 162 Rush Green Road, Romford, Essex RM1 (0708) 761047
**Rory O'Brien** 134 North Street, Romford, Essex (0708) 41588
**Ubique Bikes** 168 Hornchurch Road, Hornchurch, Essex (04024) 74644

# INNER NORTH

*Incorporating Postal Districts N1, N2, N4–N8, N10, N15–N19,
N22*

## FOOD SHOPS AND EVERYDAY PRODUCTS *including:*
*cleaning items, cosmetics, recycled paper and energy-efficient
electrical goods*

**Akisan** 1 Hornsey High Street N8
  African and Caribbean wholefoods and take-aways
**Alara** 58 Seven Sisters Road N7 (071) 609 6875
**Anubam Sweet Mart** 69 Turnpike Lane N8
**Barbaras Health Food Centre** 113 Turnpike Lane N8 (081) 348 5000
  Organic flour, biscuits, vegetable juices and some wholefood
**Barnsbury Health Foods** 285 Caledonian Road N1 (071) 607 7344
**Bennett and Luck** 54 Islington Park Street N1 (071) 226 3422

**Body Shop** 7 Upper Street N1 (071) 354 0565
**Body Shop** 85 High Road, Wood Green N22 (081) 881 3717
**Bread and Roses Food** 316 Upper Street N1 (071) 226 9483
**Bumblebee Natural Food Store** 30 Brecknock Road N7 (071) 607 1936
**Caledonian Health Food Shop** Caledonian Road N5
**Dormen Natural Foods** 541 Green Lanes N4 (081) 340 1869
    Organic rice cakes and some wholefoods
**Dormen Natural Foods** 7 Marlborough Walks, Cornwallis Road N19
    (071) 272 5605
**Earth Exchange** 213 Archway Road N6 (081) 340 6407
    Basic range of fruit and vegetables. Also organic bread, soya milk and
    organic wines and ales
**Food for All (London)** 3a Cazenove Road N16 (081) 806 4138
**Food for Thought** Unit 80, Wood Green Shopping City N22 (081) 881 2009
**J. Freeman** 9 Topsfield Parade N8 (081) 340 3100
**Freemans Butchers** Crouch End Broadway, Crouch End N8
    Supplies organic meat including beef, lamb, sausages, mince and poultry
**Fruit 'n' Veg** Muswell Hill Broadway, Muswell Hill N10
    Mainly a fruit and vegetable shop, with some other foods towards the back
**Goodlife** 7 Broadway Parade N8
    Organic foods including beans, wheatflakes, rice cakes and soya milk plus
    some wholefood
**The Haelan Centre** 41 The Broadway N8 (081) 340 4258
    Organic foods including cereals, teas, cakes, bread and dairy produce. Also
    stocks organic fruit
**Health Care** 11 Crescent Road N22 (081) 889 6012
    Stocks a good range of wholefoods and organic produce including baby food
    and cereals
**Holland & Barrett** 452 Holloway Road N7 (071) 607 3933
**Holland & Barrett** 121 Muswell Hill Road N10 (081) 883 1154
**Highbury Health Foods** 25/27 Highbury Corner N5 (071) 609 9471
**Isis Health Food Shop** 362 High Road, Tottenham N17 (081) 808 6401
    Stocks a good range of wholefood and organic produce
**Kamakarsini** 34 West Green Road N15 (081) 802 8082
    Stocks a good range of wholefoods and organic produce
**Lemondt & Co. Ltd** 30 Baron Street N1
**Losandes** 4 Bradbury Street N16 (071) 254 7533
**Maranatha Health Foods Ltd** 38/40 Church Road N17
**Muswell Hill Natural Foods** 243 Muswell Hill Broadway N10 (081) 444 7717
**Natural Foods** 242 Muswell Hill Broadway, Muswell Hill N10
    Good range of wholefoods and organic produce
**Natural Revival** 51a Carysfoot Road N16 (071) 254 9116
    Wholefood importer/wholesaler
**Neals Yard at The Garden Centre** Alexandra Park N22 (081) 444 4533
**Paradise Health Foods** Broadway Mews, 154 Stamford Hill N16
**Peacemeal Wholefoods** 10 Caledonian Road N1
**Peppercorn's Wholefood and Granary** 193/195 West End Lane, West
    Hampstead NW6 (071) 328 6874
**Purkis Fishmongers** Crouch End Broadway, Crouch End N8
    Sells undyed smoked kippers and haddock
**St. Ann's Dairy** 329 St. Ann's Road N15 (081) 874 1890
**The Spice House** Market Hall, Wood Green Shopping Centre N22

Good range of wholefoods and some organic produce including brown rice,
flour and vegetable juices

**Sunpower** 198 Blackstock Road N5 (071) 704 0247

**Taylor's Fine Food Delicatessen** 85 Muswell Hill Broadway, Muswell Hill N10
(081) 883 2904
Organic apple juice, brown rice, bread and rice cakes

**Unique Butchers** 217 Holloway Road N7 (071) 609 7016
Organic chicken, lamb, pork and additive free beef. Delivers bulk

**Wholesome** 124 High Road , East Finchley N2
Good range of wholefoods and organic foods including honey, sultanas,
soya milk, sunflower and olive oils

## EATING OUT – Restaurants, cafés and take-aways

**Anand Vegetarian Restaurant** 6 Grand Parade, Green Lanes, Haringey N4
(081) 802 9581
Unpretentious counter-service Indian Restaurant run by vegetarians. Good
food at reasonable prices. Vegans well catered for

**Bhelpoori House** 92/93 Chapel Market, Angel, Islington, N1 (071) 837 4607
Vegetarian restaurant. Vegans catered for

**Earth Exchange** 213 Archway Road, N6 (081) 340 6407
Earth Exchange is a café, food shop, community centre, art exhibitionery and
entertainment point. Most diets catered for. Take-away service

**The Fallen Angel** 65 Graham Street N1 (071) 253 3996
Pub serving vegetarian dishes

**Jai-Krishna** 161 Stroud Green Road N4 (071) 272 1680
Indian vegetarian restaurant

**Jazz Café** 56 Newington Green, N16 (071) 359 4936
Café, wine bar, vegetarian restaurant and jazz venue. International
vegetarian cuisine. Vegans catered for

**Le Mercury** 140a Upper Street, Islington, N1 (071) 354 4088
Licensed restaurant using wholefood/organic produce. Menus change daily
and have a French bias. Vegetarian dishes served

**Millward's Restaurant** 97 Stoke Newington Church Street N16 (071) 250 1025
Voted 'Best Restaurant in London' by *City Limits'* readers in 1988, this
licensed restaurant offers continental vegetarian/vegan food using organic
produce whenever possible. Take-away service

**Something Else** Cross Street N1
Popular restaurant serving vegetarian and vegan dishes

**Spices** 30 Stoke Newington Church Street N16 (071) 241 3857
Vegans catered for

**St. George's Café** Tufnell Park Road N7

**Suruchi** 18 Theberton Street N1 (071) 359 8033
Reasonably priced vegetarian restaurant offering simple but engaging
menus. Take-away service

## CHARITY SHOPS

**Age Concern** 296 High Road N15 (081) 808 1000

**British Red Cross Society** 3 Market Square, Edmonton Green N19
(081) 807 6379

**British Red Cross Society** Little Lodge, Grove Lodge, 6 Muswell Hill N10

Open Monday–Friday 10.00–3.30pm
**Helping Hand** 32 Topsfield Parade, The Broadway, Hornsey N8 (081) 341 2779
**Helping Hand** 318/320 St. Paul's Road, Highbury N1 (071) 226 0565
**Helping Hand** 124 Muswell Hill Broadway, Muswell Hill N10 (081) 883 2061
**Help the Aged** 155 Stoke Newington High Street N16 (071) 241 2642
**Imperial Cancer Research** 13 The Broadway, Crouch End N8 (081) 341 0057
**Imperial Cancer Research** 72 Highgate High Street, Highgate N6 (081) 341 6330
**Imperial Cancer Research** 161 Muswell Hill Broadway, Muswell Hill N10
    (081) 444 6688
**MIND** 329 Archway Road N6 (081) 341 1188
    Open Mon–Sat 10.00–4.00
**North London Hospice** 734 Lordship Lane N22
**NSPCC Charity Shop** 164 High Road, Wood Green N22 (No telephone)
**Oxfam** 233 Muswell Hill Broadway, Muswell Hill N10 (081) 883 2532
**Oxfam** 12a The Broadway, Wood Green N22 (081) 881 6044
**Oxfam** 29 Islington High Street N1 (071) 837 2394
**Red Cross** 6 Muswell Hill N10 (081) 883 9717
**RSPCA** 334 Hornsey Road (071) 272 0142
**Samaritans** 21 Lymington Avenue N22 (081) 889 1761
**The Spastics' Society** 46 Seven Sisters Road, Holloway N7 (071) 607 7779
**The Spastics' Society** 236 Stamford Hill N16 (081) 809 1306
**Sue Ryder** 88 Upper Fore Street, Edmonton N18
**Sue Ryder** 129 Muswell Hill Broadway, Muswell Hill N10

## WOOD

**Eco Timber** Unit 34, 560/568 High Road N17 (081) 365 0222
    Timber merchants
**Futon Factory Ltd** 192 Balls Pond Road, Islington N1 (071) 226 4477
    Furniture manufacturer and retailer
**Greenheart Co-op** 19 Pleshey Road, Tufnell Park N7
    Timber merchants, both recycled and sustainably produced tropical
    hardwood. Manufacturer of toys, furniture and household goods
**Habitat** 38/42 High Road, Wood Green N22 (081) 888 3343
**The Pine Shop** 311/323 Muswell Hill Broadway N10
    Retailer of pine furniture
**Bill Tyler ARIBA** 22 Southern Road N2
    Architects

## BIKE SHOPS

**Bike UK** 242 Pentonville Road N1 (071) 833 3917
**Daycock Cycles** 146a Seven Sisters Road N7 (071) 272 6302
**Daycock Cycles** 143 Stoke Newington Road N16 (071) 254 3380
**Days** 570 Lordship Lane, Wood Green N22 (081) 888 2686
**Halfords** 45/47 High Road N22 (081) 888 1329
**Halfords** 165 Fore Street N18 (081) 807 2585
**Mosquito Bikes** 123 Essex Road N1 (071) 226 8841
**Mosquito Bikes** 10 Bradbury Street, Dalston N16 (071) 249 7915
**Riders** 481 Hornsey Road, Upper Holloway N19 (071) 263 5601
**Robert's Rebuilds** 2 Middle Lane Mews N8 (081) 348 7621

**Victory Cycles** 90 Tottenham Lane N8 (081) 348 3132
**Yellow Jersey Cycles** 62 Drayton Park N5 (071) 359 1971

# OUTER NORTH

*Incorporating Postal Districts N3, N9, N11–N14, N20, N21, EN1, EN5*

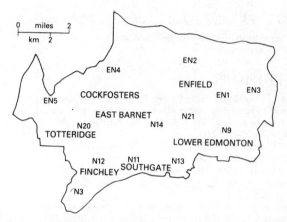

## *FOOD SHOPS AND EVERYDAY PRODUCTS including: cleaning items, cosmetics, recycled paper and energy-efficient electrical goods*

**Acorns** 17 Church Hill Road, East Barnet, Herts EN4
**Alternatives** 1369 High Road N20 (081) 445 2675
**Back to Nature** 6 Long Lane, North Finchley N3 (081) 349 2514
**Barleycorn** 120 Lancaster Road, Enfield, Middlesex EN2 (081) 363 2956
   Good selection of organic vegetables, cheeses, eggs, wines and dry goods.
   Home deliveries also available
**Body Shop** 1 Church Street, Enfield, Middlesex EN2 (081) 363 6847
**Brimarks** 241 East Barnet Road, East Barnet, Herts EN4 (081) 449 5416
**Countryside Wholefoods Ltd** 27 Russell Road, Enfield, Middlesex EN2
**Finchley Health Food Centre** 745 High Road N12  (081) 445 8743
   Fresh organic produce delivered on Friday
**The Health & Beauty Food Shop** 42 High Street, Southgate N14 (081) 886 1990
   Sells organic fruit and vegetables from a farm in Norfolk. Additive-free free-
   range eggs
**Holland & Barrett** 7 North Mall N9 (081) 807 6711
**Holland & Barrett** 332 Green Lanes N13 (081) 886 6769
**Just Meat** Lytton Road, New Barnet EN5 (081) 449 4087

Real meat stockists
**J.J. Monaghan** 60 Chase Side N14 (081) 886 3789
**Moore & Son** 1275 High Road N20 (081) 445 2828
**Natural Health** 339 Ballard's Lane N12 (081) 445 4397
**W. Sawyer** 62 Hoppers Road N21 (081) 886 0972
**Victoria Bakery** 83 High Street, Barnet EN5 (081) 449 0790
Delicious organic wholemeal loaf
**Whole Health** 8 Onslow Parade, Hampden Square N14 (081) 361 8630

## EATING OUT – *Restaurants, cafés and take-aways*

**Rani** 3/5 Long Lane, Finchley N3 (081) 349 2636
Vegetarian restaurant

## CHARITY SHOPS

**Barnardo's** 15 Greenhill Parade, Barnet, Herts EN5 (081) 449 6542
**Barnardo's** 802 High Road, North Finchley N12 (081) 445 5433
**British Red Cross Society** Houndsfield Road, Edmonton N9
Open Fridays 10.30–12.00
**British Red Cross Society** 31 Armfield Road, Enfield EN2
Open Tuesdays 10.00–2.00
**British Red Cross Society** 259 Green Lanes, Palmers Green N13
**Cancer Research Campaign** 781 High Road, Finchley N12
Opening spring 1990
**Helping Hand** 88 High Street, Barnet, Herts EN5 (081) 441 9710
**Helping Hand** 157 Hertford Road, Enfield, Middlesex EN3 (081) 804 2442
**Helping Hand** 59 Chaseside, Southgate N14 (081) 886 5433
**Imperial Cancer Research** 25 The Town, Enfield, Middlesex EN1 (081) 366 9320
**Imperial Cancer Research** 276 East Barnet Road, East Barnet, Herts EN4
(081) 449 0850
**Imperial Cancer Research** 69 Ballards Lane, Finchley N3 (081) 349 4962
**Imperial Cancer Research** 91 High Street, High Barnet, Herts N5 (081) 441 9694
**Imperial Cancer Research** 353 Green Lanes, Palmers Green N13 (081) 882 8031
**Imperial Cancer Research** 90 Chase Side, Southgate N14 (081) 882 7969
**Oxfam** 724 High Road, North Finchley N12 (081) 446 1981
**Oxfam** 326 Green Lanes, Palmers Green N13 (081) 882 8176
**Oxfam** 132 High Street, Barnet, Herts EN5 (081) 441 7664
**Oxfam** 55 Ballards Lane, Finchley N3 (081) 346 3870
**Oxfam** 54 Church Street, Enfield, Middlesex EN2 (081) 367 7728
**Oxfam** 40 Chaseside, Southgate N14 (081) 882 4752
**Oxfam** 836 Green Lanes, Winchmore Hill N21 (081) 360 3604
**Red Cross** 259 Green Lanes N13 (081) 886 2251
**The Spastics' Society** 304 Green Lanes, Palmers Green N13 (081) 886 3340

## WOOD

**The Pine Shop** 2/3 St. Onge Parade, Southbury Road, Enfield, Middlesex
Retailer of pine furniture

## BIKE SHOPS

**Dare** 155 Bowes Road N11 (081) 888 2304
**Day's** 940 Green Lanes, Winchmore Lane N21 (081) 360 8285
**Halfords** 73 Chase Side N14 (081) 886 8265
**Oscroft Brothers** 191 Woodhouse Road, Friern Barnet N12 (081) 368 2914
**Shorter Rochford** 65 Woodhouse Road N12 (081) 445 9182

# INNER NORTH-WEST

*Incorporating Postal Districts NW1–NW3, NW5, NW6, NW8, NW10, NW11*

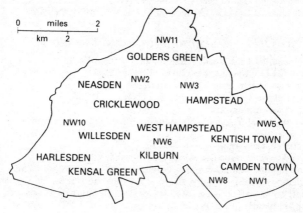

## FOOD SHOPS AND EVERYDAY PRODUCTS *including: cleaning items, cosmetics, recycled paper and energy-efficient electrical goods*

**Abundance Natural Foods** 246 Belsize Road NW6 (071) 328 4781
   Comprehensive range of organic fruit, vegetables and dry goods
**Bee's** 67 Chetwynd Road NW5 (071) 267 5275
**Body Shop** High Street, Hampstead NW3 (071) 431 3862
**Buzz Wholefoods** 10 Inverness Street NW1
**Flints Wholefoods** 14 Fortess Road NW5
**Food Sense** Unit K, Canada House, Blackburn Road NW6
**Grub Tub** High Street, Willesden NW10 (081) 451 7581
**Hampstead Health Shop Ltd** 57 Hampstead High Street NW3 (071) 435 6418
**Healthy Living** 1 Masons Avenue, Willesden NW10
**Holland & Barrett** Unit Plaza House Development, 191/200 High Street,
   Camden NW1 (071) 485 9477
**Holland & Barrett** 81 Golders Green Road NW11 (081) 455 5811
**Holland & Barrett** 55 St. John's Wood High Street NW8 (071) 586 5494

**Holland & Barrett** 14 Northways Parade NW3 (071) 722 5920
**Holland & Barrett** 17 Temple Fortune Parade NW11 (081) 458 6087
**Keshava Natural Foods** 84 Willesden Lane, Kilburn NW6
**Les's Natural Foods** 25 Malvern Road NW6
**Meeras Health Food Centre** 2 High Street, Willesden NW10 (081) 965 7610
**Nature's Delight** 90 Drummond Street NW1
**Peppercorn's Wholefood & Granary** 2 Heath Street NW3 (071) 431 1251
    Wide range of fruit and vegetables. Also organic cheeses and wines
**Peppercorn's Wholefood and Granary** 193 West End Lane NW6 (071) 328 6874
**Rainbow Health Food Store** 71 Chamberlayne Road NW10 (081) 960 2686
**Revital Health Shop** 35 High Road, Willesden NW10 (081) 459 3382
**Sesame Health Foods** 128 Regents Park Road NW1 (071) 586 3779
**South End Green Health Foods** Hampstead NW3
**Sunburst Natural Foods** 20 Cricklewood Lane NW2 (081) 208 2052

## EATING OUT – Restaurants, cafés and take-aways

**Bhajia House** 151 High Road, Willesden NW10 (081) 459 1310
**Chutneys** 124 Drummond Street NW1 (071) 388 0604
    Vegetarian Indian restaurant - diwana bhelpoori
**Diwana Bhelpoori** 121 Drummond Street NW1 (071) 387 5556
    Vegetarian restaurant
**Manna Wholefood Vegetarian Restaurant** 4 Erskine Road, Primrose Hill NW3
    (071) 722 8028
    Vegetarian restaurant
**Naturally Yours** 855 Finchley Road NW11 (081) 455 0692
    Serves an international range of vegetarian and vegan dishes using
    wholefood/organic produce. Based at the International Jewish Vegetarian
    Society's HQ so food is prepared under strict rabbinical supervision
**The Raj Bhelpoori House** 19 Camden High Street NW1 (071) 388 6663
    South Indian restaurant with a take-away service. Vegans catered for
**Ravi Shankar** 133/135 Drummond Street NW1 (071) 388 6458
    Vegetarian Indian restaurant – bhelpoori
**Sabras** 263 High Road, Willesden Road NW10 (081) 459 0340
**Surya** 59/61 Fortune Green Road, W. Hampstead NW6 (071) 435 7486
    Vegetarian Indian restaurant

## CHARITY SHOPS

**Age Concern** 120 Craven Park Road NW10 (081) 965 5975
**British Red Cross Society** 170 High Street, Willesden NW10 (081) 459 3813
    Open Monday–Friday 10.30–12.30
**Help the Aged** 247 Kentish Town Road NW5
**Imperial Cancer Research** 81 Camden High Street, Camden NW1
**Imperial Cancer Research** 66 The Mall, Ealing W5 (081) 840 1197
**Imperial Cancer Research** 871 Finchley Road, Golders Green NW11
    (081) 458 6914
**Imperial Cancer Research** 187 Kilburn High Road, Kilburn NW6 (071) 625 8515
**Imperial Cancer Research** 234 West End Lane, West Hampstead NW6
    (071) 433 1962
**MIND** 115/117 Chamberlayne Road NW10 (081) 968 7394

Oxfam 61 Gayton Road, Hampstead NW3 (071) 794 4474
Oxfam 120 Golders Green Road NW11 (081) 455 4335
Oxfam 61 St. John's Wood High Street NW8 (071) 722 5969
Oxfam 246 West End Lane, West Hampstead NW6 (071) 435 8628
Oxfam 166 Kentish Town Road NW5 (071) 267 3560
Oxfam 89 Camden High Street NW1 (071) 388 3953
Oxfam 1049 Finchley Road, Temple Fortune NW11 (081) 458 6449
The Spastics' Society 73 Camden High Street NW1 (071) 380 1455
The Spastics' Society 24 Ballards Lane, Finchley NW2 (081) 346 4147
The Spastics' Society 139 Kilburn High Road NW6 (071) 624 7798
The Spastics' Society 214 West End Lane NW6 (071) 431 5531
War on Want 301 Finchley Road NW3

# WOOD

Betham Associates 105/111 Euston Street NW1
    Architects
The Futon Centre Kingsgate Workshop, 110 Kingsgate Road NW6
    Retailer of futon bases
Gilway Interior Designs 81 Fortress Road NW5
    Retailer of kitchen units
IKEA 255 North Circular Road NW10
    Home furnishings retailer
Habitat 191/217 Finchley Road NW3 (071) 328 3444
Integrated Design & Development Ltd 33a Maresfield Gardens NW3
    Architects
Christopher Jones 16 Queen's Grove NW8
    Architect
Madigan & Donald Architects 2 Primrose Mews, Shardeshall Street NW1
    Architects
Martin Pottinger Associates 150 Regents Park Road NW1
    Architects
Rick Mather Architects 121/123 Camden High Street NW1
    Architects
The Pine Shop 176/184 West End Lane NW6
    Retailer of pine furniture
Stroud Furnishing Ltd 152 Kentish Town Road NW5 (071) 482 4163
    General furniture retailer
Porter Wright 85 Parkway NW1 (071) 482 2444
    Architects and designers

# BIKE SHOPS

Bell Street Bikes 73 Bell Street, Marylebone NW1 (071) 724 0456
Beta Bikes 275 West End Lane NW6 (071) 794 4133
Camden Bikes 3 Camden Road NW1 (071) 485 1372
Chamberlaines 71 Kentish Town Road NW1 (071) 485 3983
Cycle & Mower Ltd 143 Fortess Road, Tufnell Park NW5 (071) 482 2225
Daycock Cycles 1/3 Glengall Road NW6 (071) 372 5740
Fudge 178 Church Road NW10 (081) 459 7343
Fudge 30 Craven Park Road NW10 (081) 965 5269
Halfords 173 Kilburn High Road NW6 (071) 624 7488

**Simpsons** 116 Malden Road NW5 (071) 485 1706
**Whisker** 80 Willesden Lane NW6 (071) 624 6375

# OUTER NORTH-WEST

*Incorporating Postal Districts NW4, NW7, NW9, HA0–HA3, HA5, HA7–HA9*

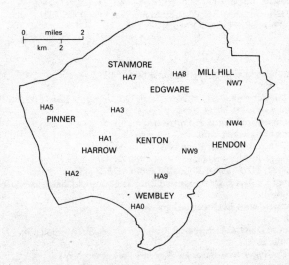

## FOOD SHOPS AND EVERYDAY PRODUCTS *including: cleaning items, cosmetics, recycled paper and energy-efficient electrical goods*

**Acorns Health Store** 17 Church Hill Road, Barnet NW7 (081) 441 2980
**V. Amin** 437 Alexandra Avenue, Harrow, Middlesex
**Body Shop** Unit 25, Brent Cross Shopping Centre NW4 (081) 202 9426
**Body Shop** 11/15 St. Anne Road, Harrow, Middlesex HA1 (081) 863 9995
**Bridge to Health** 25c Bridge Road, Wembley, Middlesex
**Brimarks & Sons** 241 East Barnet Road, Barnet NW7 (081) 449 5416
**Edgware Centre for Natural Health** 128 High Street, Edgware, Middlesex HA8 (081) 952 9566
**Healthways** 36a The Broadway NW7 (081) 959 0771
**Hendon Health Food Centre** 125 Brent Street NW4 (081) 202 9165
**Holland & Barrett** Unit W16 Shopping Centre NW4 (081) 202 8669
**Holland & Barrett** 151 Field End Road, Eastcote, Middlesex HA5
**Holland & Barrett** 14 The Promenade, Edgware, Middlesex HA8 (081) 958 2657
**Holland & Barrett** 22/24 College Road, Harrow, Middlesex HA1 (081) 427 4794
**Holland & Barrett** Unit 21 Central Square, High Road, Wembley, Middlesex

HA9 (081) 902 6959
**Kenton Whole Foods** 215 Kenton Road, Harrow, Middlesex HA1
**Krantex Health Foods** 211 Station Road, Harrow, Middlesex HA1
  (081) 863 8073
**Mother Nature** 40 The Broadway, Stanmore, Middlesex HA7 (081) 954 0686
**Orchard Fayre** Alexandra Avenue, South Harrow HA2
**Pinner Health Foods** 61 Bridge Street, Pinner, Middlesex HA5 (081) 429 1336
**Pure and Simple Whole Foods** Pickwick Walk, 286 Uxbridge Road, Hatch End,
  Middlesex HA5 (081) 421 3821
**Rowans** 6 Letchford Terrace, Off Headstone Lane, Harrow, Middlesex HA3
**Scotch Beef Centre** 14 Bittacy Hill NW7 (081) 346 1055
  Delivers free

## *EATING OUT* – *Restaurants, cafés and take-aways*

**Yum Yums** 5 Boot Parade, High Street, Edgware HA8 (081) 952 4512

## *CHARITY SHOPS*

**Barnardo's** 9 Love Lane, Pinner, Middlesex (081) 866 1159
**Barnardo's** 172 Field End Road, Eastcote, Middlesex HA5 (081) 866 2072
**Barnardo's** 118 Station Road, Edgware, Middlesex (081) 952 5132
**British Red Cross Society** St. Albans Road, Barnet NW7 (081) 449 8969
  Open Wednesdays 9.30–3.30
**British Red Cross Society** 37 Vivian Avenue, Hendon NW4 (081) 202 9669
**British Red Cross Society** 563 High Road, Wembley, Middlesex HA9
**Imperial Cancer Research** 179 Station Road, Edgware , Middlesex HA8
  (081) 951 3000
**Imperial Cancer Research** 22 Watling Avenue, Burnt Oak, Edgware, Middlesex
  HA8 (081) 952 1821
**Imperial Cancer Research** 2 Granville Parade, 34 College Road, Harrow,
  Middlesex HA1
**Imperial Cancer Research** 63 Brent Street, Hendon NW4 (081) 202 1205
  Shop acquired, opening 1990
**Imperial Cancer Research** 37 The Broadway, Mill Hill NW7 (081) 906 4628
**Imperial Cancer Research** 26 Bridge Street, Pinner, Middlesex HA5
  (081) 866 4989
**Imperial Cancer Research** 310 Northolt Road, South Harrow, Middlesex HA2
  (081) 864 4515
**Oxfam** 11 St. John's Road, Wembley, Middlesex HA9 (081) 903 0566
**Oxfam** 358 Rayners Lane, Pinner, Middlesex HA5 (081) 866 9616
**Oxfam** 103 The Broadway, Burnt Oak, Middlesex HA8 (081) 951 1720
**Oxfam** 155 Station Road, Edgware, Middlesex HA8 (081) 951 1548
**Oxfam** 361 Uxbridge Road, Hatch End, Middlesex HA5 (081) 428 0428
**Oxfam** 50 The Broadway, Mill Hill NW7 (081) 906 4499
**Oxfam** 241 Station Road, Harrow, Middlesex HA1 (081) 863 9842
**Oxfam** 8 Peterborough Road, Harrow, Middlesex HA1 (081) 422 4285
**Oxfam** 2 Buckingham Parade, Stanmore, Middlesex HA7 (081) 954 6269
**Oxfam** 19 Bridge Street, Pinner, Middlesex HA5 (081) 429 0926
**Save the Children** 551 Pinner Road, Harrow North, Middlesex HA2
**The Spastics' Society** 12 Vivian Avenue, Hendon NW4 (081) 202 2569
**The Spastics' Society**, 4 Central Square, Wembley, Middlesex HA9

(081) 902 6363
**Sue Ryder** 504 High Road, Wembley HA9 (081) 863 9695

## BIKE SHOPS

**Bittacy Cycles** 18 Bittacy Hill, Mill Hill NW7 (081) 346 5784
**Broadway Bikes, Hendon** 242 The Broadway NW9 (081) 202 4671
**Buntings** 7 Masons Avenue, Wealdstone (081) 427 5136
**Clark Howard & Son Ltd** 509 Kingsbury Road NW9 (081) 204 4165
**The Cycle Shop** 511 Pinner Road, North Harrow, Middlesex (081) 427 5454
**Cycle Systems** 45b Bridge Street, Pinner, Middlesex (081) 868 2918
**Cycle Systems** 35/39 Lowlands Road, Harrow, Middlesex HA1 (081) 864 0668
**Deesons** 138 Burnt Oak Broadway, Edgware HA8 (081) 951 0421
**Halfords** Unit 1, Silk Bridge Building, 1 The Hyde, Hendon NW9 (081) 200 8588
**Pedalers** 388 Northolt Road, South Harrow, Middlesex HA2 (081) 422 5807
**Rohans** 451 Rayners Lane, Pinner, Middlesex HA5 (081) 868 6262

# THE GREEN GUIDE TO RECYCLING

# THE GREEN GUIDE TO RECYCLING

Despite the fact that Britain still lags behind many other European countries, both in the organisation of recycling on a large scale, and in the provision of local services, there has been a considerable upsurge in interest and activity in the last year or so. Most councils now provide bottle banks; many, paper banks or collection points; and at an increasing number of civic amenity sites, facilities are available for the recycling of a range of other products including metals, CFCs, oil, textiles and old furniture. In addition, many charitable organisations and local groups have found recycling to be an excellent way of raising funds, as well as doing their bit to protect and enhance the environment.

Information about recycling in general and a list of useful contact addresses for those interested in setting up their own recycling schemes are given in the chapter on Capital Issues: rubbish, litter and recycling, on pp 29-52.

We have surveyed the whole of the capital to provide a comprehensive guide to recycling facilities throughout the Greater London area. Because of the increasing activity in this field, many more facilities are likely to be added during 1990 and you local authority Cleansing Department, Environmental Health Department or Recycling Officer (if there is one) will be able to give you further details. Their telephone numbers are given under each borough in the How Green is Your Council? section, pp 81-168.

Again, because people live their everyday lives in a locality, rather than being constrained by borough boundaries, we have divided London into fifteen geographical areas, as outlined in the map on p170.

# WEST END AND CITY

*Incorporating Postal Districts EC1–EC4, WC1, WC2, W1*

## RECYCLING FACILITIES

Cleansing depots at:
* 118/200 Drury Lane, W1.  (071)798 2062.
* Dufours Place, Soho, W1.  (071)798 2012.
* 21 Farm Street, W1.  (071)798 1395.

## MINI-RECYCLING CENTRES
* Charing Cross Road, opposite Cavell House - bottles.
* Covent Garden Piazza, Royal Opera House side - bottles.

* Dufours Place, outside cleansing depot - bottles.
* Judd Street, junction with Cromer Street - bottles.
* Langham Street, junction of Great Portland Street - bottles.
* Sutton Row, off Soho Square - bottles.
* Tottenham Court Road, near Grafton Way - bottles.
* Cockpit Yard, Northington Street, off Grays Inn Road - Camden Recycling Project, funded by Manpower Services - collects electrical goods (videos, TVs etc), furniture repaired and resold.
* Wigmore Street - bottles.
* Tavistock Street - by Monkey Business, by Rumours and by Jubilee Market - bottles.
* Crown Court - bottles.
* Warwick Street, back of Regent's Street - bottles.
* Newport Place car park - bottles.
* Charing Cross Road, junction with Goslett Yard - bottles.
* Westmoreland Street, by National Heart Hospital - bottles.
* Macclesfield Street, by Shaftesbury Avenue - bottles.
* Great Portland Street, by Langham Street W1 - bottles.

# CENTRAL WEST

*Incorporating Postal Districts SW1, SW3, SW5 - SW7, SW10, W2, W8 - W11, W14*

## RECYCLING FACILITIES

* Cleansing depot at Gatliff Road SW1. (071) 798 2154.
* Cleansing depot at 23 Wharf Road, W2. (071) 798 1470.
* Civic amenity site, Cremorne Wharf, 27 Lots Road, Chelsea. (071) 352 9402, oil, glass, paper.
* Civic amenity site, Ebury Bridge Road, - paper, cardboard, glass.
* Page Street Council Depot SW1.

## MINI-RECYCLING CENTRES

Hammersmith & Fulham Borough Council operate a weekend skip service at various locations throughout the Borough. Please contact Engineering Department, Bagleys Lane Depot on (081) 748 3020 Ext. 3214 for full details.
**Chelsea**
* Townmead Road, Chelsea harbour, opens early 1990 - bottles.
* 51 Townmead Road, Sainsbury's car park - bottles and cans.
* Denyer Street - bottles (paper in 1990).
**Earls Court**
* Cromwell Road, in Sainsbury's car park - bottles.
**Fulham**

* Coomer Place, off North End Road - bottles.
* New Kings Road, Eelbrook Common, opposite service station paper and bottles.
* Heckfield Place, Safeway car park - bottles and paper.
* High Street, nr. Station Approach - bottles and paper.

**Kensington**
* Warwick Road, Sainsbury's Homebase car park - bottles.

**North Kensington**
* Ladbroke Grove, Sainsbury's car park - bottles.

**City of Westminster**
* Lancaster Gate W2, outside church - bottles.
* Princes Square W2, by Hereford Road - bottles.
* Porchester Gardens W2, by Inverness Terrace - bottles.
* Warwick Avenue W2, next to taxi rank - bottles.
* Edgware Road W2, outside Parsons House - bottles.
* Maida Vale station W9, by Elgin Avenue - bottles.
* Upper Tatchbrook Street (south), outside Reyniers Wine Bar - bottles.
* Junction of Meanwhile Gardens and Elmstone Road SW6 - bottles.
* Junction of Sussex Gardens and Edgware Road W2 - bottles.
* Royal Albert Hall, near refuse chamber SW7 - bottles.
* Churchill Gardens SW1, by Churchill Club - bottles.
* Claverton Street SW1 - bottles.
* Eccleston Square SW1, South Side - bottles.
* Junction of Warwick Way and Sutherland Street SW1 - bottles.
* Tatchbrook Street Market SW1 - bottles.
* Ebury Street SW1, by Ebury Wine Bar - bottles.
* Erasmus Street, by Herrick Street SW1 - bottles.
* Rochester Row SW1, by petrol station - bottles.

# INNER WEST

*Incorporating Postal Districts W3–W7, W12, W13*

## RECYCLING FACILITIES

* **Acton** - Stirling Depot, Stirling Road W3. Open October to March, 8am - 4pm, seven days a week - bottles and scrap metal.

## MINI-RECYCLING CENTRES

Hammersmith & Fulham Borough Council operate a weekend skip service at various locations throughout the Borough. Please contact Engineering Department, Bagleys Lane Depot (081) 748 3020 Ext 3214 for full details.
**Acton**

* Crown Street - bottles.
* High Street, opposite Bumbles Wine Bar - bottles.
* Stirling Road, future civic amenities site - bottles.
* Victoria Road/Western Avenue (Elizabeth Arden) - bottles.
* Church Street/Salisbury Street - bottles.

**Chiswick**
* Chiswick Common - paper.
* Chiswick Police Station - bottles.
* Grove Park Hotel - bottles.

**Ealing**
* Hastings Road, (wine bar) - bottles.
* Longfield Avenue, near Town Hall - bottles and cans.
* Singapore Road, behind Marks & Spencer - bottles and cans.
* Ealing Road, by South Ealing underground station - bottles.
* ASDA, Park Royal Industrial Estate, Park Road - bottles.
* Fox & Goose pub, Hanger Lane - bottles.
* Springfield Sports Ground, Ealing - bottles.
* St. Mary's Road, Conservative Club - bottles.

**Ealing Common**
* Caernarvon Hotel - bottles.
* South Ealing Road, off Dorset Road - bottles.

**Hammersmith**
* Emlyn Road, outside Lucas Building - paper.
* Glenthorne Road, outside NCP car park - bottles and paper.
* Goldhawke Road, Majestic Wine Warehouse car park - bottles.
* Hammersmith Grove, near market - bottles.
* Queen Carolyn Street, peninsular under flyover - bottles.
* Town Hall, Nigel Playfair Avenue - bottles and paper.

**Hanwell**
* Hanwell Broadway/York Avenue - bottles.
* Hanwell Clock Tower, top of Boston Road - bottles.

**Shepherds Bush**
* Askham Court - paper.
* Bloemfontein Road, outside swimming pool - bottles and paper.
* Rockley Road, outside Atlantic House - bottles and paper.
* Uxbridge Road - bottles.

**Wormwood Scrubs**
* Old Oak Common Lane, outside Woolworths - bottles.
* Scrubs Lane, Wormwood Scrubs car park - bottles.

# OUTER WEST

*Incorporating Postal Districts UB1–UB10, HA4, HA6, TW3–TW8, TW13, TW14*

# RECYCLING FACILITIES

* **Feltham** - Space Waye civic amenity site - cardboard, textiles, tins, metal and motor oil.
* **Greenford** - civic amenities site, Greenford Road - open every day except Christmas Day. This depot has separate skip facilities for bottles, cans, newspapers, cardboard, rags, scrap metal, batteries and sump oil. Any member of the public may drive in.
* **Harefield** - civic amenity site at New Years Green Lane - glass, oil, textiles, paper, metal, cans and cardboard.
* **Hayes** - Rigby Lane civic amenity site - glass, oil, metal.
* **Ruislip** - civic amenity site at Victoria Road - glass, oil, textiles, paper, metal, cans.
* **Southall** - Waste and Recycling Centre, Gordon Road depot - bottles and scrap metal.

# MINI-RECYCLING FACILITIES

**Bedfont**
* Staines Road, by disused toilets - paper and bottles.

**Brentford**
* Albany Parade - bottles.

**Eastcote**
* Devonshire Lodge car park - bottles.

**Feltham**
* Elmwood Avenue, at junction of High Street - paper.
* Highfield Street - bottles.

**Greenford**
* 2-4 Oldfield Lane, next to Sainsbury's - bottles and cans.
* Oldfield Lane, British Legion HQ - bottles.
* Oldfield Lane (North), Soltenwar Co. - bottles.
* Perivale Lane, Ealing Golf Club - bottles.

**Grove Park**
* Spencer Road, at junction of Bolton Road - paper.

**Hayes**
* Pump Lane Car Park - bottles.

**Hayes End**
* Junction of West Drayton and Uxbridge Road - bottles.

**Heston**
* New Heston Road, near library - paper.
* New Heston Road, Elm Tree pub - bottles.

**Hillingdon**
* Junction Western Avenue and Long Lane Hill - bottles.

**Hounslow**
* Civic Centre, bus lay-by near car park - paper.
* School Road car park - paper.

**Hounslow West**

*     Car park, Bath Road - paper.
*     Pay & Display car park - bottles.

**Isleworth**
*     Isleworth Boys Club, Twickenham Road - paper.
*     BR station, London Road - bottles.

**Northolt**
*     Church Road, off White Hart roundabout - bottles.
*     Oldfield Circus - opposite Greenwood pub - bottles.

**Ruislip Manor**
*     Lindon Close - bottles.

**Southall**
*     Gordon Road Depot (future civic amenities site) - bottles.
*     Norwood Green car park - bottles.
*     Southall High Street, opposite police station - bottles.

**Uxbridge**
*     Christian Aid, 37 Warren Road, Ickenham - collect newspapers, magazines and computer paper.
*     Paved area of George Street - bottles.
*     Forecourt of Brookfield Resident Home, Park Road, facing Belmont Road - paper (mixed).

**Yiewsley**
*     Otterfield Road - bottles.

# INNER SOUTH-WEST

*Incorporating Postal Districts SW2, SW4, SW8, SW9, SW11–SW20*

## RECYCLING FACILITIES

*     **Wimbledon** - Weir Road - glass, paper, cardboard, oil, rags, metal and cans.
*     **Wandsworth** - civic amenity site, Smugglers Way
    - cans, paper, oil, rags, metal, bottles and CFC removal from old fridges.

## MINI-RECYCLING CENTRES

**Balham**
*     149/151 Balham High Road, next to Sainsbury's - bottles.
*     Culmore Cross - bottles and paper.
*     Balham Centre Car Park - bottles and paper.

**Barnes**
*     Rocks Lane Car Park, by tennis courts - bottles, cans.
*     Approach Road, near Skew Arch, West Barnes bottles.

**Battersea**
  * Battersea Park Road, opposite Forfar Road - bottles and paper.
  * Central car park, Battersea Park - bottles and paper.
  * Lavender Hill, Gateway car park - bottles and paper.

**Brixton**
  * Acre Lane, outside Town Hall - glass.
  * Cowley Road/Normandy Road - glass.
  * Loughborough Park, outside council depot - bottles.

**Clapham**
  * Clapham Common, Old Town bus terminal - glass.

**Colliers Wood**
  * Singlegate Primary School, South Gardens (081) 542 6503 - paper.
  * Savacentre Car Park - bottles and paper.

**East Sheen**
  * Sheen Lane Centre - bottles.

**Merton**
  * Savacentre, in car park - bottles and cans.

**Morden**
  * Morden Road - bottles and paper.
  * Green Lane, opposite St. Helier Station - paper and bottles.
  * Crown House - bottles.

**Nine Elms**
  * 62 Wandsworth Road, in Sainsbury's car park - bottles.

**Raynes Park**
  * Approach Road - bottles.
  * Coombe Lane, opposite Durham Road - bottles.
  * St. John's Playgroup, 12 Blenheim Road, (081) 543 2347 - paper.

**Streatham**
  * Streatham High Road, outside Cannon cinema - glass.

**Tooting**
  * Public car park, Dr. Johnson Avenue - bottles and paper.
  * Tooting Leisure Centre car park - bottles and paper.

**Wandsworth**
  * 45 Garrett Lane, in car park adjacent to Sainsbury's - bottles and cans.
  * Wandsworth Recycling Centre, 64 Kimber Road - collect household and office furniture, and renovate it.
  * Western Riverside, Smugglers Way - oil.

**Wimbledon**
  * Alexandra Road, car park of B&Q - bottles and paper.
  * Hartfield Road, by car park - bottles and paper.
  * Herbert Day Nursery, 52 Park House, Dundonald Road (081) 542 7416 - paper.
  * William Wilberforce School, Camp Road - paper.
  * Wimbledon Park Primary School, Havana Road (081) 946 5050 - paper.

## WASTE PAPER COLLECTIONS

**Barnes**
* Sun Inn, Church Street, newspapers only. First Saturday every month. Barnes Community Association

**Clapham**
* High Street, bus garage forecourt, FoE collection first Saturday each month.

**Mortlake**
* Station car park. Newspapers only. Third Sunday every month - Richmond Liberal Democrats

**Nine Elms**
* FoE collection in Sainsbury's car park, Pascal Street, last Saturday each month.

**Streatham**
* FoE collection in Safeway car park second Saturday each month.

# OUTER SOUTH-WEST

*Incorporating Postal Districts TW1, TW2, TW9–TW12, KT1–KT6, KT9*

## RECYCLING FACILITIES

* **Kew** - Townmead Road civic amenity site - glass, cans, metals, rags and soft furnishings, old sump oil, newspapers and stapled magazines, cardboard, bric-a-brac.
* **Kingston** - Athelstan Road civic amenity site - bottles, tins, rags, oil, metal, paper.

## MINI-RECYCLING CENTRES:

**Chessington**
* Hook Road - bottles
* Bridge Road - bottles

**Ham and Petersham**
* Ashburnham Road car park - bottles, cans, rags, paper.

**Hampton**
* Nursery Lands car park, near Sainsbury's - bottles, cans, paper, rags.

**Hampton Hill**
* Hampton Road car park - bottles, cans, paper, rags.

**Hampton Wick**
* Old Bridge Street car park - bottles.
* Station forecourt, over bridge - paper.

**Kingston**
* Fairfield East - bottles.

* City Kingstonian, Shell garage, 160 Richmond Road - oil.
* Lower Ham Road - bottles.

**Motspur Park**
* Station Road, by the station - bottles.

**New Malden**
* Cocks Crescent - bottles.
* Tesco car park - bottles.

**Richmond**
* Old Deer car park - bottles, cans, paper, rags.
* Kew Road, entrance to London Welsh RFC - paper.
* Queen's Road, Black Horse pub - bottles, paper, rags.

**Surbiton**
* The Crescent - bottles.
* Wimbledon Metal Co. Ltd., 105/7 Brighton Road - metal and batteries - will collect large quantities.

**Teddington**
* North Lane car park behind Tesco's - bottles, cans.
* Station car park, off Adelaide Road - paper.
* Cedar Road car park - bottles, rags.

**Tolworth**
* Kingston Road - bottles

**Twickenham**
* Sixth Cross Road, opposite Fountain pub - bottles, paper.
* South Road, Great Mills DIY Store car park - bottles, paper rags.
* Holly Road car park - bottles, cans, rags.
* Heath Road, Red Lion pub car park - bottles.
* Richmond Road, outside York House Gardens - paper.

**East Twickenham**
* St. Margaret's Hotel car park - bottles.

**Whitton**
* Nelson Road, Library car park - bottles, cans, paper, rags.
* Nelson Road, Threshers off licence - paper.
* Percy Road, Heathfield Library - bottles, paper, rags.

## WASTE PAPER COLLECTIONS

**Ham and Petersham**
* House collections once a month. Newspapers, anything. Ham and Petersham Liberal Democrats.

**Richmond**
* Old Deer car park - newspapers only. Collections third Sunday of every month - Richmond and Barnes Liberal Democrats.

**Twickenham**
* House collections, newspapers only. First Sunday every month. Twickenham Liberal Democrats.
* Heatham House, Whitton Road. All waste paper. Mornings, last Sunday every month. Richmond and Twickenham FoE.

**Hampton**
* Football Club, Station Road. Newspapers and books. Continual collection. Hampton Football Club.

**Hounslow**
* Hounslow FoE, 34 Smithland Way - paper collection once a month.

# OUTER SOUTH

*Incorporating Postal Districts SM1–SM6, CR0, CR2, CR4*

## RECYCLING FACILITIES
* **Morden** - Garth Road - glass, metal, oil, paper, rags and cans.
* **New Addington** - Fishers Farm, North Down Crescent - bottles and metals.
* **Purley Oaks** - Brighton Road, council site - oil, glass, paper, metals, rags.
* **Sutton** - Oldfields Road civic amenity site - glass, cardboard, metal, oil and car batteries.
* **West Croydon** - Factory Lane - paper, metals, bottles, oil and rags.

## MINI-RECYCLING CENTRES
**Carshalton**
* Wrythe Lane, Carshalton, Co-op supermarket - bottle bank opening early 1990.
* High Street car park - glass and paper.
* Ruskin Road Scout site - paper.
* Denmark Road car park - glass and paper.
* Queen Mary's Hospital for Children - glass and paper.
* Diamond Riding Centre - bottles.
* Ecology Centre, Honeywood Walk - glass and paper.

**Carshalton Beeches**
* Banstead Road shops - glass and paper.

**Cheam**
* Kingsway Road car park - glass and paper.
* Malden Road Scout site - paper.
* Spring Close Lane - paper.

**Coulsdon**
* Lion Green Road car park - bottles.

**Croydon**
* Barclays Road, back of Fairfield Halls - bottles.
* Lansdowne Road, by public toilets - bottles.
* Marlow Way, ASDA - bottles and paper.

* Junction of Norbury Avenue and London Road - bottles.

**Mitcham**
* Fair Green, by Langdale Parade - bottles and paper.
* London Road, by Elm Nursery car park - bottles and paper.
* Alfred Mizen Primary School, Abbotts Road (081) 679 3707 - paper.
* Centre One, Phipps Bridge Youth Centre, Cobham Court, Haslemere Avenue (081) 640 2119 - paper.
* Gorringe Park Middle School, Sandy Lane - paper.
* Raven Waste Paper Co. Ltd., Unit 3, Batsworth Road (081) 640 9210 - paper.

**Morden**
* Abbotsbury Primary School, Abbotsbury Road (081) 640 1010 - paper.
* Crown House, in car park - bottles - coloured glass only.
* Green Lane, opposite St. Helier Station - bottles.
* Merton Community Scrap Scheme, Chaucer Building, Canterbury Road, Morden, Surrey (081) 640 9510 - a registered charity open for membership to any community group in Merton, Sutton and surrounding areas.
* Morden Road, near library - bottles.
* Senior Citizens Wednesday Club, 326 Lynmouth Avenue - offcuts of paper, calendars.

**New Addington**
* Central Parade - bottles.

**North Cheam**
* London Road car park - glass and paper.
* Stonecot Hill shops - glass and paper.
* London Road, near Staines Avenue - glass and paper.

**Purley**
* High Street, opposite cinema - bottles.

**Rosehill**
* Rosehill car park - glass, paper and cans.
* Co-op Supermarket car park - glass.

**Roundshaw**
* Alcock Close car park - glass and paper.

**Sanderstead**
* Limpsfield Road car park - bottles.

**Selsdon**
* Selsdon Triangle car park - bottles.

**Sutton**
* ASDA Superstore, Beddington Lane - glass and paper.
* Bushey Road, Sutton Green - glass and paper.
* Camden Road car park - glass.
* The Quadrant, Brighton Road - glass and paper.
* Abacus Self-Storage, Westmead Road - bottles.

**Thornton Heath**
* Parchmore Road, by the clock tower - bottles.

**Wallington**
- * St. Elphege's, Stafford Road - glass and paper.
- * Shotfield car park - glass and paper.
- * Wallington High School for Boys - paper.
- * Woodcote Road car park - glass and paper.

**Worcester Park**
- * Stone Place car park - glass, paper and cans.

# INNER SOUTH-EAST

*Incorporating Postal Districts SE1–SE28*

## RECYCLING FACILITIES

- * **Deptford** - Creekside Waste Recycling Centre - glass, paper, rags, cans and oil.
- * **Norwood** - Rommany Civic Amenity Site - glass, paper, rags, cans and oil.
- * **Thamesmead** - Greenwich Civic Amenity Site, Nathan Way - glass, paper, rags, cans and oil.
  Will also take old electrical appliances, fridges, cookers etc.
- * **Southwark** - Manor Place Depot, Occupation Road - paper, cans, metal, oil, cardboard.

## MINI-RECYCLING CENTRES

**Bermondsey**
- * Junction of Albion Street and Temeraine Street - bottles.
- * Alexis Street, grassed area - bottles.

**Blackheath**
- * Lee Road, Blackheath Concert Hall - bottles.
- * Tudway Road - bottles.

**Brockley**
- * Brockley Cross - paper

**Catford**
- * Bromley Road, outside bus garage - bottles.
- * Rockbourne Road, junction with Standstead Road - bottles.
- * South London Children's Scrap Store, 163 Verdant Lane - scrap store.
- * Town Hall, Civic Suite entrance - paper.
- * Whitefoot Lane, outside Governor General pub - bottles.

**Charlton**
- * Bugsby Way, ASDA car park - glass, paper and cans.

**Deptford**
- * Avonley Road, Crown & Anchor public house - bottles.

* Town Hall, New Cross Road - paper
* Goldsmiths College, New Cross Road - paper
* Grove Street, near shopping area - paper and bottles.
* New Cross Road - paper
* Pepys Estate, Grove Street - paper

**Dulwich**
* Junction of Gallery Road and Thurlow Road - bottles.
* Junction of Sunray Avenue and Herne Hill Road - bottles.

**East Dulwich**
* Crystal Palace Road - bottles.

**Eltham**
* 1a Philiport Path, in car park adjacent to Sainsbury's - bottles, cans, paper.
* Eltham Road, Blackheath Wanderers Sports Club - bottles.
* Eltham Green School, Queenswood Road - cans.

**Forest Hill**
* Brockley Rise, junction with Codrington Hill - paper and bottles.
* Dartmouth Road, junction with Willow Way - bottles.
* 44/48 London Road, in car park adjacent to Sainsbury's - bottles and paper.
* Pearcefield Avenue car park - bottles and paper.
* Vancouver Road, junction with Woolstone Road - bottles.

**Greenwich**
* Greenwich High Road, Davy's Wine Bar - bottles.
* Royal Hill - bottles.
* Westcombe Hill - bottles.

**Grove Park**
* Riddons Road, junction with Chinbrook Road - bottles.

**Kennington**
* Oval Way, outside LBC depot - glass.

**Lee**
* Baring Road, outside bus terminal - bottles.
* Baring Road, junction with Harland Road - bottles.
* Burnt Ash Road, junction with Upwood Road - bottles.
* Eltham Road, junction with Leyland Road - bottles and paper.
* Upwood Road - paper.
* Riddons Road, junction with Chinbrook Road - paper.

**Lewisham**
* Albion Way - bottles.
* George Lane, junction with Hither Green Lane - bottles.
* 209 Lewisham Road, in Tesco car park - bottles.
* Molesworth Street, by multi-storey car park - bottles and paper.
* Lewisham High Street, by library - paper.

**New Cross**
* Avonley Road, Crown & Anchor pub - bottles.
* Brockley Road, outside Breakspears Arms pub - bottles.
* Deptford Town Hall - paper and bottles.

* New Cross Road, Raffles Wine Bar - bottles.

**Norwood**
* Christchurch Road, International supermarket - glass.

**Peckham Rye**
* Holly Grove, outside public toilets - bottles.

**Plumstead**
* Abery Street - bottles.
* Ravine Grove, Plumstead Common Working Men's Club - bottles, paper.
* London Transport bus garage - cans.

**Sydenham**
* Girton Road car park - bottles and paper.
* Sydenham Road, next to Home Park public conveniences - bottles.
* Britannic House Social Club - bottles.
* Outside R.M. Simpson, Willow Way - paper.
* St. Christophers Hospice, Lawrie Park Road - paper.

**South Norwood**
* Portland Road, by the swimming baths - bottles.

**Southwark**
* Junction of Union Street and Flat Iron Square - bottles.

**Thamesmead**
* Arnott Close - bottles.
* Thamesmere Pool, Thamesmere Drive - bottles and paper.

**Waterloo**
* National Theatre - bottles.
* Belvedere Road, opposite Royal Festival Hall - bottles.
* Junction of Waterloo Bridge and Stamford Street - bottles.

**Woolwich**
* Anchor and Hope Lane, Makro car park - bottles and paper.
* Bugsby Way, ASDA car park - bottles, cans, paper.
* 25 Calderwood Street, outside Sainsbury's - bottles and cans.
* Charlton car park, Charlton Village - bottles, paper.
* Ha Ha Road, Woolwich Barracks - bottles.
* Stadium Road, Queen Elizabeth Military Hospital - bottles.
* Greenwich Recycling Workshop, 1st Floor, 34 Bowater Road, Westminster Industrial Estate, Woolwich - furniture and renovation.

# WASTE PAPER COLLECTIONS

**Lewisham**
* Slagrove Place, Ladywell - FoE collect waste paper the first Saturday of each month.

**West Lewisham**
* Sydenham High Street, by Post Office - Labour Party collect waste paper the second Saturday of each month.

**Woodside**
* Lambeth FoE, 77 Anthony Road - two paper collections once a month.

# OUTER SOUTH-EAST

*Incorporating Postal Districts BR1–BR7, TN16, DA5–DA8, DA14–DA18*

## RECYCLING FACILITIES
* **Bromley** - Waldo Road civic amenity site - glass, oil, rags, paper, light metals, wood, cans, fridges and hardcore re-used.
* **Beckenham** - Churchfields Road civic amenity site - glass, oil, rags and fridges.
* **Crayford** - Thames Road civic amenity site - metal, oil, rags, glass, paper and cardboard.
* **Footscray** - Maidstone Road civic amenity site - metal, oil, rags, glass, paper and cardboard.

## MINI-RECYCLING CENTRES
**Beckenham**
* St. George's Road car park - bottles.
* Harvington Estate car park, South Eden Park Road - bottles.
* Marian Vian Primary School (081) 658 6524 - aluminium foil.
* Beckenham Hospital, Croydon Road - paper. Limited access so check with hosts when it is best to bring paper.

**Beckton**
* ASDA, Tollgate Road, off North Circular Road - bottles.

**Bexleyheath**
* ASDA, The Broadway - bottles.
* Beside Townley Road toilets - bottles.
* Car park opposite civic offices - bottles.
* Car park rear of civic offices - bottles.

**Biggin Hill**
* FoE (0959) 73951 - cans.

**Blackfen/Sidcup**
* The Oval Shopping Parade - bottles.

**Bromley**
* Downham Way, junction with Bromley Road, Downham - bottles.
* Downham Way, outside Downham Tavern pub - bottles.
* Old Bromley Road, Downham - bottles and paper.
* Norman Park (Hayes Lane entrance) - glass.
* The Hill multi-storey car park, Beckenham Lane - bottles.
* Roslin Way car park, Burnt Ash Lane - bottles.
* Rochester Avenue, The Civic Centre - paper.

*     Highfields Infant School, Shortlands - paper.
*     Raglan Infants School, Raglan Road (access in Jaffray Road) - paper.
    Restricted access so check with hosts when it is best to bring paper.
*     Langley Park boys' school - paper.
*     FoE (081) 460 1329 - cans.
*     Guide Dogs for the Blind (081) 460 6432 - ring-pulls and aluminium foil.
*     19th Bromley Scouts, Methodist Central Church - aluminium foil.
*     Bromley & Downham Boys Brigade, Valeswood Road - paper.
    Limited access so check with hosts when it is best to bring paper.
*     Fairacres Residents Association, Fair Acres - paper. Limited access so check with hosts when it is best to bring paper.
*     Southborough Primary School, Southborough Lane - paper. Limited access so check with hosts when it is best to bring paper.

**Crayford**
*     Sainsbury's Homebase car park - bottles.

**Crystal Palace**
*     Crystal Palace Park (Thicket Road entrance) - glass.

**Erith**
*     Pier Road car park - bottles.

**Orpington**
*     Orpington College of Further Education, The Walnuts, High Street (access in Lych Gate Road) - paper.
*     Poverest Primary School, Tillingbourne Green, St. Mary Cray - paper. Limited access so contact hosts when is best time to bring in paper.
*     Ramsden Primary School, Dyke Drive - paper.

**St. Paul's Cray**
*     Cotmandene Crescent car park - bottles.
*     Leesons Day Centre, Chipperfield Road - paper.

**Sidcup**
*     Grassington Road car park - bottles.

**Upper Belvedere**
*     Nuxley Road car park - bottles.

**Welling**
*     Co-op car park, 71/79 High Street - bottles.
*     Springfield Road car park - bottles.

# WASTE PAPER COLLECTIONS

**Biggin Hill**
*     FoE (0959) 73951 collect all papers and mazagines.

**Bromley**
*     St. Augustine's Church, Southborough Lane collect newspapers only, in a skip sited on church car park from first Tuesday in each month for seven days.

**Orpington**
*    Crofton Oaks Scouts collect newspapers and magazines at their compound, open weekends 10-6.
*    Orpington Fire Station, Avalon Road, collects all papers and magazines.

**West Wickham**
*    6th West Wickham Scouts at St. Mary's Church in The Avenue - collect any waste paper.
*    Hawes Down Infant School (081) 777 4420 - ring pulls and aluminium foil.
*    Glebe School (081) 777 4540 - aluminium foil.

# INNER EAST

*Incorporating Postal Districts E1 - E18*

## RECYCLING FACILITIES

*    **Chingford** - Suffield Road Depot - bottles, rags, paper, metal and oil.
*    **Walthamstow** - South Access Road civic amenity site, near Low Hall depot - bottles, rags, paper, metal and oil.
*    **East Ham** - Jenkins Lane civic amenity site - oil, rags, metal, bottles, asbestos sheet, CFC removal from old fridges planned for early 1990.
*    Northumberland Wharf civic amenity site, Prestons Road - paper and oil.

## MINI-RECYCLING CENTRES

**Becton**
*    ASDA car park, Tollgate Road - bottles.
**Bethnal Green**
*    Bethnal Green Road - bottles.
*    Clairedale House - bottles.
*    Commercial Street - bottles.
*    Dinmont Estate, Pritchards Road - bottles.
*    Spitalfields Farm - bottles.
*    Whitechapel High Street - bottles.
*    Lea Bridge Road roundabout, near Lower Clapton Road - bottles.
*    Town Hall, Mare Street - bottles.
     (The council plan to introduce paper banks and can banks at the above sites and additional sites early in 1990.)

**Bow**
*    Stroudley Walk - bottles.

* St. Stephen's Road, junction with Roman Road - bottles.
* Bow Road, opposite Bow Road underground station - bottles.

**Canning Town**
* Rathbone Market, Barking Road - bottles.

**Chingford**
* Richmond Road - bottles.
* Chingford Road, Leo Superstore car park - bottles.

**East Ham**
* Inside main gates of Town Hall - bottles.
* Wakefield Street, by BHS - bottles.

**Forestgate**
* Romford Road, outside the old cinema - bottles.

**Globe Town**
* Roman Road, Market Square, near Bonner Street - bottles.

**Hackney**
* Dalston Lane, near Mare Street - bottles.
* Homerton High Street, by Isabella Road - bottles.
* Lea Bridge Road roundabout, near Lower Clapton Road - bottles.
* Town Hall, Mare Street - bottles.
* Hackney Kids Scrap Store, 137 Homerton High Street - scrap store.

**Isle of Dogs**
* East Ferry Road in ASDA car park - bottles.

**Leyton**
* Auckland Road - bottles.
* Lea Bridge Road car park, near Post Office - bottles.
* Bromley Road car park - bottles.

**Leytonstone**
* High Road, rear of Leo's Store - bottles.

**Manor Park**
* Corner of Church Road and High Street - bottles.

**Plaistow**
* Queens Square, Green Street- bottles.
* Corner of St. Stephens Road and Plaistow Road - bottles.

**Poplar**
* Chrisp Street market - bottles.
* Yabsley Street municipal rubbish tip - paper, textiles, scrap metal, waste oil and glass.

**Stepney**
* Ben Jonson Road - bottles.
* Whitehorse Road - bottles.

**Stratford**
* The Broadway - bottles.

**Stoke Newington**
* Stoke Newington Church Street - bottles.

**Stratford**
* Stamford Hill, by Amhurst Park, outside supermarket - bottles.
* Stamford Hill, by Manor Road, opposite Safeway - bottles.

**Walthamstow**
* South Grove car park - bottles.
* Stockfields Road - bottles

**Wanstead**
* High Street - bottles.

**Wapping**
* Dean Cross Street/Commercial Road - bottles
* Wapping Sports Centre, Tench Street - bottles

## WASTE PAPER COLLECTIONS

**Bethnal Green**
* FoE have a skip every first Saturday of the month in Globe Town Market, Roman Road.

**Globe Town**
* Market Square, FoE collect paper on first Saturday of each month - not glossy magazines.

# OUTER EAST

*Incorporating Postal Districts RM1–RM3, RM5–RM14, IG1–IG6, IG8, IG11*

## RECYCLING FACILITIES

* **Woodford Green** - Chigwell Road civic amenity site - bottles, paper, cardboard.
* **Dagenham** - Frizlands Lane depot, Rainham Road North - bottles, glass, oil, metal, textiles.
* **Upminster** - Gerpins Lane - glass, oil, asbestos sheet, rags and metal.

## MINI RECYCLING CENTRES

**Barking**
* Axe Street - bottles.
* Faircross Parade, Putney Lane - bottles.

**Barkingside**
* Fairlop Waters - bottles.
* Forest Road - bottles.

**Chadwell Heath**
* High Road - bottles.
* Tudor Parade - bottles.
* Tesco supermarket, High Road - bottles.

**Collier Row**

*     Rex car park - bottles.

**Cranham**
*     Front Lane car park - bottles.
*     Car park (Social Hall ground) - bottles.

**Dagenham**
*     Mill House Social Club, New Road - bottles.
*     Whalebone Lane South, near junction with Broadway - bottles.

**Elm Park**
*     Elm Park Hotel car park - bottles.
*     Station Parade, site of former toilets - bottles.

**Goodmayes**
*     Green Lane - bottles.

**Hainault**
*     Staggart Green - bottles.

**Harold Hill**
*     Hilldene Avenue - bottles.

**Harold Wood**
*     Tesco car park, Gallows Corner - bottles.

**Hornchurch**
*     Fentiman Way - bottles.
*     Queens Theatre - bottles.
*     Station Parade, Elm Park - bottles.
*     Ladbrokes, Mercury Hotel on A127 - bottles.
*     Tesco car park, Toneo Corner - bottles.

**Ilford**
*     Chase Lane, Barkingside, adjacent to Sainsbury's car park - bottles.
*     High Road - bottles.
*     Chapel Road, Sainsbury Supermarket - bottles.

**Marks Gate**
*     Rose Lane - bottles.

**Newbury Park**
*     Sainsbury's - bottles.

**Rainham**
*     Bridge Road car park - bottles.
*     Cherry Tree lorry park, by Cherry Tree pub - bottles.

**Romford**
*     Dagenham Road - bottles.
*     Angel Way - bottles.
*     Rex car park, Collier Row - bottles.
*     Adams Yard - along Market Link frontage.

**Redbridge**
*     Redbridge Children's Scrap Store, Claybury Park Church, 62 Harewood Drive - scrap store.
*     Harvester Pub car park, Beehive Lane - bottles.

**Seven Kings**
*     High Road - bottles.

**South Woodford**
* Derby Road - bottles.
**Upminster**
* Gaynes Road - bottles.

# INNER NORTH

*Incorporating Postal Districts N1, N2, N4–N8, N10, N15–N19, N22*

## RECYCLING FACILITIES

* **Tottenham** - Park View Road depot - bottles, oil, CFC removal on old fridges.
* **Islington** - Queensland Road civic amenity site - paper, cardboard, oil, glass, metals, computer paper and CFC removal on old fridges.

## MINI-RECYCLING CENTRES

**Edmonton**
* Fore Street - bottles.
* Knightstone - bottles.
* Monmouth Road car park - bottles (paper in 1990).

**Finsbury Park**
* Endymion Road entrance - proposed bottle bank opening 1990.
* Seven Sisters Road Gates - proposed bottle bank opening 1990.
* Salisbury pub, Green Lanes - bottles.
* Haringey Stadium old site, next to Sainsbury's - bottles.

**Hornsey**
* Alexandra Park, Priory Road Gates - bottles, cans.
* Hornsey Library, Haringey Park - bottles and paper.
* Priory Road, outside tennis courts - bottles.
* Texas, Green Lanes - bottles.

**Islington**
* Wallis Road, outside station - bottles.
* Stroud Green Road, outside Tesco - bottles.
* Junction Road, outside shopping mall - bottles.
* Seven Sisters, outside Safeway supermarket - bottles.
* Holloway Road, outside Selbys - bottles.
* Newington Green, East Side - bottles.
* Upper Street, outside municipal offices - bottles.
* Islington Green, Essex Road side - bottles.
* Caledonian Road/corner Carnegie Street - bottles.
* 222 Old Street, outside Argos - bottles.
* Highbury Crescent - bottles.

* Upper Street, on High Pavement near Angel - bottles.
* Essex Road/corner Rotherfield Street - bottles.
* St. John's Street, outside Finsbury Library - bottles.
* Holloway Road, near Majestic Wine Warehouse - bottles.

**Muswell Hill**
* The Avenue, Alexandra Park Road - bottles.
* Colney Hatch Lane, Tesco Superstore - cans.
* Muswell Hill Road - bottles.

**Seven Sisters**
* Haringey Furniture project, Seaford Road, Tuesday and Thursday (081) 802 0495 - collect household furniture.

**Tottenham**
* Church Lane - bottles.
* Colina Mews, Green Lanes - bottles.
* Downhills Park, Philip Lane - bottles.
* Footway, High Road - bottles.
* Middlesex Polytechnic, White Hart Lane - bottles.
* Rheola Close, High Road - bottles.
* Tottenham Town Hall - proposed bottlebank opening 1990.

**Wood Green**
* Central Library, High Road - bottles.
* Civic Centre, High Road - bottles.
* Civic Centre, Trinity Road - bottles.
* Lymington Avenue, next to Sainsbury's - bottles.
* New River Sports Centre, White Hart Lane - bottles.
* Turnpike Lane underground station - bottles.

## WASTE PAPER COLLECTIONS
**Muswell Hill**
* Muswell Hill FoE and Haringey Green Party organise monthly paper collections in Wood Green and Muswell Hill.
* 4 Lanchester Road, East Finchley - clean pie trays, milk bottle tops for Guide Dogs for the Blind.

# OUTER NORTH
*Incorporating Postal Districts N3, N9, N11–N14, N21, EN1, EN5*

## RECYCLING FACILITIES
* **Enfield** - Caterhatch Lane - rags, paper, oil and bottles.
* **Finchley** - Summers Lane civic amenity site.

# MINI-RECYCLING CENTRES

**Barnet**
* Refuse tip, Summers Lane - cans.

**Bounds Green**
* Bounds Green underground station - bottles.

**Bush Hill**
* Bush Hill Park Station, Trinity Avenue - bottles.
* Junction of Oakwood Parade and Queen Anne's Place - bottle-bank opening early 1990.

**Cockfosters**
* Junction of Cockfosters Road and Westpole Avenue - bottles.

**Edmonton Green**
* Monmouth Road - paper.

**Enfield**
* Brick Lane, Enfield High Way car park - bottles.
* Chaseside, junction with Nuns Road near Jewson Yard - bottles.
* Little Park Gardens car park - bottles.
* Southbury Road, near Copocabana - bottles.
* Junction of Church Street and Ridge Avenue, outside bakery - bottles.
* Southbury Road, Enfield Football Club - bottles.
* Junction of Lancaster Road and Baker Street - bottles.

**Enfield Wash**
* Unity Road, near Co-op supermarket - bottles.

**Finchley**
* 21/49 Ballards Lane, in Tesco car park - bottles.
* Summers Lane - bottles.
* Lodge Lane - bottles.
* Back of Tesco's, Finchley Central - bottles.

**Friern Barnet**
* Friern Barnet Lane by Tesco's - bottles.

**Hadley Wood**
* Hadley Wood Golf Club, Beech Hill - bottles.

**High Barnet**
* Stapleton Road car park - bottles.

**New Barnet**
* 66 East Barnet Road, near Sainsbury's - bottles.

**North Finchley**
* Coppetts Centre, North Circular Road, in Tesco car park - bottles.

**Ponders End**
* The Post Office, Ponders End High Street - bottles.
* South Street, near Alma Road junction - bottles.

**Southgate**
* 80/82 Chase Side, near Sainsbury's - bottles.
* ASDA, 130 Chase Side - bottles.
* Winchmore Hill, outside Capitol House - bottles.

* Linwood Grove, near Salisbury pub - bottles.
* Bowes Road, outside Arnos Grove underground station - bottles.
    * The Green, outside Cherry Tree pub - bottles.
* Southgate Circus, near roundabout - bottles.

# INNER NORTH-WEST

*Incorporating Postal Districts NW1–NW3, NW5, NW6, NW8, NW10, NW11*

## RECYCLING FACILITIES

* **Jamestown Recycling Centre**, 28 Jamestown Road, NW1 - metal, paper, cardboard, glass, oil, rags, soft plastics.
* **Brent Cross** - Tilling Road civic amenity site.

## MINI RECYCLING CENTRES

**Hammersmith & Fulham Borough Council** operate a weekend skip service throughout the Borough. Please contact Engineering Department, Bagleys Lane Depot (081) 748 3020 Ext 3214 for full details.

**Camden**
* Agar Grove, junction with Murray Street - bottles.
* Eversholt Street, near Euston station - bottles.
* Inverness Street, junction with Arlington Road - bottles.
* Robert Street, junction with Albany Street - bottles.
* Marylebone Station, NW1 - bottles.

**Hampstead**
* Regents Park Road, junction with King Henry's Road - bottles.
* Rosslyn Hill, opposite Belsize Lane - bottles.
* Swiss Cottage, underground station - bottles.

**Harlesden**
* Western Road, ASDA car park - bottles and tins.

**Kensal Green**
* Kensal Green Station, junction Harrow Road - paper.

**Kentish Town**
* Highgate Road, opposite Forum Dance Hall - bottles.
* Malden Road, opposite Grafton Terrace - bottles.

**Kilburn**
* Fortune Green Road, by Prince of Wales pub - bottles.
* Kilburn High Road, outside old Grange Cinema - bottles.
* West End Lane, opposite Fire Station - bottles.
* Victoria Road - bottles and cans.
* Stafford Road, outside South Kilburn Community School - paper.
* Aylestone Avenue, inside gates of Aylestone Community School - paper.

> * Furness Road, junction Rucklidge Avenue - paper.

**Neasden**
* Great Central Way, in Tesco car park - bottles.
* Neasden Shopping Centre - bottles, paper and cans.

**St. John's Wood**
* Wellington Place, by Wellington Road - bottles.
* Abbey Road, NW8 - bottles.

**Willesden Green**
* Station Parade - bottles.
* Crownhill Road, junction Harlesden High Street - bottles.
* Tesco's, Brent Park - bottles.

# OUTER NORTH-WEST

*Incorporating Postal Districts NW4, NW7, NW9, HA0–HA3, HA5, HA7 - HA9*

## RECYCLING FACILITIES

* **Wealdstone** - civic amenity site, Kenmore Avenue - paper, bottles, cans (proposed from January 1990). Fridges and freezers are accepted free-of-charge or collected from residents for a fee of £10. CFCs are removed before scrapping. n.b. The civic amenity site will be relocated in Spring 1990 to Forward Drive, Wealdstone.
* **Wembley** - Civic Amenity Site, Alperton Lane - oil, metal, glass, rags, paper, cans, foil, furniture, batteries, bric-a-brac.

## MINI-RECYCLING CENTRES

**Alperton**
* Central depot, Marsh Lane - paper.
* Ealing Road, Alperton High School - paper.

**Belmont**
* Belmont School, Hibbert Road, outside main entrance - paper
* St. Joseph's School, Belmont, outside school - paper.

**Colindale**
* ASDA, Capitol Park Industrial Estate, Capitol Way - bottles.

**Harrow**
* The civic centre - paper.
* Greenhill Road, outside Debenhams rear entrance - paper and bottles.
* Kenton Road, outside Waitrose - paper and bottles.
* Grange School, Welbeck Road, outside school - paper.
* Greenhill College, Lowlands Road, inside main gate - paper.
* Longfield First School, Raynors Lane, outside school - paper.

* Newton Farm School, Raynors Lane, inside playing fields - paper.
* Queensbury Circle, Honeypot Lane, outside garage next to Honeypot pub - paper.
* St. George's School, Sudbury Hill, inside school - paper.
* Weldon Park School, Kingsley Road, outside school - paper.
* Cedars Middle School, Whittlesea Road, outside main entrance - paper.
* Cedars First School, Whittlesea Road - paper.
* Raynors Lane, outside old cinema - paper and bottles.
* Earlsmead School, Arundel Drive, inside school - paper.
* Elmgrove Road, on pavement outside office block - paper.

**Kenton**
* Woodcock Hill, junction Draycott Avenue - paper.

**Kingsbury**
* 634 Kingsbury Road, outside Sainsbury's - bottles and paper.
* Princess Avenue, Kingsbury High School - paper.
* Stag Lane, Kingsbury High School (annexe) - paper.
* Queensbury Station Parade - paper.

**Harrow on the Hill**
Paperbanks only:
* Grove Road.
* Harrow Park.

**North Harrow**
* Station Road, outside bowling alley - paper and bottles.
* St. John Fisher School, outside school - paper.

**West Harrow**
* Vaughan School, outside school - paper.

**Harrow Weald**
* College Avenue, outside Red Lion pub - paper and bottles.

**Pinner**
* Bridge Street, outside Safeway - paper and bottles.
* Chapel Lane car park - paper and bottles.
* Pinner Park School, Headstone Lane, outside school - paper.
* Canon Lane School, Cannonbury Avenue, inside school - paper.
* Pinner Wood School, Latimer Gardens, outside main school gate - paper.

**Stanmore**
* The Broadway - paper and bottles.
* Wemborough Road, alongside Canon Hall - paper.
* North London Collegiate School, Dalkeith Grove - paper only.

**Wembley**
* Goodwill Industries, 282 Water Road - collect and renovate office furniture and equipment.
* 6th Wembley Scout Group, 116 Carlton Avenue West - collect newspapers once a month.
* St. John's Road - bottles and paper.

*     Wembley Stadium Complex - paper.
*     Blackbird Hill, junction Chalkhill Road - paper.
*     Town Hall, Forty Lane - paper.
*     Cecil Avenue, outside Copland Community School - paper.
*     Barnhill, junction Barn Way and West Hill - paper.
*     Norval Road, junction Audrey Gardens - paper.
*     Outside Hillcrest, Preston Hill - paper.
*     Barham Park Library, Harrow Road - paper.
*     Preston Road Library, Carlton Avenue East - paper.
*     Ealing Road Library, Ealing Road - paper.
*     East Lane, car park Sudbury Court Sports - paper.

# ENTRY FOR THE 1991 GREEN GUIDE

*Nominations of shops, businesses and services to be included in the 1991 Green Guide To London*

I would like to nominate:

Name of shop/restaurant/service/business:

.......................................................................................

Full address: ...................................................................

.......................................................................................

.......................................................................................

.......................................................................................

Telephone number: ........................................................

for inclusion in the 1991 *Green Guide to London*.

*(For criteria for inclusion, please see page 171)*

Brief details of activities and specialities:

.......................................................................................

.......................................................................................

.......................................................................................

.......................................................................................

Your name and address:

.................................................................

.................................................................

.................................................................

.................................................................

.................................................................

.................................................................